lonely planet

Where To Go When

Hiking

The Ultimate MONTH-BY-MONTH Trip-Planner
for Hikes, Walks & Treks

Contents

INTRODUCTION 4
INDEX 322
CREDITS 327

● **JANUARY** 6
Machame Route, *Kilimanjaro, Tanzania* 9
GR132 Circular, *La Gomera, Canary Islands* 13
Waitukubuli Trail, *Dominica* 16
Queen Charlotte Track, *South Island, New Zealand/Aotearoa* 19
Ciudad Perdida Trek, *Sierra Nevada de Santa Marta, Colombia* 23
Pekoe Trail, *Central Highlands, Sri Lanka* 26
Island Trails, *Madeira, Portugal* 29
Camino de Costa Rica, *Central Costa Rica* 32

● **FEBRUARY** 34
W Trek, *Patagonia, Chile* 36
Berliner Mauerweg, *Berlin, Germany* 39
Snowies Alpine Walk, *New South Wales, Australia* 42
Mt Kenya Traverse, *Mt Kenya National Park, Kenya* 45
Lake Waikaremoana Track, *North Island, New Zealand/Aotearoa* 48
Manaslu Circuit, *North-central Nepal* 51
Camino Francés, *Northern Spain* 55
Mt Kinabalu, *Sabah, Malaysian Borneo* 58

● **MARCH** 60
Fishermen's Trail, *Alentejo & Algarve, Portugal* 63
El Mirador Trek, *Petén, Guatemala* 68
88 Temple Pilgrimage, *Shikoku, Japan* 69
Otter Trail, *Western & Eastern Cape, South Africa* 72
Dry Stone Route, *Mallorca, Spain* 75
Three Capes Track, *Tasmania, Australia* 78
Lycian Way, *Southwest Anatolia, Türkiye* 81
Santa Barbara Cammino, *Sardinia, Italy* 84

● **APRIL** 86
Giant's Cup Trail, *KwaZulu-Natal, South Africa* 89
Dutch Mountain Trail, *Zuid-Limburg, Netherlands* 92
Dana to Petra Trail, *Western Jordan* 95
Scenic Rim Trail, *Queensland, Australia* 98
South West Coast Path, *Southwest England* 101
Rogue River Trail, *Oregon, USA* 104
Moselsteig, *Moselle Valley, Germany* 107
Singalila Ridge, *West Bengal, India* 110

NEXT Hiking the first leg of Patagonia's Huemul Circuit from El Chaltén, Argentina.

CONTENTS

● MAY 112

- Gold Coast Hinterland Great Walk, *Queensland, Australia* 114
- West Highland Way, *Western Scotland* 117
- Toubkal Circuit, *Atlas Mountains, Morocco* 121
- Tiger Leaping Gorge, *Yunnan, China* 124
- Juliana Trail, *Northwest Slovenia* 127
- Grand Canyon Rim-to-Rim, *Arizona, USA* 130
- Jomolhari Trek, *Jigme Dorji National Park, Bhutan* 133
- Cordillera Huayhuash Circuit, *Northern Peru* 136

● JUNE 138

- Mare è Monti Nord, *Corsica, France* 141
- Greenstone Ridge Trail, *Michigan, USA* 144
- Via Dinarica, *Bosnia & Hercegovina/Montenegro* 147
- Michinoku Coastal Trail, *Honshū, Japan* 150
- Dingle Way, *County Kerry, Ireland* 153
- Thorsborne Trail, *Queensland, Australia* 156
- East Coast Trail, *Newfoundland, Canada* 159
- Via Transilvanica, *Transylvania, Romania* 162

● JULY 164

- ViaBerna, *Canton of Bern, Switzerland* 166
- John Muir Trail, *California, USA* 169
- Markha Valley Trek, *Ladakh, India* 172
- Chemin de Stevenson, *Southeast Massif Central, France* 175
- Fish River Canyon Trail, *Southern Namibia* 178
- Archipelago Trail, *Fyn Archipelago, Denmark* 181
- West Coast Trail, *Vancouver Island, Canada* 184
- Adlerweg, *Tyrol, Austria* 187

● AUGUST 190

- Kungsleden, *Swedish Lapland* 193
- Wonderland Trail, *Washington, USA* 196
- Laugavegur, *Southern Iceland* 199
- Lužnice Valley Trail, *Bohemia, Czechia* 202
- Larapinta Trail, *Northern Territory, Australia* 205
- K2 Base Camp & Concordia, *Baltistan, Pakistan* 208
- Baltic Coastal Hiking Trail, *Western Lithuania* 211
- Malmveien Historical Trail, *Trøndelag, Norway* 214

● SEPTEMBER 216

- Karhunkierros Trail, *Northern Finland* 218
- Choquequirao Trek, *Southern Peru* 221
- Premužić Trail, *Velebit Mountains, Croatia* 224
- Jeju Olle Trail, *Jeju-do, South Korea* 227
- Kalalau Trail, *Kaua'i, Hawai'i* 230
- Cape to Cape Track, *Western Australia* 233
- Traversée de Charlevoix, *Québec, Canada* 236
- Alta Via 1, *Dolomites, Italy* 239

● OCTOBER 242

- Coast to Coast, *Cumbria & Yorkshire, England* 245
- Appalachian Trail, *Tennessee & North Carolina, USA* 248
- Andros Route, *Cyclades, Greece* 251
- Island Walk, *Prince Edward Island, Canada* 254
- Via Francigena, *Switzerland & Northern Italy* 257
- Kangaroo Island Wilderness Trail, *South Australia* 260
- Kumano Kodō, *Honshū, Japan* 263
- Malerweg, *Saxony, Germany* 267

● NOVEMBER 270

- Routeburn Track, *South Island, New Zealand/Aotearoa* 273
- Menalon Trail, *Peloponnese, Greece* 276
- MacLehose Trail, *Hong Kong, China* 279
- Strandloper Trail, *Eastern Cape, South Africa* 282
- Langtang & Helambu Trek, *Northern Nepal* 285
- Trans-Catalina Trail, *California, USA* 288
- Grampians Peaks Trail, *Victoria, Australia* 291
- Quilotoa Loop, *Cotopaxi Province, Ecuador* 294

● DECEMBER 296

- Huemul Circuit, *Patagonia, Argentina* 298
- GR92 Sendero del Mediterráneo Cataluña, *Catalonia, Spain* 301
- Outer Mountain Loop, *Texas, USA* 304
- Santo Antão Trails, *Cabo Verde* 307
- E35, *Eastern Hajar, Oman* 310
- Rakiura Track, *Stewart Island/Rakiura, New Zealand Aotearoa* 313
- Batongguan Traversing Trail, *Yushan National Park, Taiwan* 316
- Via Algarviana, *Algarve, Portugal* 319

INTRODUCTION

LONELY PLANET'S WHERE TO GO WHEN HIKING

Hiking is all about freedom...

Freedom to roam wild expanses, drinking in views of snow-clad peaks or surf-pounded shores. To encounter unfamiliar cultures, to spy charismatic animals in their natural habitat, to savour solitude or enjoy the company of fellow trekkers. Mostly, freedom to wander where you will – though not necessarily when. Because timing is key.

Sure, we all know the old saying coined by legendary English ambler Alfred Wainwright: 'There's no such thing as bad weather, only unsuitable clothing.' But the truth is that walking in dismal conditions can be soul-sapping or downright dangerous. Some trails are accessible or safe only when high mountain passes are snow-free, or when paths aren't quagmires mid-monsoon. So, it pays to know when's best to head out. And that's not always about sun or rain: it can be worth hiking outside what's typically deemed the 'best', sunniest or driest period in order to bag discounts, catch a seasonal wildlife spectacle or dodge the crowds.

Of course, your 'when' may be fixed – when you can take time off work, say. To help you decide where to spend your precious leave or long weekend, we've curated this collection of the world's greatest hikes organised by month, each containing routes of varying durations. At the start of each chapter, you'll find a flow chart helping you choose your ideal trail according to time available and the main feature or style of the walk.

Got a week free in October? You could get cultural on Japan's Kumano Kodō trail, or artsy on Germany's Malerweg (Painters' Way). Aiming for a longer adventure in February? Head for the heights on the Manaslu Circuit in the Nepalese Himalaya, or enjoy a peaceful pilgrimage on the Camino Francés to Santiago de Compostela.

Naturally, there are other considerations to ponder. Do you prefer to sleep in comfy guesthouses, absorb the bonhomie of rustic mountain huts or bed down under canvas? Are you looking for a strolling safari, watching wildlife as you walk, or keen to sample local specialities? Our entries kick off with notes on the dominant styles, landscapes and themes of each route, as well as distance, duration and challenge level, and other suitable months you could walk it. You'll also find basic logistical information to get you started, covering transport, accommodation, supplies and other planning essentials.

Along with the where, when and how, you also want to know why – what makes each hike unmissable? That's the main goal of this book: to provide inspiration, to tempt you to discover something or somewhere new. Rather than simple day-by-day descriptions of routes, these pages are filled with pen-portraits of walks spanning six continents, bringing to life the diverse experiences you can expect. So, dip in, browse, explore, ponder – and find your own trails of the unexpected, just when you need them.

– SARAH BAXTER & PAUL BLOOMFIELD

JANUARY

La Gomera's GR132 Circular affords glimpses of Mt Tiede on neighbouring Canary Isle Tenerife (page 13).

JANUARY

I WANT A HIKE THAT'S A...

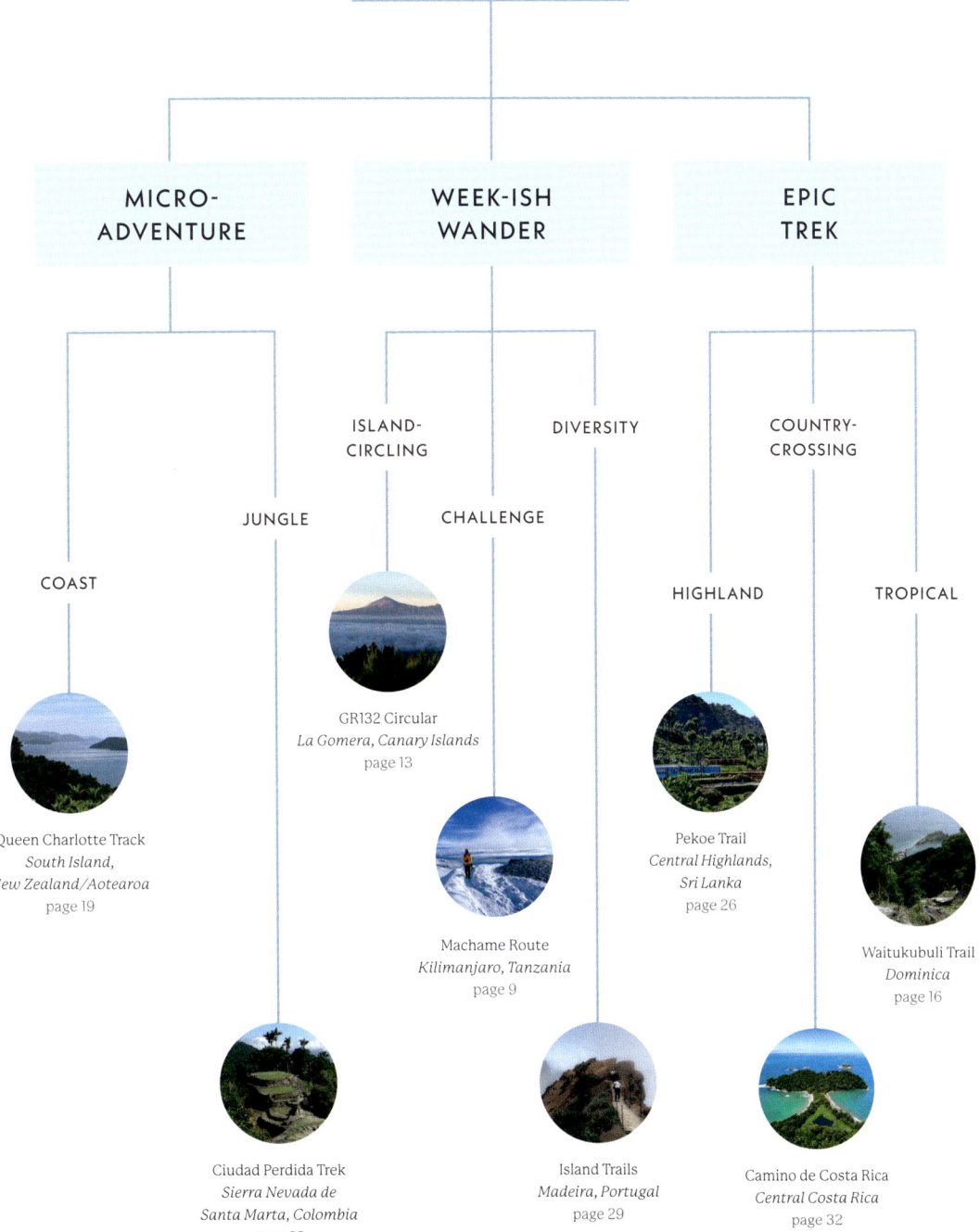

MICRO-ADVENTURE

WEEK-ISH WANDER

EPIC TREK

ISLAND-CIRCLING

DIVERSITY

COUNTRY-CROSSING

JUNGLE

CHALLENGE

COAST

HIGHLAND

TROPICAL

GR132 Circular
La Gomera, Canary Islands
page 13

Queen Charlotte Track
*South Island,
New Zealand/Aotearoa*
page 19

Pekoe Trail
*Central Highlands,
Sri Lanka*
page 26

Machame Route
Kilimanjaro, Tanzania
page 9

Waitukubuli Trail
Dominica
page 16

Ciudad Perdida Trek
*Sierra Nevada de
Santa Marta, Colombia*
page 23

Island Trails
Madeira, Portugal
page 29

Camino de Costa Rica
Central Costa Rica
page 32

NATURE / CAMPING / MOUNTAIN

Machame Route

KILIMANJARO, TANZANIA

Gird your loins for a metaphorically – and literally – breathtaking summit attempt on this gargantuan mountain, to stand atop the 'Roof of Africa'.

Is there a more tantalising prospect for the avid trekker? Mighty Kilimanjaro stands on the Tanzanian savannah only a few clicks south of the equator, looming large and lonely as a god, the highest thing in all Africa. It practically bellows: c'mon then, if you dare.

This dormant volcano is the ultimate achievable challenge. Kilimanjaro rises a lung-scraping 5895m (19,340ft) above sea level but, unlike other peaks of such stature, demands no technical climbing skills – just a good level of fitness, a bit of patience and hefty doses of grit and determination. To get to the top – to stand, jubilant, at Uhuru (Freedom) Peak – all you must do is walk *pole, pole* (slowly, slowly), acclimatise to the altitude and dig in.

The first person known to climb Kili was German geology professor Hans Meyer, in 1889. Many have followed in his footsteps since – an estimated 50,000 people now attempt it each year. Around a third of them don't complete the climb: even the fittest can be hit by headaches, nausea and dizziness – the telltale symptoms of altitude sickness.

You can increase your chances of success, and have a better time all round, by tackling the mountain in optimal weather conditions. The dry seasons are the best time to hike, with the 'shorter dry' (January to early March) offering not only mostly clear, rain-free days but also quieter trails than during the peak 'long dry' from June to September. The 'shorter dry' is when you're more likely to see this equatorial behemoth under a sparkling cloak of snow, too.

START
Machame

FINISH
Mweka

DISTANCE
60km (37 miles)

DURATION
Six to eight days

CHALLENGE LEVEL
★ ★ ★ ★ ★

WHEN TO WALK
January–March
& June–October

LEFT Hike the Machame Route to summit Tanzania's Mt Kilimanjaro, the 'Roof of Africa'.

Which route to choose? There are several established trails. Whichever you pick, independent trekking is not permitted. You'll be accompanied by a guide and porters, who carry phenomenal loads so you don't have to — and will overtake you despite their hefty burdens. Marangu is the shortest and busiest route, with the lowest success rate. Rongai starts near the Kenyan border, and offers a steady climb. Machame is an excellent choice: it's popular, incredibly scenic, and is doable in a week.

The Machame ascent starts in lush, leafy montane forest, which is liable to be wet and sticky whatever the season — but also offers chances to spot bright birdlife and colobus monkeys. As you gain altitude the trees disappear, replaced by alien-looking giant lobelias and barren plateaus of volcanic rock; you'll wind up via the dramatic Lava Tower, tackle the craggy Barranco Wall and, with luck, will enjoy epic views above the clouds. The air thins with every upward step.

ACCOMMODATION
Camping (Marangu is the only route with huts).

FOOD
Breakfast, lunch, dinner and snacks are provided on organised tours. Meals usually comprise large portions of carb-heavy fare such as porridge, rice and pasta.

GETTING THERE
Kilimanjaro Airport is between Moshi and Arusha; tour companies in both towns offer climbing trips.

PLANNING
Independent climbing isn't allowed. Tours should include permits, park fees, guides, porters, food and equipment.

SAFETY
Altitude sickness is the biggest danger. Know the symptoms, take time to acclimatise, follow your guide's lead, and stay well fuelled and hydrated.

INFO
tanzaniaparks.go.tz

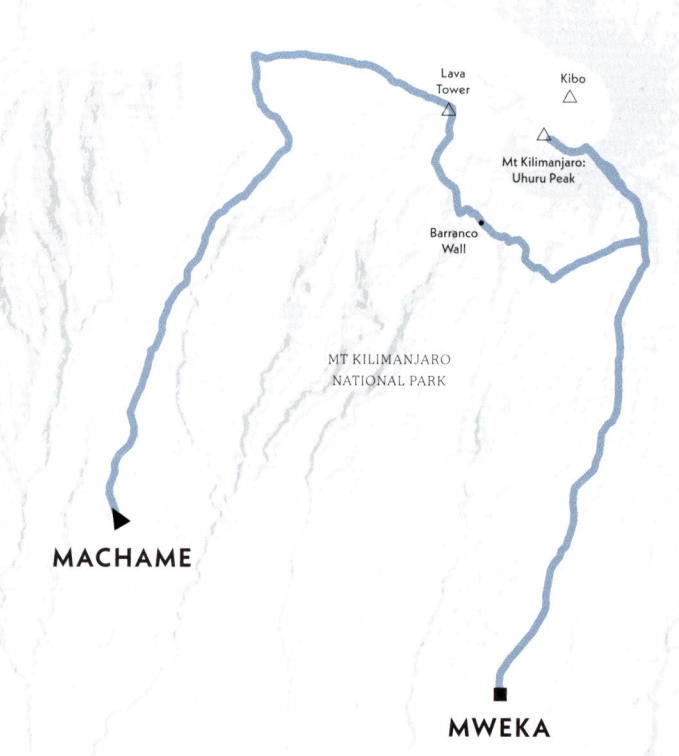

LEFT Otherworldly giant lobelia flourish on Kili's mist-swathed flanks. **RIGHT** Karanga Camp on the Machame Route, sitting pretty at around 3995m (13,106ft).

'KILIMANJARO'S NAME MAY COME FROM THE SWAHILI WORD *KILIMA* (MOUNTAIN) AND THE KICHAGGA WORD *NJARO* ('SHINING' OR 'WHITENESS'), ALLUDING TO THE SNOW ON ITS SUMMIT.'

The big challenge comes on summit night: a midnight wake-up call followed by a slow, monotonous, soul-destroying tramp behind a procession of head-torches snaking into the night. It's a lung-testing grind in the biting-cold darkness that never seems to end. The aim? To make it over the crater rim, past the receding glaciers and to the summit in time to witness an epic sunrise.

Then there's the task of getting down, another day and a half of knee-punishing descent sweetened by the euphoria of having — albeit briefly — crested a continent.

The snows of Kilimanjaro

IN 1848, German missionary Johannes Rebmann became the first European to see Kilimanjaro. When he sent back reports of snow on the equator, scholars sneered; the president of the Royal Geographical Society declared it 'a great degree incredulous'. But Rebmann was right. Kilimanjaro, which sits just 3° south of the Earth's equator, is still topped by glaciers — just. Between 1912 and 1989, the ice cover decreased by 75%. Some scientists predict it could be gone by 2030.

SPAIN

NATURE / CAMPING / COAST

GR132 Circular

LA GOMERA, CANARY ISLANDS

Climb to volcanic peaks, plunge into ravines, and then do the same over and over again on a wild loop of this compact but craggy Canary Isle.

There's a popular image of Spain's Canary Islands that's all holiday resorts rammed with sunseeking tourists. Then there's La Gomera. Like the archipelago's other westerly isles, it's less about beach-flopping than boot-yomping. Because the whole of this mountainous, gorge-sliced, sparsely populated Atlantic outcrop is designated a UNESCO Biosphere Reserve, and it's riddled with some 600km (370 miles) of walking routes. Chief of these is the GR132.

This Gran Recorrido (Spanish for 'long route') completes a loop of La Gomera, with hikers typically starting and ending in east-coast capital San Sebastián. You could walk it at any time – the Canaries are blessed with great weather year-round. But summers do get hot, pushing 30°C (86°F). The cooler winter months, with average highs just over 20°C (68°F) and very little rain, are most pleasant for hefting up-down on the trails.

The GR132 isn't easy. This is a volcanic island, with barely a flat stretch. It's rough underfoot, riven with geological ructions and plummets into steep *barrancos* (ravines). Over its full length, the trail racks up around 8000m (26,247ft) of elevation gain; for the same reason, it's spectacular right out of the box. Within metres of climbing out of San Sebastián, you'll drink in joyous views back over the town's hill-clinging homes; a couple of kilometres later you're up on high, looking across the surrounding rugged ridges and over to massive Mt Teide, rising from the neighbouring isle of Tenerife.

Most hikers head anticlockwise, following waymarks towards the north coast – La Gomera's cooler, windier, more humid

START/FINISH
San Sebastián

DISTANCE
133km (83 miles)

DURATION
Six to eight days

CHALLENGE LEVEL
★★★★

WHEN TO WALK
October–May

LEFT En route to La Gomera's Mirador de Abrante for picture-perfect views of Tenerife's Mt Tiede.

SPAIN

Up, not around

A SHORTER alternative is the 44km (27-mile) GR131, a well-signed trail that crosses the island from the southeast to the north coast, linking San Sebastián and Playa de Vallehermoso. It runs via nose-diving ravines, volcanic plugs, fertile valleys and 1487m (4879ft) Alto de Garajonay, the island's highest point – from here, on a clear day, you can see Teide on Tenerife, plus La Palma and El Hierro islands. The trek takes two or three days.

'INSCRIBED ON UNESCO'S ORAL AND INTANGIBLE HERITAGE OF HUMANITY LIST, THE ISLAND'S WHISTLING LANGUAGE, SILBO GOMERO, IS USED TO COMMUNICATE ACROSS MOUNTAINS.'

side. Day one sees the trail rise from the port, cross the wild innards of Parque Natural de Majona – all plunging rockscapes and ancient laurel forest – before dipping to the sea. And it's a rhythm this flower-shaped route repeats on every stage: climb from sea level, tick off a variety of microclimates, traverse *barrancos*, lava fields and palm-edged farming terraces, then dip back towards the ocean (but note that though the black-sand and pebble beaches look tempting for swims, currents can be strong and dangerous).

As the GR132 progresses, the challenge doesn't let up – you'll need to be fit and sure-footed. But the scenery is literally out of this world: it looks a little alien, all crumpled, cacti-prickled and raw. It's also often empty and remote. You will pass villages – for

TOP The volcanic plg of Roque de Agando in central La Gomera. **LEFT** The island's dramatic lava-sculpted coastline. **RIGHT** Hillside homes in Hermigua, northeast La Gomera.

ACCOMMODATION
Hotels and guesthouses in some villages. Theoretically, wild camping is illegal; in reality, it's sometimes the only option.

FOOD
Villages with shops/cafes most days. Natural water sources are limited – fill up whenever possible and purify.

GETTING THERE
La Gomera doesn't have an international airport. Ferries from Tenerife to San Sebastián take one hour.

PLANNING
By tweaking the route or arranging transfers it's possible to stay in guesthouses each night. Book in advance.

SAFETY
Shade is limited. Paths can be rocky and uneven – take trekking poles. Research locations of water sources.

INFO
lagomera.travel
rundwanderung-lagomera.de

instance, colourful little spots such as Agulo or Alajeró, and time-warp Vallehermoso. But there are just enough facilities en route to stop for the odd cold *cerveza* (beer) and replenish supplies each day. There aren't, though, quite enough spots directly on the route where you can sleep in a bed each night – so, though wild camping is technically illegal, it's how many hikers complete this trail, and is generally tolerated as long as you camp away from settlements and leave no trace; ask permission where possible. While that involves carrying more equipment, it also means waking up alone, on deserted beaches or high plateaus, to watch pink-purple sunrises cracking the clouds. And it means drifting off beneath glittering galaxies – the Canary Islands have some of Europe's cleanest, clearest, most star-spangled skies.

NATURE / CULTURE / MOUNTAIN / COAST

Waitukubuli Trail

DOMINICA

START
Scotts Head Peninsula

FINISH
Cabrits

DISTANCE
185km (115 miles)

DURATION
10–14 days

CHALLENGE LEVEL
★★★

WHEN TO WALK
January–April

Blaze your way across the Nature Isle on the Caribbean's only long-distance hiking trail, experiencing a very different side to this traditionally beach-focused region.

Dominica's Indigenous Kalinago name, Waitukubuli — 'tall is her body' — is a nod to the fact that nowhere here is really flat; the landscape is forever rearing up or plummeting down, often at precipitous angles. This is one of the Caribbean's wildest outposts — a place where nine 'potentially active' volcanoes simmer, rainforest runs rampant and beaches come in inky black rather than region-regulation white-gold. It's also home to the Caribbean's first — and so far sole — long-distance walking route.

Just 47km (29 miles) top to bottom, 26km (16 miles) wide, Dominica somehow squeezes a 185km (115 mile) trail into its luscious confines. Stringing together paths historically used by the Kalinago and by Maroons (escapees from enslavement), and divided into 14 sections, the route wiggles from 18th-century Fort Cachacrou on the southerly Scotts Head Peninsula to Fort Shirley in Cabrits, in the northwest. Along the way it takes in pools and waterfalls, the Wotten Waven hot springs, the bird-twittered forest of Morne Trois Pitons National Park, the fizzing Atlantic coast and the foothills of Morne aux Diables (Devil's Peak). It also cuts through Kalinago country, giving this trail real cultural chops. A key aim of the Waitukubuli is to bring people to villages that rarely see visitors, delivering tourist dollars to their guesthouses and cafes while showing hikers a different side to the Caribbean.

The project was dealt a hammer blow by Hurricane Maria in 2017, which destroyed infrastructure, rerouted rivers and even altered ecosystems. But the Waitukubuli is now walkable again, with the help of local guides. Tackle it in the dry season, when humidity is lower, temperatures slightly cooler and storms less likely.

JAN

ACCOMMODATION
Options, including homestays, accessible from most sections.

FOOD
Pack snacks and seek out local cafes en route. Look for callaloo soup and cassava bread.

GETTING THERE
Scotts Head is a 40-minute drive/taxi ride from Dominica's capital, Roseau.

PLANNING
It's advisable to walk with a local guide. Hikers should register with the Forestry, Wildlife & Parks Division before tackling any segment of the trail.

SAFETY
Be prepared for steamy tropical conditions and slippery, overgrown paths.

INFO
discoverdominica.com

LEFT The Waitukubuli cuts through Dominica's lush, waterfall-fed interior rainforest. **TOP** Hiking through Morne Trois Pitons National Park.

NEW ZEALAND/AOTEAROA

NATURE / CULTURE / CAMPING / COAST

Queen Charlotte Track

SOUTH ISLAND, NEW ZEALAND/AOTEAROA

Trace the fractal shoreline of the Marlborough Sounds, following historic bridlepaths through emerald forests, past limpid inlets and along soaring ridges.

Meretoto has the sense of a beginning. Jumping off the boat onto the wooden pier, you can't miss the gleaming white memorial, stark against lush green forest, commemorating the arrival in 1770 of Captain James Cook – the first European to set foot on South Island, dubbing this spot Ship Cove. More alluring are the intricately carved *pou whenua* (wooden poles) representing the great Polynesian navigator Kupe and the *iwi* (tribes) who foraged these shores and waters for centuries after his legendary arrival. Aptly, at the back of the beach you'll find the start of a tempting trail through the foliage, following bridlepaths forged by European settlers.

This is the Queen Charlotte Track, taking its name from the adjacent sound known to Māori as Tōtaranui, rechristened by Cook to honour the British King George III's consort. A hike along its generous curves offers an immersion into Indigenous, colonial and natural history. Unlike the more-famous routes designated Great Walks, it doesn't rely only on Department of Conservation huts or campsites for accommodation; the trail is studded with comfortable lodges and homestays, and boats transfer luggage. The lack of that official tag means the path is quieter and easier to book, too, even during the blissful summer days of January.

The route starts as it means to go on – with a climb, initially in the welcome shade of native trees. But though undulating, it never ascends much above 400m (1312ft); any moderately fit hiker will lap up the terrain – and the many rewards. After that first haul, you'll gaze out over Resolution Bay and Queen Charlotte Sound/Tōtaranui beyond: with your eyes, trace

START
Meretoto/Ship Cove

FINISH
Anakiwa

DISTANCE
73.5km (45.6 miles)

DURATION
Three to five days

CHALLENGE LEVEL

WHEN TO WALK
October–April

LEFT The Queen Charlotte Track is named for the superlative sound known to Māori as Tōtaranui.

NEW ZEALAND/AOTEAROA

ACCOMMODATION
Simple DOC campsites on the route, plus private campsites, resorts, homestays, lodges, huts and cabins.

FOOD
There are a few restaurants and cafes along the way; otherwise bring supplies from Picton.

GETTING THERE
Various boat operators link Picton with Meretoto/Ship Cove and other points on the trail, transfer luggage between overnights and offer return transport from Anakiwa to Picton.

PLANNING
A pass is required for sections crossing private land; fees support track maintenance, and the app (qctlc.com/buy-passes) has useful information.

SAFETY
Mountain bikers share the track (Meretoto/Ship Cove to Kenepuru Saddle closed to cyclists December–February).

INFO
qctrack.co.nz

endless gnarled fingers of land, tree-cloaked promontories lining up one after the other. And so it continues, as ridge sections reveal dramatic prospects along Kenepuru Sound to the north of the trail.

Interpretation boards detail aspects of the area's diverse past. At Endeavour Inlet, for example, a short detour leads to a disused antimony mine, which thrived during the latter part of the 19th century. The gentle shoreline stretch to Camp Bay leads past a burgeoning forest of lofty tōtara trees that lent the sound its Māori name. Later sections weave between nīkau palms, mānuka trees and profuse ferns hosting all manner of birdlife. Listen for the glissando chimes of korimako/bellbird and the R2-D2 chirrups, churs and cheeps of tūī; greet friendly fantails and inquisitive flightless weka emerging from the shadows; and watch herons, oystercatchers and kingfishers feeding along the shore, perhaps with a sideshow of porpoises.

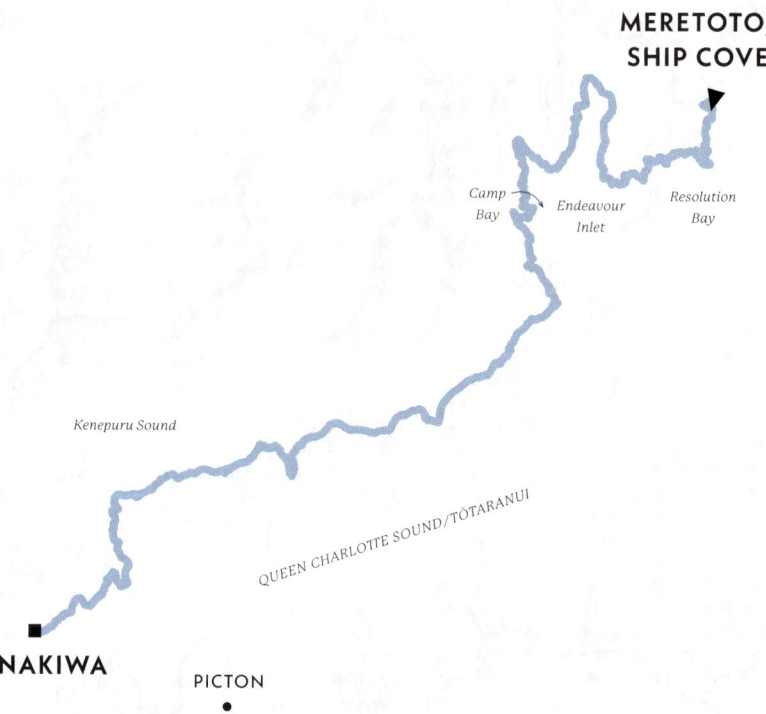

LEFT Trampers along the Queen Charlotte Track. BELOW Māori *pou whenua* at Meretoto. RIGHT Tree ferns frame trailside views near Camp Bay.

'MĀORI HAVE INHABITED TŌTARANUI (QUEEN CHARLOTTE SOUND) FOR CENTURIES, LIVING IN SEASONAL CAMPS OR VILLAGES, AND HARVESTING *KAI MOANA* (SEAFOOD) AND BIRDS.'

After three or four days' walking, the climbs seem less steep, the so-swimmable water yet more magnetic, the peace more mesmerising. Finally you reach, Anakiwa — formerly a Māori settlement that, two centuries ago, was 'a populous place and picturesque in the extreme... Quite a fleet of canoes lay there, ready for use,' as diarist John Salisbury recounted in 1853. Today, you'll see sailboats bobbing at anchor rather than those traditional *waka*, but echoes of the past remain long after you've boarded the boat back to Picton.

Māori myths

THIS REGION is steeped in Māori legends. One tells of the great Pacific navigator Kupe — by convention, the Polynesian ancestor who first arrived in these islands — battling a giant *wheke* (octopus), whose thrashing tentacles gouged out the Marlborough Sounds. Another claims the Sounds formed from the shattered prow of a *waka* (canoe) rowed by gods. Māori have occupied the area for at least eight centuries, and *pou whenua* (carved poles) commemorate their presence at Meretoto.

NATURE / CULTURE / CAMPING / MOUNTAIN

Ciudad Perdida Trek

SIERRA NEVADA DE SANTA MARTA, COLOMBIA

Tackle a challenging hike through the Colombian jungle to discover the remains of the ancient 'Lost City' of Teyuna, high in the Santa Marta Mountains.

Some treks are more tales than trails. Tramping these paths, you feel as if you're a character in a swashbuckling adventure story, each kilometre a fresh episode being written, each day a new chapter on an epic quest. Hence the allure of the hike to the ancient site known to Indigenous people as Teyuna (Mother Nature), but more commonly dubbed La Ciudad Perdida (the 'Lost City'), which rises from the mountainous jungle of the Sierra Nevada de Santa Marta in northern Colombia.

This is real adventure-movie stuff. For some four centuries the site lay hidden from view, swathed in thick jungle and remembered only by local tribespeople. Then, in the 1970s, *guaqueros* (looters) searching for pieces of intricately decorated goldwork – like others found in the region and sold on the black market – stumbled upon the remains of a series of round plazas and terraces high above the Buritaca River. Word got out, and in 1976 archaeologists began excavating and then restoring the site, built by the Tairona people from around 800 CE onwards – centuries before the Aztecs constructed Tenochtitlán or the Incas Machu Picchu.

That was then. Today, Ciudad Perdida can be reached only by way of a challenging return trek from the nearest road. The drier season (December–April) is the time to traverse the humid rainforest, though trails can still be muddy and slippery. It's a couple of days' hike to the camp beneath the ruins, largely along the river – a delicious boon in this sticky climate, with detours to cascading waterfalls and dips in shady pools perfect for cooling off during and after a sweaty day on the trail.

START/FINISH
Typically Machete Pelao

DISTANCE
44km (27 miles) approx.

DURATION
Three to six days

CHALLENGE LEVEL
★ ★ ★

WHEN TO WALK
December–April

LEFT Tagua palms sway above the terraces and plazas of mountaintop Ciudad Perdida, the 'Lost City'.

COLUMBIA

ACCOMMODATION
Hammocks, mattresses and bunks (with mosquito nets).

FOOD
Your guide should provide meals and snacks. Purify drinking water from sources en route.

GETTING THERE
The nearest town is Santa Marta, where tour companies offer guided trips including transfers to a trailhead, usually Machete Pelao village.

PLANNING
The trek must be undertaken with a reputable tour company that can arrange permits. A limited number of hikers are permitted to access Ciudad Perdida each day.

SAFETY
Biting insects are rife – bring lightweight clothes with long sleeves and legs, plus insect repellent. Consult your doctor or travel clinic about vaccinations (particularly yellow fever) and malaria prophylaxis.

The forest is alive with birds, insects, monkeys, peccaries and more. Perhaps more significantly, the region is home to communities of the Indigenous Kogi, Wiwa, Arhuaco and Kankuamo people who may be descended from the ancient Tairona; meeting them and learning about their traditions is a highlight of the trek. You might even encounter a spiritual leader who could explain a little about the rituals conducted at the site, notably in September when it's closed to tourists.

The hike culminates in a challenging climb up some 1200 stone steps to the city itself, at an altitude of around 1000m (3280ft) – and if you weren't puffing after the ascent, the views will take your breath away. Tagua palms sway high above scores of terraces carved into the mountainside and circular plazas upon which wooden buildings once stood – the remains of a metropolis spanning over 30 hectares (80 acres) that may have been home to several thousand Tairona people in its pre-Hispanic

LEFT Ancient staircases link the Ciudad Perdida plazas. **BELOW** The jungle-swathed mountain trail to the Lost City. **RIGHT** Kogi Indigenous village in the Santa Marta range.

'RECHARGE POST-TREK WITH DOWNTIME IN PARQUE NACIONAL NATURAL TAYRONA, HOME TO GOLDEN CARIBBEAN BEACHES AND A WEALTH OF WILDLIFE, FROM JAGUARS TO VIVID MACAWS.'

heyday. Probably the political capital of a complex society based on agriculture and trade, it was equipped with storehouses and water channels, and linked to dozens more settlements in the area as evidenced by a map carved into a stone slab at the site.

No longer an isolated secret, the dry season sees dozens of intrepid trekkers tackling the trail each day – though numbers are limited to preserve the physical and spiritual integrity of this mysterious and magical place.

Tairona legacy

HAVING SETTLED Teyuna around 800 CE, the Tairona are believed to have developed a network of some two dozen towns and villages across the region, cultivating crops on terraced slopes and trading with coastal communities. Spanish colonisation in the 16th century saw them decimated and dispersed by conflict and introduced diseases, but the Kogi people who now inhabit the area are thought to be descendants of the ancient Tairona, and still perform rituals at Ciudad Perdida.

NATURE / FOOD & DRINK / CULTURE

Pekoe Trail

CENTRAL HIGHLANDS, SRI LANKA

START
Hanthana, near Kandy

FINISH
Nuwara Eliya

DISTANCE
323km (201 miles)

DURATION
10–22 days

CHALLENGE LEVEL
★ ★ ★

WHEN TO WALK
December–April

Roam the tea plantations, villages and peaks of Sri Lanka's vivid green heartland to escape the crowds and discover rural life.

Love tea? Sri Lanka's newest long-distance hike will be just your cup of — well, you know. It's in the name: Pekoe is high-grade black tea made with young leaves plucked from plants in Sri Lanka's Central Highlands. And the route winds through tea country, exploring its landscapes, history, culture, food and, of course, drink.

It's a little over two centuries since British colonial incomers recognised ideal tea-growing conditions here (humid, sunny, plenty of rain); the first plantation was established at Loolecondera in 1867 by Scotsman James Taylor. Sri Lanka became a tea-growing powerhouse, with swathes of *Camellia sinensis* carpeting the highlands, and indentured labourers from India drafted in to work the estates.

Tracks and footpaths were created to enable these workers to access the plants, and to transport tea to train stations and on to capital Colombo for shipping. By linking these, Spanish expat Miguel Cunat wove together the Pekoe Trail, aiming to encourage visitors to discover rural life, bring incomes to small highland communities, and meet villagers and 'tea artisans' who pick and produce the drink.

You can hike all 22 stages alone, but it's more enjoyable with a guide — who can identify flowers and plants, spot wildlife and introduce the customs of the people you meet — and most comfortable before late April, when the southwest monsoon rolls in and temperatures climb. Using local buses and attractive rail routes, it's also possible to stitch together shorter stretches, or base yourself in one spot while covering multiple legs. En route you'll visit tea estates and factories, spot sambar deer, macaques and endemic birds in Horton Plains National Park and drink in vistas from viewpoints including Ella Peak. A deliciously refreshing trek.

ACCOMMODATION
Hotels and homestays.

FOOD
Buy lunch supplies at local shops and bakeries, dinners at hotels or restaurants.

GETTING THERE
Kandy is 2½ hours by train from capital Colombo, less by taxi, or a 30-minute flight. Nuwara Eliya–Colombo buses take under five hours.

PLANNING
Buy a Trail Pass (US$10/stage) to access the dedicated app and contribute to the organisation. Joining a local guide or tour operator is recommended.

SAFETY
Consider leech socks and repellent. Carry a hat, sunscreen and plenty of drinking water (purify from sources en route).

INFO
thepekoetrailsrilanka.com

LEFT Picking tea on Sri Lanka's emerald terraces. **TOP** Surveying the Central Highlands from the track to Ella Peak.

MOUNTAIN / COAST / FOOD & DRINK

Island Trails

MADEIRA, PORTUGAL

There's no one route that totally sums up this ruggedly handsome Atlantic outpost – but a week of winter walking showcases its trails at their sunny best.

It's absurd, really, that an island as hiker-friendly as Madeira doesn't have any recognised multiday walking trails. Where's the Madeira Camino? Or the Coast to Coast Traverse? But maybe this tells you all you need to know about this wild isle.

Although Madeira has something of a reputation as a genteel, sedate sort of place, its topography is anything but. Fashioned from black basalt, it's perpetually piercing upwards, diving down, rippling, rucking, rupturing and ravine-ing. The airport had to be built on a platform in the sea because there wasn't a stretch of land flat enough for a runway.

There *is* a cross-island route of sorts. Over the past couple of decades, Madeira has gained popularity among trail runners; the Madeira Island Ultra Trail, which runs for around 115km (70 miles) from Porto Moniz on the northwest coast to Machico in the far east, is a fixture on the global ultramarathon scene. But the MIUT route changes a little every year – in 2024, wildfires ravaged the central mountains, leading to significant alterations – and it isn't waymarked or well-serviced for walkers. Maybe that'll happen one day – but, until then, the best option is to scheme a week of day-walks to enjoy the island's varied terrain.

It's especially appealing as a winter walking option. While much of Europe shivers in January, Madeira – closer to Africa than its Portuguese motherland – promises highs of up to 20°C (68°F). It does rain a fair bit, and conditions can be markedly different depending on which of the island's many microclimates you're in, but you'll likely find decent weather somewhere, whenever you hike.

START/FINISH
Various

DISTANCE
From 3km (2 miles)

DURATION
Seven days

CHALLENGE LEVEL
★★

WHEN TO WALK
Year-round

LEFT Windswept laurel trees near the Laurissilva Forest, on Madeira's PR13 Vereda do Fanal hiking route.

PORTUGAL

Porto Santo

MADEIRA'S LITTLE SISTER
Porto Santo, just a 2½-hour ferry ride northeast, is home to the archipelago's best beach, a long sweep of golden sand running virtually the full length of the island. It's not just a place of tranquil pleasures, though: hikers stretch their legs on the PS PR1 (5.4km/3.3 miles return), a former mule track that leads across the craggy rocks of the Rocha Quebrada up to 450m (1476ft) Pico Branco, the island's second-highest point.

'KNOW THE LINGO: A 'LEVADA' WALK IS A TRAIL ALONGSIDE AN IRRIGATION CHANNEL; A 'VEREDA' IS A MOUNTAIN PATH; 'PR' ROUTES ARE WAYMARKED AND GOVERNMENT-MAINTAINED.'

But where to walk? There are trails everywhere: up amid the jagged mountains, through the precious UNESCO-listed laurel forests, along the historic irrigation channels known as *levadas*. After Madeira was claimed by Portuguese explorers in 1419, it quickly became a major producer of sugarcane, with these artificial channels carrying water to the thirsty fields. Today, more than 2000km (1240 miles) of *levadas* lace the island, and the footpaths running alongside them enable hikers to reach Madeira's most inaccessible spots.

Top trail choices include the moderate-rated PR13 Vereda do Fanal (10.8km/6.7 miles). It starts at the Assobiadores trailhead and crosses the high Paúl da Serra plateau to reach Fanal's mystical, moss-bearded Laurissilva Forest, with views down to the

TOP Beach-blessed Porto Santo is a short ferry hop from Madeira. **LEFT** En route to Porto Santo's Terra Chã on the PS PR1 hike. **RIGHT** The Vereda do Pico Ruivo route includes the ascent of Madeira's highest peak.

PORTUGAL

ACCOMMODATION
Capital Funchal is a good base, with a range of accommodation. Consider moving around the island to access other hiking areas more easily.

FOOD
Local specialties include *espetada* (skewered beef), scabbardfish, *queijada* (curd-cheese pastries) and honey cake.

GETTING THERE
There's a good bus network, but not all trailheads are bus accessible. You may need to use taxis or a hire car.

PLANNING
Non-residents must pay a €3 fee per route to walk Classified trails, in advance online (simplifica.madeira.gov.pt) or on site. Guided tours are available.

SAFETY
Weather varies greatly by altitude and microclimate – be prepared for every eventuality.

INFO
visitmadeira.com

Ribeira da Janela and Chão da Ribeira valleys. The PR8 Vereda da Ponta de São Lourenço (6km/3.7 miles return) explores Madeira's easternmost peninsula, where an arid, otherworldly finger of rock points out into the crashing waves; the brave can take a dip at Cais do Sardinha (winter sea temperatures average around 18°C/64°F).

Combining the popular PR6 Levada das 25 Fontes (8.6km/5.3 miles return) and PR6.1 Levada do Risco (3km/1.8 miles return) showcases the lushness of the interior, following water channels to cascades and secret-feeling, forest-tucked springs. Or stand atop everything by hiking the PR1.2 Vereda do Pico Ruivo (5.6km/3.5 miles return), which tackles 1862m (6109ft) Ruivo, the island's highest point.

NATURE / CULTURE / COAST / CAMPING

Camino de Costa Rica

CENTRAL COSTA RICA

START
Parismina

FINISH
Quepos

DISTANCE
280km (174 miles)

DURATION
10–16 days

CHALLENGE LEVEL
★★★☆☆

WHEN TO WALK
December–April

Hike coast-to-coast across a whole country from the seashores to the wildlife-rich rainforests, providing a boost to rural communities en route.

The Camino de Costa Rica is an amazing adventure and a grand vision: a two-week hike from the Caribbean Sea to the Pacific Ocean across one of the planet's most biodiverse countries, linking a host of offbeat places most travellers just don't reach. It traverses multiple eco-zones, passes though Indigenous settlements and shows off Costa Rica's squawking, howling, buzzing green-ness at its greatest, while helping to support local communities.

The caveat: the trail's in its infancy. It was set up in 2018 by the non-profit Asociación Mar a Mar, which focuses on rural development and works closely with villages along the route. It's not well waymarked or uniformly well-serviced, but a local guide (mandatory for sections in Indigenous reserves) will not only lead the way but organise nights in village houses, cook-ups of *gallo pinto* (traditional beans and rice) made by local people, and even off-trail excursions to raft rapids or soak in hot springs.

Rain is pretty much guaranteed at some point – the country is so green for a reason. But tackling this trek in the 'dry' – December to April – reduces the chances of experiencing too many downpours.

From seaside Parismina, accessible only by boat or plane, the Camino plunges west across palm-tickled coastal plains, into cloudforests and rainforests, and up and over the Continental Divide, reaching its highest point at 2365m (7760ft). It visits wildlife-rich Pacuare Reserve, offers insights into Cabécar culture in the Cabécar Nairi-Awari Indigenous Reserve, crosses the Fila Balalaica range for expansive views, cuts through sugarcane fields and coffee plantations, delves into the Valle de Orosi (a good place to learn about renewable energy) and, finally, finishes on the Pacific's shores.

ACCOMMODATION
Camping platforms and simple guesthouses en route.

FOOD
Some villages have restaurants, many don't – guides can organise meals. Carry plenty of water.

GETTING THERE
Buses run from San José to Siquirres, then to Caño Blanco; from there, taxi ferries connect with Parismina.

PLANNING
The trail isn't well marked. Hire a guide or book a tour.

SAFETY
Some Spanish is helpful. Solo hikers should notify Asociación Mar a Mar before starting.

INFO
caminodecostarica.org

LEFT Hiking a palm-shaded pathway on the country-crossing Camino de Costa Rica. **TOP** Rugged Pacific coastline in Parque Manuel Antonio, near the route's end in Quepos.

FEBRUARY

Approaching Charlotte Pass on the Snowies Alpine Walk, Australia (page 42).

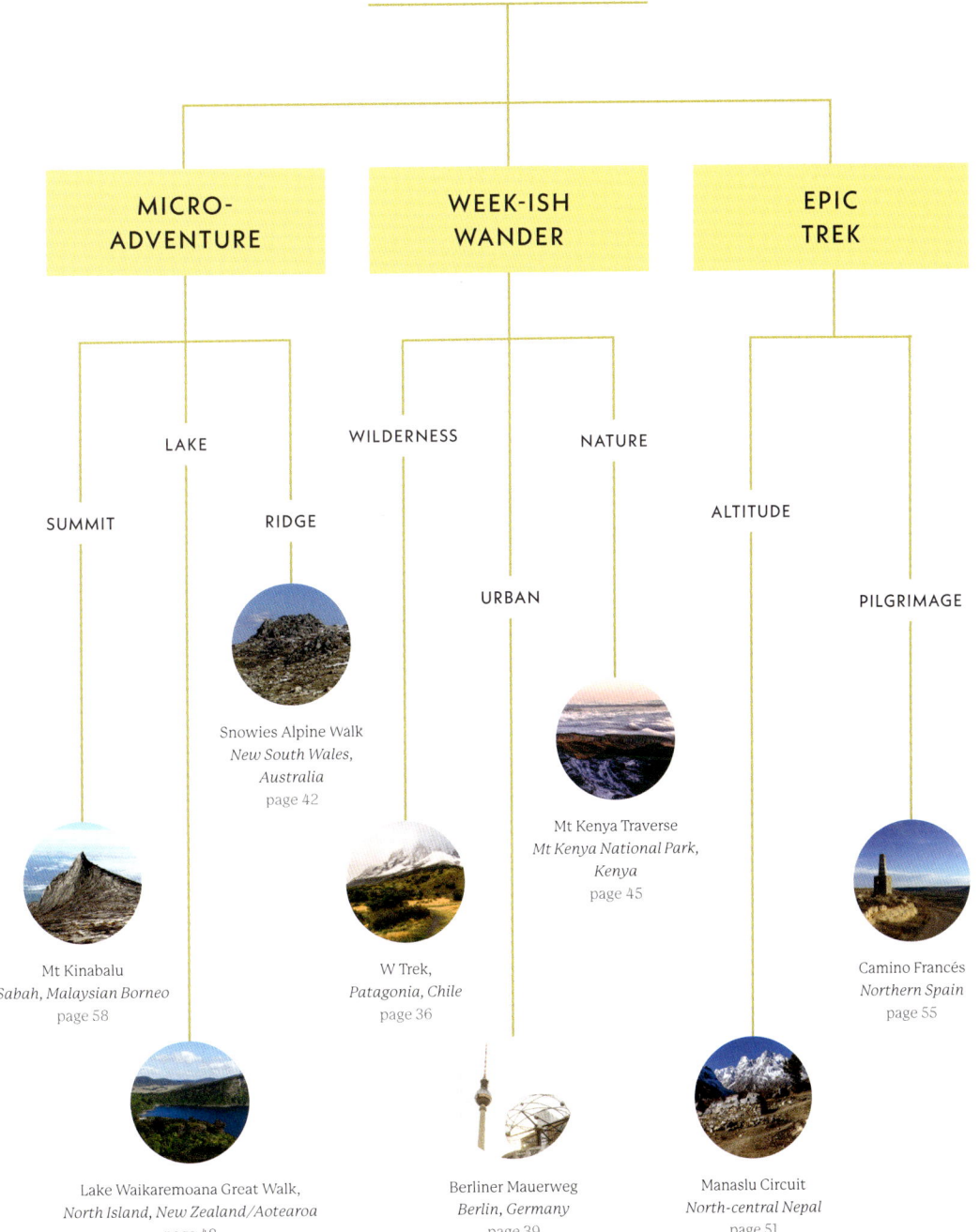

CHILE

NATURE / CAMPING / MOUNTAINS

W Trek

PATAGONIA, CHILE

START
Central Sector, Laguna Amarga

FINISH
Lago Grey

DISTANCE
74km (46 miles)

DURATION
Four to five days

CHALLENGE LEVEL

WHEN TO WALK
October–May

Walk beneath soaring rock pinnacles and alongside glittering glacial lakes, admiring guanacos and other wildlife in this wildest corner of Patagonia's Torres del Paine.

Patagonia isn't quite the end of the Earth – but boy, does it feel a long way from anywhere. And the the epic rock pinnacles, glaciers and glimmering lakes and lagoons of Parque Nacional Torres del Paine are suitably out of this world. They form the backdrop to one of the world's finest short treks: the 'W'.

That letter reflects its shape on a map – but arguably also the wind that buffets hikers as they tramp between the peaks for which the park is named. This region is renowned for weather that changes minute by minute, though the December–February austral summer brings the longest, warmest days (as well as peak tourist numbers: book accommodation well ahead). 'W' could also mean 'wild': you're nigh on guaranteed to encounter guanacos, forebears of domesticated alpacas and llamas, and might even spy puma, huemul deer, flightless rhea – or condor soaring overhead.

That's if you can tear your eyes away from the scenery. Starting – as most do – from Central Sector near the park entrance at Laguna Amarga, the route veers northwest along the Valle Ascencio to the viewpoint for the famed 'blue towers' themselves, soaring pinnacles that glow gold at sunrise but smokey blue at other times. Returning to Central, head southwest alongside milky-turquoise Lago Nordenskjöld and beneath the granite 'horns' of the Cuernos del Paine to the Refugio and Camping Francés. From here, day three leads up Valle Francés on the W's middle stalk, with glimpses of peaks including Hoja (Blade), Espada (Sword) and Fortaleza (Fortress), ending at Paine Grande on Lago Pehoé. Finally, complete the W along the eastern shore of Lago Grey to vast Grey Glacier – an unusually drab moniker to end a trek that's anything but.

ACCOMMODATION
Camping or *refugios* (simple lodges or hostels), which rent camping gear; some hotels.

FOOD
Meals and cooking facilities at *refugios*; carry lunch and water.

GETTING THERE
Puerto Natales–Laguna Amarga buses take about two hours; the return from Lago Grey is three hours.

PLANNING
Buy Parque Nacional Torres del Paine permits online (pasesparques.cl) and book accommodation in advance.

SAFETY
Patagonian weather is notoriously fickle; bring clothing and gear for all conditions.

INFO
torresdelpaine.com

LEFT The jagged horns of the Cuernos del Paine from Lago Pehoé. **TOP** Hiking the W through Parque Nacional Torres del Paine.

FOOD & DRINK / CULTURE

Berliner Mauerweg

BERLIN, GERMANY

Follow what's left of the infamous Cold War barricade around the western half of the German capital for a sobering but fascinating off-season stroll.

Hiking? In Berlin? In February? OK, it is likely to be overcast, damp and certainly chilly (temperatures range from below freezing to 'highs' of around 4°C/39°F), but the German capital is always a fascinating, stimulating place to visit. And it has one of the most thought-provoking of long-distance hiking trails, which can be followed at any time of year – the dour days of winter adding extra poignancy.

The Berliner Mauerweg (Berlin Wall Trail) follows the footprint of the infamous barrier that once encircled the western half of the city. In the aftermath of WWII, when Germany was split in two, Berlin ended up wholly within communist East Germany – even though a portion of the city was part of democratic West Germany. That segment found itself a far-adrift enclave in a politically divergent land. As time progressed, more and more East Germans defected via West Berlin so, from 1961, an increasingly nasty barricade of concrete and barbed wire was built around that patch – a bulwark that wasn't fully demolished until 1992.

Little remains of the wall these days, but hiking the Berliner Mauerweg still immerses you in this not-so-ancient history. It's an easy but emotional route, divided into 14 stages, with public transport serving the ends of each leg. This is useful in winter – if the weather turns truly awful it's easy to hop on a train and retreat to your warm hotel or a cosy Kneipe (neighbourhood pub) instead.

As the trail is a loop it can be started anywhere, though the obvious place to begin is Potsdamer Platz. Once Berlin's busiest square, it was decimated by Allied bombs then bisected by the

START/FINISH
Potsdamer Platz

DISTANCE
160km (100 miles)

DURATION
Seven to 10 days

CHALLENGE LEVEL

WHEN TO WALK
Year-round

LEFT The view to the east through Berlin's signature Brandenburger Tor.

wall and left to fester; today, thankfully, it's buzzing once more. The wall era is easier to imagine at nearby Niederkirchnerstrasse, where a 200m-long (656ft) section of pitted concrete has been preserved and the site of the Gestapo HQ has become the Topography of Terror exhibition. Nearby stands a recreation of the Checkpoint Charlie border crossing, as well as a memorial to teenager Peter Fechter: shot by East German guards while trying to abscond in August 1962, he lay bleeding to death for an hour before his body was moved.

Following the 40km (25 miles) of the trail that zigzag through the heart of the city is a great way to get acquainted with Berlin. It passes the Reichstag and Brandenburger Tor as well as the East Side Gallery – the longest continuous remaining stretch of wall, now daubed with street art – and the chilling fortifications at Bernerstrasse, the only section complete with its original 'death strip' (the multilayered wall's heavily guarded border zone).

ACCOMMODATION
Hotels, hostels and apartments. The trail could be completed as day walks from one base.

FOOD
Readily available along the route. Good on-the-go snacks include currywurst and *Pfannkuchen* (Berlin doughnuts), as well as kebabs, falafel and shawarma.

GETTING THERE
The beginning and end of each section is served by S-Bahn, subway and/or regional trains.

PLANNING
The trail is divided into 14 sections of between 7km (4.5 miles) and 21km (13 miles). Consider buying a daily/weekly transport ticket.

SAFETY
Be aware that cyclists also use the trail. Wrap up warm in cold weather, when surfaces can get icy and slippy.

INFO
berlin.de/mauer/en/wall-trail

LEFT Brezhnev and Honecker embrace in Dmitri Vrubel's iconic East Side Gallery piece. **BELOW** Brutalist brilliance near the Spree River. **RIGHT** The East Side Gallery's *Worlds People* by Schamil Gimajew depicts 40 years of German history.

'WALK PAST THE PARLAMENT DER BÄUME (PARLIAMENT OF TREES), NEAR THE BUNDESTAG – A VERDANT MEMORIAL THAT REMEMBERS THOSE WHO DIED TRYING TO CROSS THE WALL.'

There are reminders out in the suburbs, too, as the trail loops out through Spandau and towards Potsdam, taking in the Grunewald forest and lake country. For instance, around Griebnitzsee and Wannsee, markers commemorate 19-year-old cadet Peter Böhme (killed while trying to escape), border guard Jörgen Schmidtchen (killed trying to prevent Peter escaping) and Herbert Mende (not trying to escape, just wrong place, wrong time). Moving and memorable for so many reasons.

What was the wall?

ON 13 AUGUST 1961, temporary barriers were erected to separate West Berlin from the Soviet sector. Barbed wire was hung, then replaced by concrete, bisecting neighbourhoods. Over time, these fortifications were reinforced and expanded: watchtowers and high fences were erected and an inter-wall no-man's land created that, in some places, was laid with 'asparagus beds' – strips of steel spikes, planted sharp end up. In one way or another, the wall claimed at least 140 lives.

AUSTRALIA

NATURE / MOUNTAINS

Snowies Alpine Walk

NEW SOUTH WALES, AUSTRALIA

START
Guthega Village

FINISH
Bullocks Flat

DISTANCE
56km (35 miles)

DURATION
Four days

CHALLENGE LEVEL

WHEN TO WALK
December–April

New South Wales' newest multiday ridge trek traces a high path through the Snowy Mountains, conquering a succession of summits including the country's tallest, Mt Kosciuszko.

Bigger doesn't always mean better — but sometimes it adds spice to a hike. So it is with this skyscraping trek, tackling some of the higher ridges and peaks of Kosciuszko National Park — including 2228m (7310ft) Mt Kosciuszko, the loftiest summit not just in New South Wales but in all Australia. This is a testing challenge on often exposed trails, involving rock-hopping across the Snowy River and some sheer climbs. But that's not the only reason why it's best walked in summer, when paths are typically clear of snow. It's also wildflower season, when meadows are spangled with purple eyebright, alpine mint, white gentian, yellow billy button and everlasting and yam daisies. Look out, too, for grazing wombats, rare mountain pygmy possums and perhaps short-beaked echidnas, more active and less elusive in the warmer months.

Though not the longest trek, the Snowies Alpine Walk is a point-to-point trail with no public transport, so you'll need to set up transfers and consider accommodation — stay at one place and tackle it in four day-long outings, or move on to a new bed each night?

Day one is an amble along the Snowy River Valley, with an exhilarating crossing of Australia's highest suspension bridge over Spencers Creek. The ante's upped on the Main Range loop, as you conquer Kosciuszko and drink in views of glimmering glacial Blue and Albina Lakes. From Charlotte Pass, the trail veers east along the ridge to the Porcupine Rocks, yielding vistas over the Thredbo Valley and traversing snow gum woodland. The final leg provides glimpses of the Ramshead Range and Monaro Plains as you descend through wildflower-strewn meadows and ash woods — a complete taster of the region's wonderfully diverse landscapes and habitats.

ACCOMMODATION
Ski lodges, resorts, hotels en route; national park cabins and campsites nearby.

FOOD
Bring supplies or eat at restaurants en route.

GETTING THERE
No public transport to trailheads; local providers (see snowymountains.com.au) offer transfers. Nearby Jindabyne is 2½ hours from Canberra by bus.

PLANNING
If driving, buy a pass for Kosciuszko National Park (not required if entering on foot).

SAFETY
Prepare for alpine terrain (including rock-hopping across rivers) and rapidly changing weather; pack accordingly.

INFO
nationalparks.nsw.gov.au

FEB

LEFT Along the Snowies Alpine Walk route through Kosciuszko National Park. **TOP** High-mountain meadowland in the Snowies range.

43

NATURE / CAMPING / MOUNTAINS

Mt Kenya Traverse

MT KENYA NATIONAL PARK, KENYA

Take on Africa's second-highest peak on a trek that combines epic scenery and wildlife-watching with an ascent like no other.

There are several reasons not to take an ascent of Kenya's roof lightly. There's the altitude, of course: its tallest prominence, Batian, soars 5199m (17,057ft) above sea level, and nearby sister Nelion is just a fraction lower. They're both technical climbing peaks requiring experience and equipment, but even the trekker's destination, Point Lenana, is at a lung-emptying 4985m (16,355ft) — easily enough to wallop incautious (or too-speedy) hikers with altitude sickness. The terrain isn't the toughest, true — but you'll likely tackle the final scramble to the summit in the small hours when temperatures plummet to -15°C (5°F), rendering fingers icy and heads swimmy.

Oh, and did we mention that you're venturing into the home of a god? According to the traditional beliefs of Kenya's Kikuyu people, this is the seat of the creator deity Ngai. In short, you might want to watch where you step. Certainly, plan your climb for drier months — February being pretty much optimal.

You'd expect a god's domain to be spectacular — and Mt Kenya doesn't disappoint. At the centre of its namesake 715-sq-km (276-sq-mile) national park — a UNESCO World Heritage Site and Biosphere Reserve — looms this long-extinct volcano. Last active some three million years ago, it's been sculpted by wind, rain and, notably, ice: a dozen glaciers have gouged valleys down Mt Kenya's slopes, exposing its volcanic core as jagged pinnacles.

Though Point Lenana is some 900m (2953ft) lower than Uhuru Peak on Africa's highest mountain, Kilimanjaro, in many ways Mt Kenya is a more rewarding hike. For one thing, it's quieter, and largely less a straight uphill slog. There are options to

START
Sirimon Gate

FINISH
Chogoria Gate

DISTANCE
52km (32 miles)

DURATION
Five to six days

CHALLENGE LEVEL

WHEN TO WALK
January–March
& July–October

LEFT Sunrise over the summit near Shipton's Camp, from where the final leg of the Mt Kenya ascent begins.

Mountain wildlife

THOUGH THIS isn't a safari, you'll encounter plentiful wildlife on Mt Kenya. Amid the lower montane forest, watch for zebras, baboons, monkeys and elephants. Eland graze on the heather-speckled moorland around Moses Hut, and charismatic bird species include alpine chats and gleaming blue-green malachite sunbirds. One animal you can't avoid is the hyrax (or dassie), a curious mammal like a cross between a rabbit and a marmot that hangs around huts hoping to beg or steal food.

'KENYA WAS NAMED FOR THE PEAK THAT LOOMS AT ITS CENTRE, KNOWN TO THE KIKUYU PEOPLE AS KĨRĨNYAGA OR KERE-NYAGA (MOUNTAIN OF WHITENESS) FOR ITS SNOWCAPPED SUMMIT.'

stay in simple huts (not viable on most Kili routes) and, importantly, it's a scenic and biodiverse delight.

Six established trails radiate out (or, rather, up to) the summits, though only three are realistic propositions for most hikers. To appreciate the best the mountain has to offer, many combine two of these, ascending from the Sirimon Gate in the northwest, then descending east to the Chogoria Gate. All hikers need a qualified, experienced guide, and most tour companies use a team of porters (monitored to ensure they're not overladen) to lug most of your kit between overnight stops; plentiful hot food is part of the package, whether you're camping or hutting.

The first stretch from Sirimon Gate traverses montane forest that gives way to bamboo, then hagenia and eventually high moorland studded with giant heather. Overnight at Old Moses

TOP Black-and-white colobus monkey, Mt Kenya National Park. **LEFT** Harris Tarn, on the path to the summit. **RIGHT** Golden hour lights up Point Lenana, Mt Kenya's highest peak.

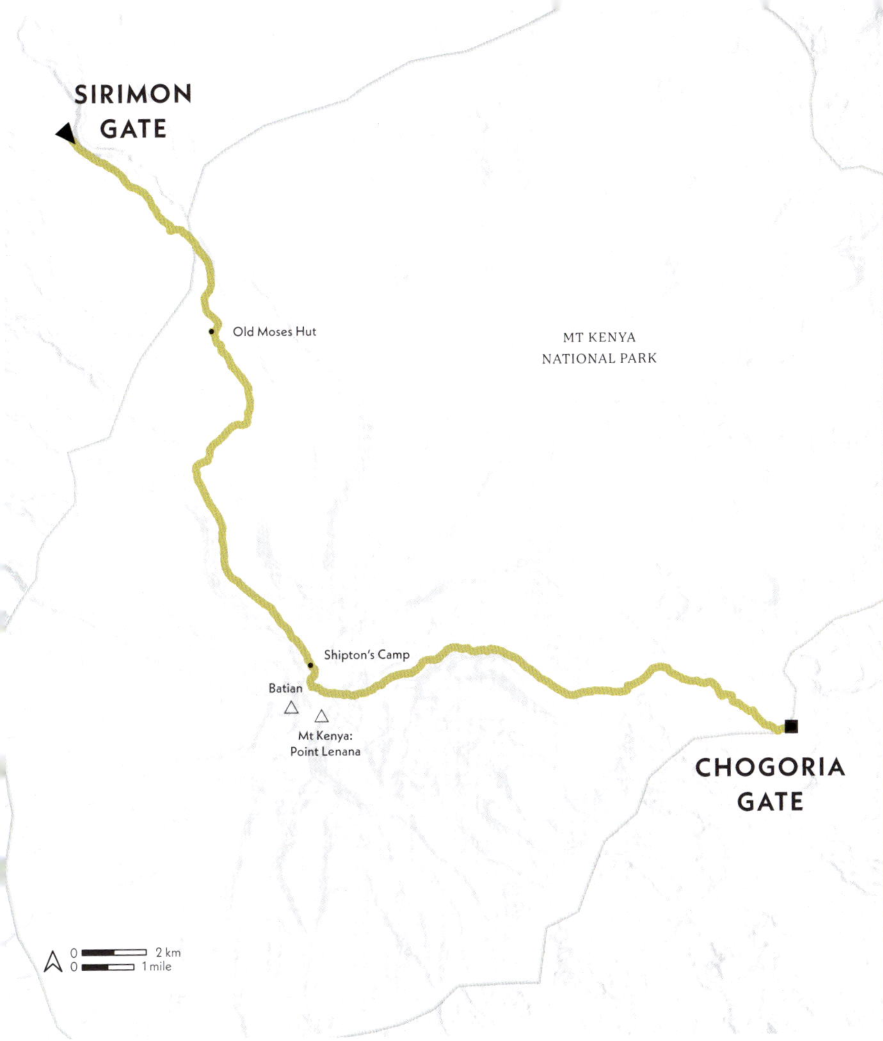

KENYA

ACCOMMODATION
Camping or very basic huts with bunks — bring a sleeping bag and warm clothes.

FOOD
Plenty of sustaining meals will be provided by your trekking support team. Bring snacks and prepare to purify water.

GETTING THERE
Sirimon Gate is around four hours' drive from Nairobi's Jomo Kenyatta International Airport; Chogoria Gate is slightly further away by road.

PLANNING
Book a guided, supported trek with a reputable operator, locally or in your home country.

SAFETY
Point Lenana is extremely cold and breath-snatchingly high — climb slowly to reduce the risk of altitude sickness, heed your guide's advice, and dress warmly.

INFO
kws.go.ke

Hut and continue up along glacial valleys populated by phalanxes of tall lobelias and giant groundsels.

Summit night is spent at Shipton's Camp, where hyrax descend to pilfer food from unwary visitors. Rise several hours before dawn to clamber up rocky slopes and scree to Point Lenana as the sun rises, setting Batian and Nelion aflame and revealing 360-degree views across park, glaciers, coffee plantations and beyond.

Descending east towards Chogoria, you'll enjoy the most dramatic landscapes: cliffs, lakes, waterfalls, cirques and the rock amphitheatre known as the Temple — a suitably heavenly end to a divine hike.

NEW ZEALAND/AOTEAROA

NATURE / CULTURE / CAMPING

Lake Waikaremoana Great Walk

NORTH ISLAND, NEW ZEALAND/AOTEAROA

START
Onepoto

FINISH
Hopuruahine (or vice versa)

DISTANCE
46km (28.5 miles)

DURATION
Three to four days

CHALLENGE LEVEL
★★☆☆☆

WHEN TO WALK
October–May

Tackle a remote Great Walk in a lush North Island wilderness that's rich in nature and Māori heritage.

Less a hike, more an extended forest-bathing experience, this lakeside route offers an immersive introduction to the human and natural history of Te Urewera — a region recognised in law as a living person. This is the traditional homeland of the Ngāi Tūhoe, the *iwi* (tribe) known as the 'Children of the Mist', who care for the tracks as well as the environment. A swathe of undulating emerald greenery, it's the epitome of New Zealand's primal wilderness, encompassing North Island's largest expanse of native forest. Midsummer, when sunshine is most likely to sparkle off Lake Waikaremoana, is the perfect time to hike.

You can start at either end of the horseshoe-shaped route, though most set out from Onepoto. 'Most' being relative: hikers are sparse compared with other Great Walks. Wildlife, though — well, that's not so scarce. Over three or four days, starting with the steady haul up to Panekire Bluffs and ridge for sweeping lake views, you'll traverse rainforest and 'goblin forest', wetland and scrub, grassy flats and shoreline stretches, misty valleys and hillsides striped with cascades. Among the rimu, red beech, tōtara, rātā and many other tree species, you might spy — or hear — almost any of North Island's native forest birds. You'll be regaled by the piping, trilling, whistling call of the tūī, and the soft cooing of the kererū (wood pigeon). Come nightfall, when you're relaxing in one of the cheerful huts or campsites en route, the repeated whistling of a male kiwi tells you that New Zealand's national bird is foraging nearby. Immersion in nature never felt so accessible or rewarding.

ACCOMMODATION
Heated huts with bunks, toilets and water, plus campsites.

FOOD
Bring supplies; purify drinking water.

GETTING THERE
You'll need to organise transport to your chosen start point; parking is most convenient near Onepoto. Water taxis (see ngaituhoe.iwi.nz) link both ends of the trail between October and April.

PLANNING
Book campsites or huts (via bookings.doc.govt.nz) as early as possible.

SAFETY
Pack for rapidly changing weather and be aware of potentially slippery trails.

INFO
doc.govt.nz

LEFT See Te Urewera from on high along the Lake Waikaremoana Track. **TOP** The pristine lakeside along a shoreline section of the route.

FEB

NEPAL

NATURE / CULTURE / MOUNTAINS

Manaslu Circuit

NORTH-CENTRAL NEPAL

Trek between Tibetan Buddhist villages and Himalayan summits, through bamboo forests, across yak-grazed meadows and over lung-busting passes in a remote and magical region.

The first rays of the rising sun catch the highest peak on the horizon. Twin fangs glow fiery red then pearly white: a beacon, a challenge, a dream. This is Manaslu, the 'Mountain of the Spirit', fulcrum of an epic trekking circuit that wheels through some of Nepal's most inspiring and diverse landscapes and settlements.

By some criteria, this is not a wealthy nation. Yet if measured by the richness of its heritage and wildlife plus awe-inspiring scenic wonders – its generous slice of the Himalaya includes eight of the world's 10 tallest peaks – Nepal has almost incomparable riches. Surging rivers powered by glacial icemelt carve dramatic valleys and gorges between those summits. Traditional villages speckle terraced slopes. Rhododendron forests and dense bamboo stands cede at higher altitudes to larch forests, then high pastures where yaks browse.

Trekkers seeking these marvels, but eager to sidestep the masses that throng better-known routes – particularly Everest Base Camp and Annapurna Circuit – are only now discovering the spectacular and gloriously diverse loop winding around the world's eighth-tallest peak, 8163m (26,782ft) Manaslu, a little southeast of the Annapurna massif. Out of bounds for foreigners until the 1990s, it was then clobbered by the devastating earthquake of 2015.

Today, though, it's a real Goldilocks option: relatively comfortable teahouse lodges have opened, yet the paths are quiet even during peak trekking season (late autumn or late winter, when

START
Machhi Khola

FINISH
Jagat

DISTANCE
175km (110 miles) approx

DURATION
12 days, plus acclimatisation days

CHALLENGE LEVEL

WHEN TO WALK
October–November & February–April

LEFT The Manaslu Circuit trek delivers ever-changing views of monumental Himalayan summits.

ACCOMMODATION
Simple teahouses (lodges) with basic bathroom facilities.

FOOD
Lots of *dal bhat* – platters of vegetable curries, lentil dal, rice and poppadom – plus occasional welcome *momos* (Tibetan dumplings) and *thukpa* (Tibetan noodle soup). Purify drinking water from sources en route.

GETTING THERE
Kathmandu to Machhi Khola is around eight hours' drive; the return from Jagat is a little longer.

PLANNING
Guides and permits are mandatory; book with a reputable tour company. Sherpas (porters) typically carry most luggage.

SAFETY
Most of the trek is above 2500m (8200ft), and the Larkya La is double that, so altitude sickness is a risk; walk slowly, drink plenty of water and always follow guides' instructions.

rain and snow are scarce and temperatures brisk but not too bitter). It's far enough from Kathmandu and Pokhara to deter casual walkers, but not too difficult to access; testing enough but with a gradual ascent for slow, steady acclimatisation.

That haul starts at a trailhead southeast of Manaslu itself, typically Machhi Khola, still relatively warm and low at around 900m (2953ft). Over the following 12 days, altitude and fitness levels gradually build as you wind anticlockwise around the massif, the route marked by subtle changes in habitat and culture. The valley narrows as you trek alongside the mineral-milky Buri Gandaki River, with bamboo thickets shading the trail and mule trains jostling for space on swaying suspension bridges.

Approaching the border, the influence of Tibetan culture becomes ever more clear: *mani* stones and walls line the path, inscribed with the ubiquitous Buddhist mantra of Avalokiteshvara. A good guide (mandatory) will share the meanings of the

LEFT Prayer flags at the breath-snatching saddle of Larkya La.
BELOW Samdo village, on the Manaslu Circuit near Larkya La.
RIGHT Pack mules cross the Buri Gandaki River, near the Manaslu trailhead at Machhi Khola

'THE MANASLU AREA'S SNOW LEOPARDS, RED PANDAS AND HIMALAYAN TAHR ARE ELUSIVE, BUT YOU'LL CERTAINLY SPOT GREY LANGUR MONKEYS AND MANY OF THE 100-PLUS BIRD SPECIES.'

colourful murals that adorn monastery walls, the rainbow-hued prayer flags fluttering overhead, the libraries of sacred texts, the huge prayer wheels rotating slowly in village shrines.

It's a journey of mind and soul as well as body – though you'll feel it in the latter, too, as legs push ever upwards and lungs are emptied ever quicker. And never more so than on the ascent of the Larkya La, a 5106m (16,752ft) saddle that snatches your breath and freezes your fingers – but also yields extraordinary views of 7000m-plus (23,000ft) peaks: Kang Garu, Himlung Himal, Annapurna II and of course Manaslu itself. The Mountain of the Spirit will surely set yours soaring.

Tibetan culture

PARTICULARLY AT higher altitudes close to the border with China, Tibetan Buddhist culture dominates. The trail is studded with *mani* stones and walls inscribed with mantras and Buddha images. Stupas are lined with prayer wheels and gateways decorated with colourful mythological murals and mandalas. Visits to Buddhist *gompas* (monasteries) and shrines are highlights; climb to Pungyen Gompa from Samagaon for insights into Buddhist beliefs and culture, and the chance to acclimatise to the thin air at altitudes of above 3500m (11,483ft).

NATURE / CULTURE / FOOD & DRINK

Camino Francés

NORTHERN SPAIN

Hike in the winter months for a calmer, less-crowded and arguably more spiritual take on the Camino de Santiago, the world's most popular Christian pilgrimage trail.

Pilgrims have been making the trek to Santiago de Compostela since soon after the remains of Saint James were (reputedly) rediscovered here in the 9th century. The practice then fell out of fashion for several centuries, till it found a new audience over the past few decades. As the desire for more meaningful, mindful travel surged, so too has the desire to walk the Camino – around half a million people now tackle it each year.

Over peak season, from late spring to autumn, in excess of 60,000 souls journey to the Galician city each month to pay their respects at the apostle's tomb and earn their certificate for completing this age-old walk. In the winter months, from December to February, that number falls below 3000.

True, pilgrim camaraderie is a significant part of this walk. But for those hankering after a more solitary, contemplative experience among far sparser crowds, winter is prime time. The way ahead will be much emptier, allowing for silent moments immersed in both nature and your own thoughts. And the bonds you make with those pilgrims you do encounter will likely be all the stronger: you are a select group who have chosen to add extra challenge to what's already an extraordinary journey. Or, rather, journeys: there are several Caminos, starting from distant points in France, Portugal, southern Spain and elsewhere.

By far the most popular of all the 'Ways of St James' is the classic Camino Francés, which begins near the French–Spanish border and wends west, taking a month or so to complete. Waymarked by scallop shells (the traditional symbol of Saint James), the Francés first crosses the Pyrenees, then snakes across

START
St-Jean-Pied-de-Port, France

FINISH
Santiago de Compostela, Spain

DISTANCE
780km (485 miles)

DURATION
30–35 days

CHALLENGE LEVEL

WHEN TO WALK
September–June

LEFT Marvellous mountain views along the Camino Francés route as it tracks through the Pyrenees.

The Winter Way

THE WINTER WAY (aka Camino de Invierno) was created in medieval times as a winter alternative to the Francés. This 263km (163-mile) route starts in the handsome town of Ponferrada, peeling away from the classic trail to take a longer but lower-altitude route to Santiago via the Ribeira Sacra region, a place of Romanesque monasteries and rolling vineyards. This lesser-tramped way avoids potentially snowy O Cebreiro as well as the busy final 100km (62 miles) of the Francés.

'OTHER POPULAR CAMINO ROUTES INCLUDE THE PORTUGUÉS, FROM LISBON THROUGH CENTRAL PORTUGAL; AND THE ATLANTIC-HUGGING PORTUGUÉS COASTAL, WHICH BEGINS IN PORTO.'

northern Spain via Navarre's hills, the vine-striped slopes of Rioja, Castilla y León's endless *meseta* plains and, finally, bucolic Galicia. En route lie ancient cities such as Pamplona, Burgos, León and Astorga (rich in Roman ruins), plus rippling fields, tiny chapels, traditional villages and a wealth of pilgrim facilities. The climax is Santiago de Compostela itself — a UNESCO-listed maze of cobbled streets leading to the flamboyant cathedral inside which Saint James rests.

LEFT The pilgrims' path alongside Burgos' UNESCO-listed Gothic cathedral. **RIGHT** Vicente Galbete's Monumento al Peregrino overlooks the Camino Francés route from its hilltop site in Navarre.

ACCOMMODATION
Albergues have dorms plus shared bathrooms and kitchens. Hotels, *hostales* and *pensiónes* offer private rooms.

FOOD
Many restaurants serve a *menú del peregrino*, typically a starter, main, dessert and drink (water/wine). Carry other supplies.

GETTING THERE
St-Jean-Pied-de-Port has a train station; connections from major hubs usually require a change of trains in Bayonne.

PLANNING
Research winter accommodation options. Hikers require a *credencial* (pilgrim's passport) to stay in *albergues*. The high-altitude Napoleon Route over the Pyrenees is closed November–March; alternatives are available.

SAFETY
Wear warm layers. Allow extra days in your schedule as a buffer in case of bad weather.

INFO
oficinadelperegrino.com

Yes, tackling the Camino in winter is a little more challenging. You can expect shorter days, frosty mornings, biting winds, temperatures perhaps below zero and higher chances of rain and snow. The good news is that, though some *albergues* (pilgrim hostels), hotels, bars and restaurants close, there is enough passing trade on this route to ensure a sufficient number remain open – you just need to plan ahead. Whenever you do come across a spot serving *café con leche* and hearty bowls of *patatas bravas* (spicy potatoes), take the opportunity to pause and warm up.

Winter here has its own beauty, too. The landscapes are laid bare, hills perhaps dusted with snow, skeletal trees and church towers brought into sharp, striking focus against crisp blue skies. As nature lies at peace before its spring reawakening, so winter pilgrims may find a similar calm before their own rebirth at trail's end. ¡*Buen Camino!*

MALAYSIA

NATURE / MOUNTAINS

Mt Kinabalu

SABAH, MALAYSIAN BORNEO

START/FINISH
Timpohon Gate

DISTANCE
16km (10 miles) round-trip

DURATION
Two days

CHALLENGE LEVEL
★★★★☆

WHEN TO WALK:
February–April

Summit Borneo's roof on a testing ascent that rewards with tropical wildlife and eye-popping views across this island of natural wonders.

A climb isn't always just a climb. Sure, to conquer Borneo's loftiest peak you'll need to tackle 20,000-plus steps (and the same on the way down, of course) – but that's hardly the point. Because the namesake park surrounding Mt Kinabalu (4095m/13,435ft), the highest summit between the Himalayas and New Guinea, is also Malaysia's first UNESCO World Heritage Site, a biodiversity hotspot packed with animal and plant species.

Various mammals inhabit the forests here – gibbons, tarsiers, slow loris, leaf monkeys, fruit bats, pygmy squirrels, orangutans – but many are shy, nocturnal or treetop-dwelling, so hard to spot. You will see some of the hundreds of species of butterflies, insects, spiders and birds – likely including the extraordinary rhinoceros hornbill. But the headline acts are flora, numbering more than 5000 species and including the world's largest flower, rafflesia, with blooms of up to 1m (3ft) across that stink of rotting flesh. And in drier February to April, you can enjoy the rainforest with a little less rain (though Borneo's never exactly arid).

That's the backdrop to a hike that ascends from the park gate at 1866m (6122ft) to the resthouse at Laban Rata, set at a breathless 3272m (10,735ft), for the pre-summit night. Fuel up well here – you'll need plenty of energy. To stand atop needle-like Low's Peak at dawn, set out around 2am. At this altitude, cold and oxygen-starved limbs complain as you trudge ever up, crossing elephant-skin-cracked igneous rock above the treeline, clambering over boulders as the sky pales and pinkens, and ridges, crags and gullies emerge from the darkness. Then the peak, and payback: the rising sun hits, mist swathes the forest, and you gaze across a sea of cloud below.

ACCOMMODATION
Private rooms and dorms at Laban Rata Resthouse and Panalaban Hostel.

FOOD
Laban Rata has a restaurant and grocery shop.

GETTING THERE
Buses from Kota Kinabalu to the park entrance take four hours, taxis under two hours.

PLANNING
Park conservation fee, climbing permit fee and registered guide mandatory; insurance additional. Book your slot in advance. Bring Malaysian ringgit cash for the overnight stay.

SAFETY
Altitude sickness is a risk. Bring suitable footwear, warm layers and a headtorch.

INFO
sabahparks.org.my

LEFT Set out from Laban Rata in the early hours to reach Mt Kinabalu's summit by sunrise. **TOP** Views of cloud-swathed Kinabalu National Park from its namesake peak.

MARCH

Cherry blossom at Ryōzen-ji, start of the 88 Temple Pilgrimage on Shikoku, Japan (page 69).

MARCH

I WANT A HIKE THAT'S A…

MICRO-ADVENTURE

WEEK-ISH WANDER

EPIC TREK

CULTURE

CLIFFS

MOUNTAINS

JUNGLE

COAST

ANCIENT WONDERS

PILGRIMAGE

FOOD

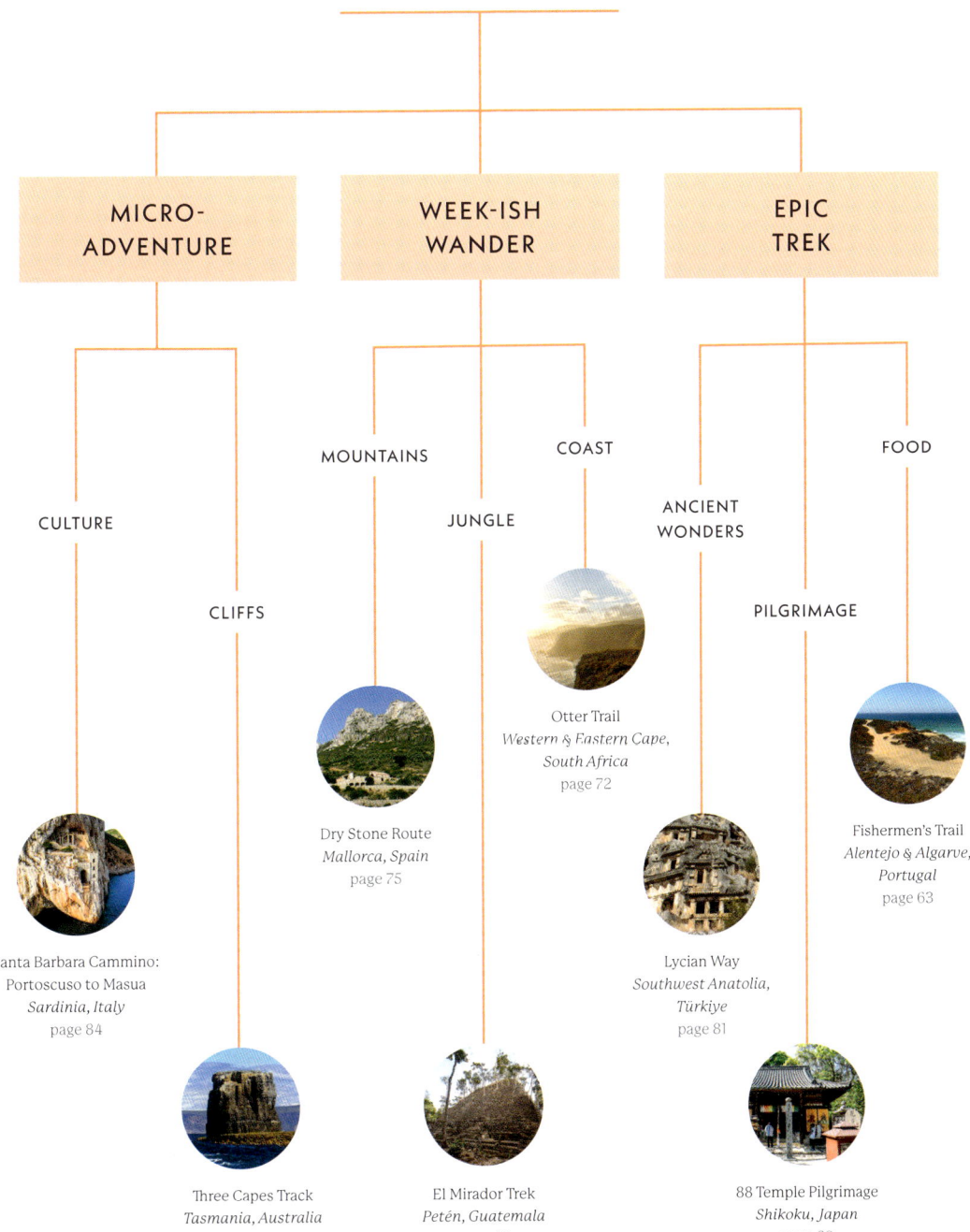

Santa Barbara Cammino: Portoscuso to Masua
Sardinia, Italy
page 84

Three Capes Track
Tasmania, Australia
page 78

Dry Stone Route
Mallorca, Spain
page 75

El Mirador Trek
Petén, Guatemala
page 68

Otter Trail
Western & Eastern Cape, South Africa
page 72

Lycian Way
Southwest Anatolia, Türkiye
page 81

88 Temple Pilgrimage
Shikoku, Japan
page 69

Fishermen's Trail
Alentejo & Algarve, Portugal
page 63

61

MAR

NATURE / FOOD & DRINK / COAST

Fishermen's Trail

ALENTEJO & ALGARVE, PORTUGAL

Hike a coastal epic, ambling wildflower-strewn clifftops, white-sand beaches and past comely fishing settlements where white storks nest, sampling sensational seafood along the way.

Portugal's southwest coast has a magnetic allure: it simply demands return visits. Just ask the white storks that come back each spring, the monogamous pairs building oversized nests atop chimneys, bell towers and rock stacks. For them, the appeal of this place is clear: ample sunshine and clean air, peace to raise their broods, and plenty of fish, frogs and invertebrates to eat.

The draws for walkers this season are not so very different. The spectacular shoreline of the Parque Natural do Sudoeste Alentejano e Costa Vicentina (Southwest Alentejo and Costa Vicentina Natural Park) intersperses golden-sand beaches and windswept cliffs with cork-oak stands, orange groves, and traditional fishing villages and towns where the freshest seafood sizzles in friendly restaurants. As spring progresses, constellations of wildflowers cover the clifftops, and more birdlife throngs the skies and seas. In short, hiking heaven.

Yet the Alentejo, sandwiched between capital Lisbon and the better-known Algarve, is strangely under-explored. Spanning nearly one-third of Portugal's land area, it's home to just 5% of its population – leaving ample empty space between its hilltop castles, ancient monuments and bijou villages for hikers to roam.

Thanks to the creation of a trail network dubbed the Rota Vicentina, launched in 2012, the Alentejo's natural, cultural and culinary delights are finally being discovered by hikers. Its flagship route, the Fishermen's Trail, rivals coastal paths worldwide for scenic spectacle, gastronomy, cultural insights

START
Praia de São Torpes (near Sines)

FINISH
Lagos (or vice versa)

DISTANCE
226km (140 miles)

DURATION
10–13 days

CHALLENGE LEVEL

WHEN TO WALK
March–June
& September–November

LEFT The Atlantic meets the Alentejo coast along the Fishermen's Trail.

and sheer walking bliss. Winding around Portugal's southwest headland to finish in Lagos, Algarve, it now covers some 226km (140 miles) – a comfortable two-week walk, but easy to break down into shorter chunks. For example, the first five sections, from Praia de São Torpes (near Sines) to Odeceixe, traverses the entire shoreline of the Alentejo – an achievable and satisfying mini-adventure.

If you've time to tackle the whole route, though, the rewards are luminous. As the name suggests, fishing boats bob off white-washed settlements – enchanting hamlets such as Entrada da Barca, jaunty towns like Porto Covo, and comely Vila Nova de Milfontes, its early 17th-century Forte de São Clemente standing sentinel above its estuary. The daily catch is cooked up into various delights, from simple grilled fish to more sophisticated dishes using favourite ingredients like eel, prawn, sardines, octopus and *percebes* (goose barnacles).

ACCOMMODATION
Guesthouses, hotels and campsites.

FOOD
Many cafes, restaurants and food stores. Unsurprisingly, fish and seafood are fantastic – try *açorda* (bread and garlic seafood soup) and *cataplana* (fish stew), washed down with a glass of crisp local Alvarinho white.

GETTING THERE
From Sines, served by buses from Lisbon (two hours), it's a 15-minute taxi or drab 1½-hour walk to Praia de São Torpes. Lagos has good public transport connections, including to the nearest airport at Faro.

PLANNING
No permits required. Navigation is straightforward: follow blue and green arrows and signs.

SAFETY
Be wary of crumbling cliff edges.

INFO
rotavicentina.com

LEFT Fishing is alive and well in the Alentejo; sample fresh-caught fruits of the sea at restaurants along the route. **RIGHT** Tantalising Alentejo views from the Fishermen's Trail.

'SPRING FESTOONS THE COSTA VICENTINA WITH WILDFLOWERS, FROM WHITE ROCK-ROSE TO A DELICATE, MAGENTA-FLOWERED KNAPWEED FOUND NOWHERE ELSE ON EARTH.'

And it's not just those storks feasting on the region's bounty. Bonelli eagles and egrets nest here; you might see fishing ospreys and red-billed choughs wheeling above the cliffs and, if you're very lucky, perhaps a lithe otter. Terrain is pleasingly diverse; steep cliffs in various hues are broken by countless beaches tempting trekkers to haul off boots and cool feet in the Atlantic surf.

The route becomes more undulating as it dips south into the Algarve, veering inland to the ancient village of Aljezur, dominated by its medieval castle ruins, and continuing to mainland Portugal's southwesternmost point, Cabo de São Vicente, whose fort was rebuilt after being destroyed by English navigator Francis Drake in 1587. All in all, a treat for feet, stomach and mind.

Vicentina variants

THIS IS one of two long-distance trails devised to nurture sustainable tourism in this long-overlooked corner. The alternative Historical Way traces a 263km (163-mile) mainly inland route between Santiago do Cacém and Cabo de São Vicente. Traversing cork-oak forests, hills, valleys and villages, and waymarked with red-and-white signs, it's a deep-dive into the cultural and natural heritage of rural Portugal. In addition, 24 circular day-walks have been mapped and waymarked (with red-and-yellow signs).

NATURE / CULTURE / CAMPING

El Mirador Trek

PETÉN, GUATEMALA

START/FINIS
Carmelita

DISTANCE
96km (60 miles) approx

DURATION
Five to six days

CHALLENGE LEVEL
★★★☆☆

WHEN TO WALK
December–April

This hike into Guatemala's tropical forests not only reveals the remnants of lost civilisations – it makes you wonder what else the jungle has to hide.

If you're going to hike into the sprawling, teeming jungle of Guatemala's Petén region, do it now, during the drier season. Trails will be less swampy, the air a smidgen cooler, the mosquitoes less rapacious – better conditions for a foray in search of a lost city.

Centuries before the flourishing of Tikal, the Maya city of El Mirador rose to prominence further north. At its peak (from 300 BCE to 150 CE), it was twice as big as Tikal – now Guatemala's headline Maya site – and home to over 100,000 people. Later, El Mirador was abandoned and eventually subsumed by the forest. Rediscovered as recently as the 1930s, it's still only partially excavated, and lies far from any roads. Unless you have a helicopter, the only way to get there is on foot.

An out-and-back route leaves from the village of Carmelita. Hire guides and muleteers here, and load up with supplies before plunging into the twitter-full, critter-full jungle – nights are atmospheric, camping out in these noisy environs. Sometimes the trail weaves amid *bajos* (swamps), straggly lianas and chechen trees (with toxic sap), soundtracked by screeching howler monkeys; sometimes it follows *sacbeob*, the Maya's raised and stuccoed 'white roads'.

There are ancient sites along the way. At El Tintal – a popular place to camp – explore the remains of some 850 structures, including a vast ball court. Or detour to the crumbling platforms, temples and causeways of Nakbé. But El Mirador is the main goal. Trekkers camp near the researchers' buildings – archaeologists conduct ongoing work in the wet season – to spend a day exploring the jungle-swallowed ruins. The highlight is the view from atop 72m-high (236ft) La Danta – the tallest Maya pyramid ever built.

ACCOMMODATION
There's a hotel in Carmelita, and campsites on the route (you'll sleep in tents or hammocks).

FOOD
Guided tours provide hearty meals. Independent hikers will need to pack all provisions and cooking kit.

GETTING THERE
A bus runs from Flores to Carmelita.

PLANNING
It's not illegal to hike solo, but joining a guided tour is highly recommended.

SAFETY
Use insect repellent, watch out for snakes and spiders, and stay well hydrated – purify all drinking water.

MAR

LEFT Muleteers and hikers trek through lush Guatemalan jungle en route to El Mirador. **TOP** Taking in the view from atop El Mirador's La Danta pyramid.

CULTURE / NATURE / COAST / MOUNTAINS

88 Temple Pilgrimage

SHIKOKU, JAPAN

This island-looping long-distance trail between a series of sacred Buddhist places is an epic walk and a deep insight into Japanese culture and beliefs.

To walk so far, with the purpose of ending up exactly where you started – that's quite the undertaking. But such is the goal of the Shikoku Pilgrimage, which completes a circuit of Japan's fourth-largest island. It's designed to visit the 88 temples that represent the 88 evils of human life, as defined by Shingon Buddhism. The founding father of this strand of Buddhism was Kūkai – also known as Kōbō Daishi – who was born in Shikoku in 774 CE, within the grounds of Zentsū-ji (Temple 75). He became an itinerant monk, wandering near and far, seeking knowledge and enlightenment in the wilderness. This historic hike follows in his spiritual footsteps.

The starting point is not important, so long as a full circuit is completed. However, as the practice of visiting all these temples became popular, guidebooks were written; a volume published in 1687 recorded the 88 temples in order and formalised a route. These days, most *aruki henro* (walking pilgrims) begin at Ryōzen-ji, in Shikoku's northeast and numbered Temple 1; they typically then walk *jun-uchi* – in a clockwise direction.

Of course, many *henro* don't complete the whole route in one go, but choose to employ the *kugiri-uchi* method. This involves covering the pilgrimage in stages, sometimes over several years, or perhaps ticking off the legs in the four prefectures – Tokushima, Kōchi, Kagawa, Ehime – over four trips. Many people don't walk at all, undertaking the pilgrimage by riding one of the popular *henro* buses.

Spring, with pleasantly mild temperatures and lower rainfall, is peak pilgrimage season; by summer, humidity is high and

START/FINISH
Ryōzen-ji

DISTANCE
1200km (746 miles)

DURATION
40–50 days

CHALLENGE LEVEL

WHEN TO WALK:
March–May
& October–November

LEFT Zentsū-ji (Temple 75) was the birthplace of Kōbō Daishi, the founding father of Shingon Buddhism.

JAPAN

Hiking style

TRADITIONAL HENRO have a certain look. They wear a conical sedge hat to protect from sun and rain, a white vest to indicate purity, and a stole or scarf, symbolic of Buddhist robes. They carry a walking staff, a rosary, a bell to ring after reciting sutras, and *osamefuda* – slips of paper bearing their name, address, date and wishes, to be placed in temple boxes. They also carry a *nōkyōchō* (pilgrim book) to collect stamps en route.

'THERE IS A TRADITION OF SHOWING GREAT RESPECT TO PILGRIMS. PEOPLE MAY OFFER *OSETTAI* (SMALL GIFTS); EXPRESS GRATITUDE BY GIVING AN *OSAMEFUDA* (NAME SLIP) IN EXCHANGE.'

typhoons arrive. March can still be chilly in the more mountainous regions but is less crowded than April or May, with the delightful bonus of – with luck – hiking through fairy-tale frills of cherry-blossom trees, which tend to bloom here from mid-March onwards. Autumn is lovely, too, when conditions are again good, and Shikoku's forests put on a colourful show of turning leaves.

The diversity of this trail is one of its joys. There are off-road sections that weave through stands of cedar, pine and bamboo, trace burbling streams, skirt wave-bashed coast and climb mountain slopes – Unpen-ji (Temple 66), the highest temple, perches at 911m (2989ft). But over half of the route is on tarmac, passing through busy towns and alongside roads. It's not a wild walk

TOP *Henro* at Ishite-ji (Temple 51), near Matsuyama. **LEFT** Hiking a bamboo grove on the 88 Temple Pilgrimage near Zentsūji. **RIGHT** Cherry trees blossom at the *torii* gates of Kumadani-ji (Temple 8).

ACCOMMODATION
Options include hotels, *minshuku* (B&Bs), *ryokan* (inns) and *shukubo* (temple stays); *zenkonyado* are free/low-cost pilgrim lodgings.

FOOD
Convenience stores, roadside stations and vending machines are ubiquitous. Bento boxes are good on-the-go options.

GETTING THERE
There are train and bus stations close to Ryōzen-ji, with connections to major cities such as Tokyo and Kyoto.

PLANNING
Walk clockwise – it's easier to follow the waymarks.

SAFETY
Look out for snakes and giant hornets, which have nasty stings. The route is largely on tarmac so take comfy shoes and blister plasters. Sections marked *henro korogashi* – 'where pilgrims fall' – are especially difficult.

INFO
henro.org/shikoku-pilgrimage

---

but a chance to engage with Shikoku's past, present, nature and, particularly, its people.

The temples themselves are largely simple structures. Some are clustered together, others are several days' walk apart, interspersed with wayside shrines and statues of Kōbō Daishi. At each temple, the same ritual should be performed: pilgrims bow to the left of the gate, wash their hands and mouths, ring the bell, place a name-slip in the box, light incense and a candle, make a donation, recite the sutras, then pray again inside the main hall. Most get a stamp in their pilgrimage books to record their progress – though this hike isn't really about visiting all of the temples. The path itself is the journey and the blessing.

NATURE / CULTURE / COAST

Otter Trail

WESTERN & EASTERN CAPE, SOUTH AFRICA

START
Storms River Mouth

FINISH
Nature's Valley

DISTANCE
45km (28 miles)

DURATION
Five days

CHALLENGE LEVEL

WHEN TO WALK
September–April

Experience the wild and wonderful Tsitsikamma coastline on South Africa's oldest official long-distance hike, watching for dolphins, whales and – of course – otters.

South Africa's premier multiday hike winds through the Garden Route National Park, with both trail and reserve straddling the Western and Eastern Cape provinces. But don't be fooled by the park's demure moniker: though there are flowers aplenty, this is far from a sedate stroll through pruned and mown greenery – and all the more spectacular for it.

The trail is named for the Cape clawless otter – the world's second-largest freshwater otter species. You might spy this lithe carnivore at river mouths along the route, using its slender, powerful tail to swim and dive for crabs, fish and frogs detected by its sensitive whiskers. It's an apt label for the hike – because to tackle this trek you'll need to be nimble and happy getting your feet wet. Though distances are relatively modest, never exceeding 14km (9 miles) on any one day, the frequent switchbacks will test calves, quads and knees. And there are river mouths to cross, too – check tide tables each day – so you'll have to splash at least a little, and may even need to swim for part of the Bloukrans River traverse.

It's not all climbs and crossings though. Right from the off, you'll discover caves and cascading waterfalls, thriving fynbos shrubland and dense gallery forest, plus empty beaches perfect for a cool dip. Spring and summer are the seasons to enjoy this trek at its best and safest, with long, warm days and clearer skies. It's also the time to admire those dazzling wildflower displays, and to spot threatened African black oystercatchers foraging along the shore. Listen out for the gruff calls of vividly coloured Knysna turacos, spot shy little blue duiker among the trees and watch for humpback whales and dolphins breaching and porpoising off the coast.

ACCOMMODATION
Mattresses in shared rooms at simple forest huts, with communal toilets, rainwater tanks and braais (barbecues); bring sleeping bag and cooking stove.

FOOD
Bring all supplies; purify drinking water.

GETTING THERE
Nature's Valley is a two-hour drive from George Airport. Park at Nature's Valley or Storms River Mouth and/or arrange transfers.

PLANNING
Book with SAN Parks well in advance. Daily conservation and community fees apply. A medical certificate is required.

INFO
sanparks.org

LEFT Trailside waterfall near the hike's start at Storms River Mouth. **TOP** Descending to the wild, river-cut Tsitsikamma coastline on the Otter Trail

NATURE / MOUNTAINS / COAST

Dry Stone Route

MALLORCA, SPAIN

The ancient trails that weave across Mallorca's rugged Tramuntana range offer both an interactive history lesson and marvellous mountain views.

Ah, early spring in Mallorca. The pinky-white blooms of almond trees are just beginning to fall as the island decisively shrugs off winter and starts to warm up. Days are lengthening, the sun is shining, the mercury nudges up to around 18°C (64°F) – but none of the beach-floppers have arrived. Altogether, it's a delightful time for hiking the GR221, aka the Ruta de Pedra en Sec – Dry Stone Route.

Mallorca is scribbled with cobbled footpaths, many of which date back centuries and help tell the story of this largest of the Balearic Isles. They were variously constructed by Arab invaders, conquering Christians, foresters, muleteers, smallholders, smugglers, anti-pirate patrollers, even an Austrian archduke. They weave between old stone walls, traverse tumbling terraces, follow irrigation canals and dip into olive groves.

The GR221 pieces together some of these old paths to cross the island along Mallorca's dramatic northern spine, the Serra de Tramuntana. This lumpy route runs for around 140km (87 miles) from the harbour of Port d'Andratx, at the island's westernmost tip, to the inland town of Pollença, in the east. We say 'around' – various figures are quoted, in part because there is a multitude of variants. For instance, some hikers detour to tick off Tramuntana peaks. But while not everyone walks the same route, most will experience a similar string of pleasures: welcoming villages, historic trails, rugged ridges and dazzling views over the Med.

From Port d'Andratx, the GR221 wends via reddish cliffs to reach the fishing village of Sant Elm. Old pilgrim paths lead through thick pines to the ruined monastery of La Trapa; a side

START
Port d'Andratx

FINISH
Pollença

DISTANCE
140km (87 miles) approx

DURATION
Seven to 10 days

CHALLENGE LEVEL
★★★☆☆

WHEN TO WALK
March–May
& September–November

LEFT Mallorca's Dry Stone Route weaves through the dramatic gorge of Barranc de Biniaraix.

ACCOMMODATION
Cheap *refugios* (mountain huts) with dorm beds at the end of most stages. Hotels in some towns and villages. Check in advance when travelling in low season to ensure places are open. Wild camping is illegal.

FOOD
Restaurants and shops in towns and villages along the route.

GETTING THERE
Buses run from Palma to Port d'Andratx in about an hour; Pollença–Palma takes just a little longer.

PLANNING
There are various possible routings – research options before setting off. Trails sometimes cross private land – always hike respectfully.

SAFETY
The terrain varies enormously: some sections are leisurely, others are challenging and suitable only for experienced hikers.

---

trip to the Devil's Pulpit viewpoint rewards with awesome vistas. Trails then cross the high plateau to the *finca* (country estate) at Ses Fontanelles and drop down to Estellencs, picturesquely perched on the hillside of Puig de Galatzó. Ahead lie historic coal miners' settlements and an old post route running into the little town of Esporles. Continue to reach the rocky heights of ancient Son Moragues estate – keep an eye out for bearded vultures – and views to the ravine-tucked village of Deià, a hub for artists and creatives.

From there, you have choices for reaching pretty Sóller: take the old smugglers' trail along the cliffs, or opt for the path leading up to the rocky Finca Muleta Gran, both yielding superb sea views. It's a challenging tramp into the higher reaches of the Serra de Tramuntana, though the gorge of Barranc de Biniaraix to the foot of the Tossal massif, with dry-stone walls threading the slopes. From the Refugi Tossals Verds, experienced mountaineers can cross the Coll des Prat and divert up lofty 1367m (4485ft) Puig de Massanella. The regular route follows another scenic trail down to 17th-century Monestir de Lluc, the island's premier pilgrimage site.

LEFT Poppy-speckled farmlands below Puig Tomir, near the end of the hike. **BELOW** Donkeys along the Dry Stone Route near Galatzó, western Mallorca. **RIGHT** Approaching comely Sóller via the old smugglers' trail along the cliffs.

'OFFICIAL *REFUGIOS* ARE MANAGED BY THE CONSELL DE MALLORCA, AND NEED TO BE BOOKED IN ADVANCE. DUVETS ARE PROVIDED; RENT SHEETS OR BRING A SLEEPING-BAG LINER.'

The final stage wends down through the woods to the foot of Puig Tomir — a worthwhile detour for summit views — before taking the pilgrims' path to the narrow alleys, Roman bridge and cafe-lined squares of Pollença, a suitably gorgeous end to a spectacular hike.

Spring celebrations

IF HIKING in March, arrive in time for the Dia de les Illes Balears (Day of the Balearic Islands), held on 1 March to commemorate the signing of the Balearic Statute of Autonomy in 1983. Celebrations centre on Palma, where a massive medieval market is held, selling traditional food, drinks and crafts. Across the island you might happen upon parades of *gigantes y cabezudos* (huge heads) and *ball de bot* folk dances.

AUSTRALIA

NATURE / CULTURE / COAST

Three Capes Track

TASMANIA, AUSTRALIA

START
Denmans Cove

FINISH
Fortescue Bay

DISTANCE
46km (29 miles)

DURATION
Four days

CHALLENGE LEVEL

WHEN TO WALK
Year-round

Sample Tasmania's epic wilderness, striding alongside dolerite cliffs, through dense forest and past pounding surf.

Boarding the boat at Port Arthur feels like release – and not just because you're departing Tasmania's most notorious former penal colony. The historic site is well worth exploring – but you're here for the eco-cruise across Port Arthur Bay, spotting cormorants and white-bellied sea eagles on an amuse-bouche for one of the island's most accessible microadventures.

Taking in two dramatic capes, this moderate hike provides a taster menu of wild Tasmania: cliffs, forest, beaches and all the animals they harbour. Walkers stay in simple cabins, and pass a series of 'encounters' – alfresco sculptures evoking natural and historic aspects of the Tasman Peninsula. This gnarled southeastern promontory is exposed to the wildest wind and waves, so many tackle the track in summer (December–February). But autumn offers ample benefits: orchids flower and whales migrate past.

From Denmans Cove, the first leg is a gentle 4km (2.5-mile) intro, delving into dense gum forest and ending at Surveyors Cabin, for views across to Cape Raoul and possible sightings of grazing Bennett's wallabies. Day two kicks off with steep stone steps climbing Arthurs Peak, rewarded with spectacular vistas along the coast to the main destination on day three: Cape Pillar. The path then weaves through stands of stringybark and white gum, across Hurricane Heath – spot scatterings of cubic wombat poo – and along the narrow, vertiginous-sided isthmus (with such reassuringly named features as the Chasm and the Blade) to the cape itself, an awesomely end-of-the-world meeting of rock, sky and roaring sea.

Day four brings the toughest test: the ascent of 490m (1608ft) Mt Fortescue, followed by the heart-in-mouth majesty of Cape Hauy and, finally, a triumphant toe-paddle at Fortescue Bay.

ACCOMMODATION
Dorms in simple but comfortable self-catering cabins.

FOOD
Cabins have cooking facilities but not crockery or cutlery. Bring all food and purify drinking water from sources on the hike.

GETTING THERE
Buses from Tasmanian capital Hobart reach Port Arthur in about 1¾ hours. The scenic 1¼-hour eco-cruise to Denmans Cove is included in the hike fee.

PLANNING
Book ahead, particularly for summer; only 48 places are available daily.

SAFETY
Paths are well made, but prepare for all weather.

INFO
threecapestrack.com.au

LEFT Tasman Island Lighthouse, offshore of the Cape to Cape Track's start point at Cape Pillar. **TOP** Towering dolerite rock pillars along the Tasman Peninsula coast

FOOD & DRINK / CULTURE / MOUNTAIN / COAST

Lycian Way

SOUTHWEST ANATOLIA, TÜRKIYE

Stride through centuries of ancient history – and the delights of rural Turkish culture – on a trek around the edge of the Mediterranean Sea.

Trace the coastline of the Teke Peninsula along the Lycian Way, and you'll share the trail with ghosts. This glorious route links pathways trodden by herders, fishers, farmers and traders for millennia. Unsurprisingly, it's littered with reminders of the region's long, storied past: funerary monuments and rock tombs adorned with finely carved decorations; temples and sanctuaries; Roman and Lycian theatres; walls of mighty cities lost to time; and remains of Ottoman settlements abandoned during the population exchanges of the early 20th century. You'll even walk sections of Roman roads.

The brainchild of British expat Kate Clow, the Lycian Way was devised, waymarked and opened at the tail end of last century, creating Türkiye's first – and most popular – long-distance trail. Despite the many ancient remains studding the path, the intention was to look not back but forwards – to share this little-visited region with outsiders, and to bring the benefits of sustainable tourism to local communities. Being welcomed by these warm people is one of the great delights of a trek, and visits to their villages provide opportunities to sample the fruits of their labours: fresh cheese, yoghurt, bread, nuts, fruits and vegetables.

Summer brings sweltering heat to Anatolia, and many facilities close in winter; best arrive in spring to enjoy wildflowers and a warm welcome, or cool autumn. The trail can be walked in either direction, heading either east or west. A long hike – typically around a month, give or take – that features some fairly remote, little-developed areas on rough, sometimes stony and steep paths, this is no small undertaking, and takes some planning.

START
Ovacık

FINISH
Geyikbayırı

DISTANCE
540km (335 miles)

DURATION
25–40 days

CHALLENGE LEVEL
★★★★☆

WHEN TO WALK
March–May
& September–November

LEFT Gelidonya Lighthouse, overlooking the island-studded eastern section of the Lycian Way.

Who were the Lycians?

IN THE 6th century BCE, the ancient region of Lycia was overrun by the Persian Achaemenid Empire. After Alexander the Great swept through in 333 BCE, an independent Lycian League flourished – until the Romans came, saw and conquered. Lycia became a Roman province in 43 CE, then part of the Eastern Roman (Byzantine) Empire, coming under the Ottoman Empire from the later Middle Ages until the birth of modern Türkiye in the 20th century.

'THE PERPETUAL FLAMES FLICKERING FROM VENTS AT YANARTAŞ (BURNING ROCK) MAY HAVE INSPIRED THE FIRE-BREATHING, GOAT-SERPENT CHIMERA MONSTER OF HOMER'S *ILIAD*.'

Though you'll find guesthouses and *pansiyons* (pensions) in villages on or near the route, and may be offered a bed in private houses, on some stretches where settlements are sparse it pays to be self-sufficient – consider bringing a tent and sleeping bag, and carry food and plenty of water.

Of course, many walkers don't hike the whole route in one go, but break down the trail into shorter sections to tackle piecemeal. The western stretch between Ovacık and Kaş can be completed in about a week or so, with highlights including the ghost village of Levissi at Kayaköy, abandoned by its largely Greek population in 1923; the aptly named Butterfly Valley (Kelebek Vadisi), where Jersey tiger moths proliferate; ancient ruins at Sidyma, with its forest of stone tombs, and at Xanthos, graced by a still-impressive amphitheatre; and the endless sweep of golden sand at Patara, where the imposing remains of

TOP Amphitheatre at the ancient city of Patara, one-time capital of Lycia. **LEFT** Hiking the the Lycian Way along the Teke Peninsula coast. **RIGHT** Strolling the dunes at picture-perfect Patara Beach.

ACCOMMODATION
Guesthouses, *pansiyons* (pensions), private villages houses and camping.

FOOD
Buy essentials at food shops in one of the cities (Fethiye or Antalya) or towns such as Ölüdeniz, Kalkan or Kaş. Top up basic supplies in villages.

GETTING THERE
Dalaman and Antalya are the nearest airports; overnight buses run to both from İstanbul and İzmir. Daily buses run from Dalaman to Fethiye, connected to Ovacık by local *dolmuş* (minibus). Infrequent buses link Geyikbayırı with Antalya. Taxis are relatively cheap.

PLANNING
Carry Turkish lira cash.

SAFETY
Watch for hornets, and shake boots for scorpions.

INFO
The Lycian Way by Kate Clow (trekkinginturkey.com)

theatres, agora, temples and tombs speak of the pomp of this historic city, birthplace of Saint Nicholas.

To the east, you can peer down at the sunken remains off Kekova; near Çıralı, climb Mt Olympos and explore the ruins of its namesake 2nd-century-BCE city, and witness the eternal flames of Yanartaş (aka Chimaera) blazing from the rocks. You'll pass ruined Roman castles and watchtowers; stroll in the shade of pine and cedar forests; and cool off in the waters of Göynük Gorge. And throughout, the limpid turquoise waters of the Mediterranean beckon just offshore.

ITALY

NATURE / FOOD & DRINK / CULTURE / COAST

Santa Barbara Cammino

SARDINIA, ITALY

START
Portoscuso

FINISH
Masua

DISTANCE
64km (40 miles)

DURATION
Four days

CHALLENGE LEVEL
★★★☆☆

WHEN TO WALK
March–May
& September–November

Hike through millennia of mining history and help support modern-day communities on the Portoscuso to Masua leg of this varied, multi-stage ramble around southwest Sardinia.

Santa Barbara is the patron saint of miners, so it's apt that the newest trail through southwest Sardinia bears her name. Not only because this is a historic mining region, but because it's hoped the Cammino will help nurture the area by reviving interest in its past industry — which dates back to ancient times — and bringing new opportunities to the communities living here today.

The full trail stretches some 500km (310 miles), looping along dirt paths, mule tracks and abandoned railways, equal parts historical, cultural and scenic. It's split into 30 stages, which range from 5km (3 miles) to 29km (18 miles), linking ancient *nuraghe* (Sardinia's curious neolithic stone towers), Roman remains, mountains, turquoise seas, tunnels blasted into the rock and comely villages. The trail is open year-round, and founding association Fondazione Cammino Minerario di Santa Barbara (CMSB) actively encourages walkers to come in quieter months. Spring and autumn are prime times: cheaper, quieter, warm but not scorching.

For those without the time or inclination to tackle the entire trail, we suggest combining stages 29, 30, 1 and 2 to make a fine four-day hike, linking the tuna-fishing port of Portoscuso with the limestone cliffs of Masua via Iglesias. Starting by the sea, you'll encounter volcanic cliffs, mining heritage and one of the island's largest Nuragic settlements. Then follow old railway tracks to Iglesias — though it's worth taking the longer alternative route to delve into the tunnels of the San Giovanni mine. From Iglesias, the Cammino leads to the town of Nebida, via chapels and churches dedicated to Santa Barbara. Finally, continue to Masua, where shafts are hewn into the rock and an idyllic beach beckons.

ACCOMMODATION
Find details of CMSB-affiliated stays on the trail website.

FOOD
Facilities vary by stage. Carry plenty of water. Local specialities include ravioli-like *culurgiones*, roast piglet and tuna.

GETTING THERE
Trains and buses run from Cagliari to Iglesias; buses connect Iglesias with Portoscuso.

PLANNING
Download the free trail app. Buy a CMSB *credenziale* (walker's passport; €5) for discounts.

SAFETY
Do not approach shepherds' dogs.

INFO
camminominerariodisanta barbara.org

LEFT Coastal mine at Nebida, southwest Sardinia. TOP The cliff-hewn mineshaft of Porto Flavia in Masua, at the end of the Santa Barbara Cammino.

APRIL

Hike through deserts and canyons on the Dana to Petra section of the epic Jordan Trail (page 95).

APRIL

I WANT A HIKE THAT'S A...

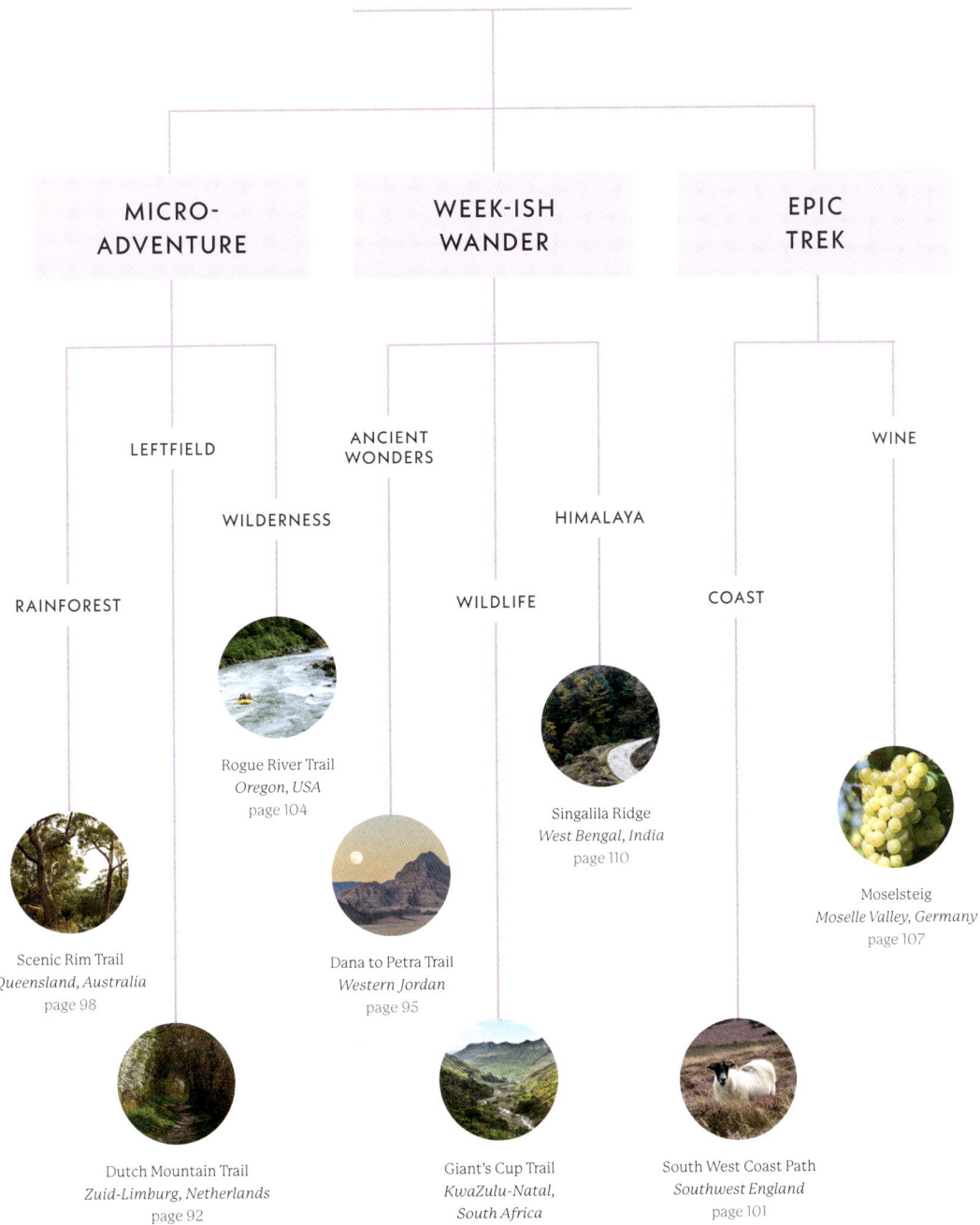

- MICRO-ADVENTURE
  - RAINFOREST
    - Scenic Rim Trail
    - *Queensland, Australia*
    - page 98
  - LEFTFIELD
    - Dutch Mountain Trail
    - *Zuid-Limburg, Netherlands*
    - page 92
  - WILDERNESS
    - Rogue River Trail
    - *Oregon, USA*
    - page 104

- WEEK-ISH WANDER
  - ANCIENT WONDERS
    - Dana to Petra Trail
    - *Western Jordan*
    - page 95
  - WILDLIFE
    - Giant's Cup Trail
    - *KwaZulu-Natal, South Africa*
    - page 89
  - HIMALAYA
    - Singalila Ridge
    - *West Bengal, India*
    - page 110

- EPIC TREK
  - COAST
    - South West Coast Path
    - *Southwest England*
    - page 101
  - WINE
    - Moselsteig
    - *Moselle Valley, Germany*
    - page 107

APR

SOUTH AFRICA

NATURE / CULTURE

Giant's Cup Trail

KWAZULU-NATAL, SOUTH AFRICA

APR

Stride out beneath the robust ramparts of the Drakensberg Mountains, through wild landscapes inhabited by San people for thousands of years.

A glance at a map can reveal so much. Look at the section covering Lesotho's eastern border and notice the name curving around the summits and ridges that forms the boundary: Drakensberg – 'Dragons' Mountains' in Afrikaans, uKhahlamba (Barrier of Spears) in Zulu. You've already got a clear picture of what's here. And that's before you spot the individual landmarks: Giant's Castle; Cathedral Peak; Organ Pipes; Amphitheatre; Devil's Hoek; Sleeping Beauty Cave.

The Drakensberg's lofty basalt buttresses, sandstone ramparts, waterfall-carved gorges and sheer-sided valleys live up to those dramatic monikers, and then some. Unsurprisingly, they form the backdrop for many of South Africa's most spectacular hikes, best undertaken in autumn (April–May) after the mist, clouds and thunderstorms of summer have eased; or spring, when you can enjoy warmer days and nights at altitudes topping 3000m (9843ft).

Arguably the finest multiday walk in this epic region, the Giant's Cup is named for the bowl-like saddle between Hodgson's Peaks, high above the southern section of Maloti-Drakensberg Park – a trans-frontier World Heritage Site encompassing some of the range's wildest swathes. Winding south through grassy foothills, the trail is clear and well-signed – watch for the white footprint markers on trees and rocks – with accommodation in simple but comfortable huts. Though only a modest challenge for experienced hikers, it's not to be taken lightly.

The route stays above 1500m (4920ft) altitude, nipping up over 2200m (7218ft), and weather can change rapidly; even

START
Ezemvelo KZN Wildlife
Makhakhe Field Ranger
Outpost, Sani Pass Rd

FINISH
Bushman's Nek

DISTANCE
60km (37 miles)

DURATION
Five days

CHALLENGE LEVEL
★★★☆☆

WHEN TO WALK
April–May
& September–October

LEFT The Amphitheatre, one of the signature sights of the dramatic Drakensberg Mountains.

SOUTH AFRICA

ACCOMMODATION
Modest huts with running water, toilets and bunks but no cooking facilities. More upmarket stays available at various points off the trail.

FOOD
Stock up before setting out; only minimal supplies are available once on the trail.

GETTING THERE
No public transport to/from either trailhead. Arrange transfers by taxi or with your accommodation in Underberg, Himeville or nearby.

PLANNING
Places in huts are limited – book in advance (via kznwildlife.com).

SAFETY
Though daily distances are relatively short, you'll need to be prepared for changeable weather, perhaps including snow. Check in and sign registers where available.

INFO
kznwildlife.com

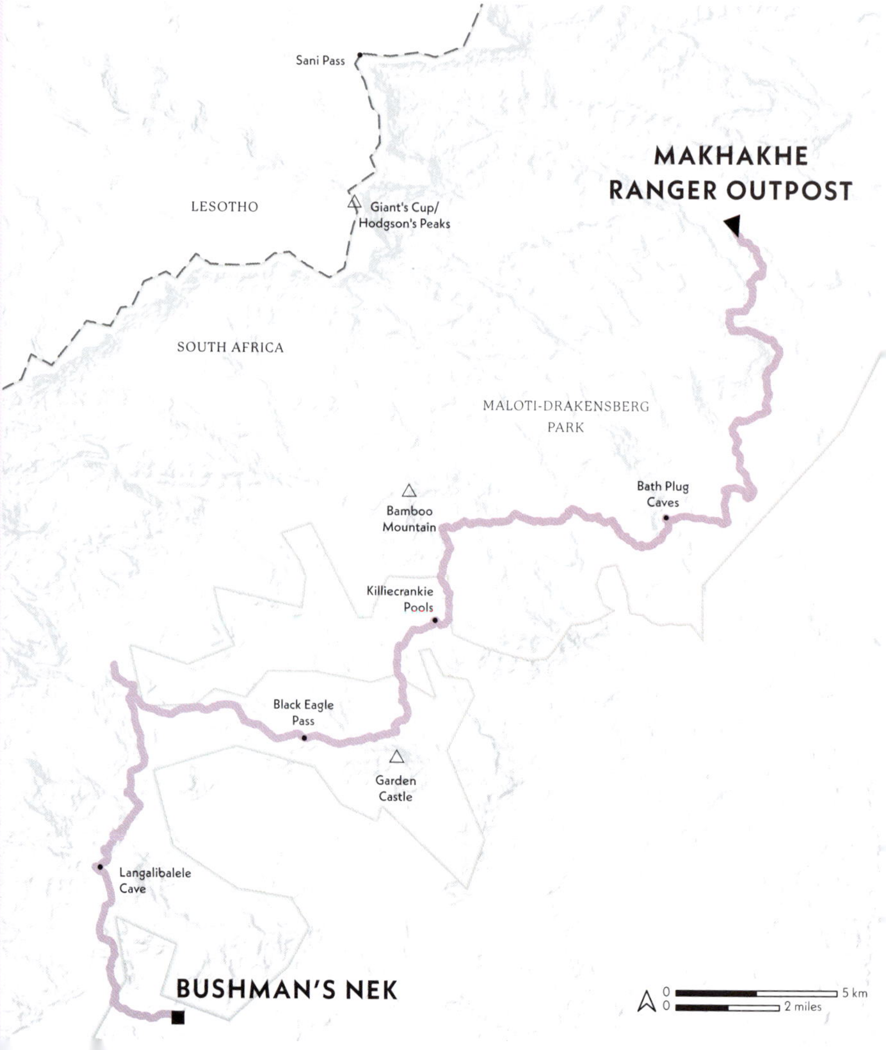

summer nights are cool, and snow is possible at any time. In short, you need to be prepared for anything – including wildlife encounters. True, you've a very small chance of coming across one of the terrestrial predators that hunt in the park – including leopard, caracal, serval and black-backed jackal. Look up, though, and you might watch Cape vultures and rare, bone-crunching bearded vultures circling overhead, along with jackal buzzard and Verreaux's eagle. You could meet baboons, elands, oribi, mountain reedbuck and dassies (rock hyrax) along the way, too.

Starting from the Sani Pass Rd (which winds on into Lesotho), the trail meanders south along streamside paths – sometimes calling for rock-hopping crossings – and soon provides views of the Giant's Cup to the west. Vistas transform hour by hour and day by day: on the second leg, you'll cross a plateau heading for Siphongweni Ridge (2151m/7057ft), near the sandstone chunks known as Tortoise Rocks. Fynbos scrub alternates with protea

LEFT Drakensburg peaks near the Sani Pass. BELOW Ancient San rock art, Maloti-Drakensberg Park. RIGHT The Giant's Cup Trail weaves through the formidable Drakensberg Mountains.

'THE FORBIDDING CLIFFS AND CRAGS OF THE DRAKENSBERG RANGE ARE CARVED FROM BASALT DEPOSITS LAID DOWN BY POWERFUL VOLCANIC ACTIVITY SOME 180 MILLION YEARS AGO.'

woodland, before the route climbs to the flanks of Bamboo Mountain, passing alpine tarns where you might catch glimpses of crested or rare blue cranes, and admire the crenellated crags of Garden Castle. You'll also pass spots providing telling nods to the nostalgia of early European settlers, sporting decidedly Scottish names: Inverness, Stromness, Killiecrankie Pools – an alluring spot for a dip on a hot day.

Traversing Black Eagle Pass, the last stretch passes close to Langalibalele Cave, adorned with astonishing San rock art – a poignant reminder that these paths were trodden for many millennia before you.

Rock art

SAN PEOPLE inhabited this region for some four millennia, and their incredible rock art is a major reason why Maloti-Drakensberg Park was inscribed onto UNESCO's World Heritage list (alongside the vulnerable wildlife it harbours). Caves and overhangs sport paintings of animals and human figures representing spiritual aspects of the lives of the San. Bath Plug and Langalibalele Caves are on the route; others make worthy side-trips. Please protect these fragile artworks – admire but don't touch.

NATURE / CULTURE

Dutch Mountain Trail

ZUID-LIMBURG, NETHERLANDS

START
Eygelshoven

FINISH
Maastricht

DISTANCE
101km (63 miles)

DURATION
Four days

CHALLENGE LEVEL
★★☆☆☆

WHEN TO WALK
April–October

This route through the notoriously un-mountainous Netherlands sounds like a contradiction in terms, but is both a satisfying stroll and a climate call-to-arms.

Don't laugh. Well, maybe a little. The creators of this 'Mountain Trail' in the famously flat Netherlands did have tongues slightly in cheeks when plotting a route via seven of the country's highest 'summits' – up to 252m/827ft – in southerly Zuid-Limburg province. But they also had some serious points to make. The trail was dreamed up in 2019 by the organisers of the Dutch Mountain Film Festival, which celebrates international alpine culture; with travel's effects on the climate becoming ever more worrying, they wanted to encourage locals to mountaineer closer to home. So they devised a route to showcase the country's lumpiest, loveliest, most alpine-like terrain – not high peaks, perhaps, but a succession of appealing hills, deep-ish valleys, wildflower meadows, cliffs and streams.

It's fascinating, too. Zuid-Limburg is sandwiched between Germany to the east and Belgium to the south and west, and the trail hops into both, adding to its cultural heft and its altitude. The top of Schneeberg, one of the seven 'peaks', is actually in Germany; along the border with Belgium, hikers are reminded of the high-voltage fence – the 'Wire of Death' – strung along here during WWI. (Perversely, the Netherlands' highest point –322m/1056ft Vaalserberg – is skipped on account of it being too touristy.)

Roughly W-shaped, the trail is split into four stages, with a total ascent of 1690m (5545ft). April is a good time to hike: it's not hot – averaging 13°C (56°F) – but it's the driest month, with days rapidly lengthening and facilities reopening. And on 27 April, the country celebrates its biggest knees-up, King's Day, in a raucous riot of orange – maybe a good moment to escape to the 'hills'?

ACCOMMODATION
There are campsites and hotels close by, though few directly on the trail – detours are required. Most campsites close from October to March.

FOOD
Pack supplies for each day; cafes and shops typically lie just off the trail.

GETTING THERE
Eygelshoven–Maastricht takes 40 minutes by train.

PLANNING
The route isn't waymarked, but a booklet is available locally. The Eijsden foot ferry runs only April to October; in winter, a detour is required.

SAFETY
Take hiking poles.

INFO
dmff.eu

LEFT Peaceful pathway along the Dutch Mountain Trail near Vaals. **TOP** The trail loops through the hill-speckled pastureland of Zuid-Limburg province.

NATURE / CULTURE / CAMPING

Dana to Petra Trail

WESTERN JORDAN

Hike through history on a path established for millennia, through arid desert and wild canyons, to enter the rose-red city of Petra through the back door.

On his 'last crusade' for the Holy Grail, Indiana Jones famously galloped to the monumental tomb called the Treasury along the Siq. That narrow, winding canyon is the front door to Petra, the fabled city hidden among (and carved from) rose-red sandstone. But it's not the only way in. The most atmospheric approach is via the back door — culmination of the region's most thrilling multiday hike.

In Petra's heyday around the turn of the first millennium CE, when its great wealth was built through trading, the route through the city would have been buzzing. Today it forms part of the Jordan Trail, a 675km (420-mile) on-foot odyssey linking ancient and restored paths running the length of the country via many of the most absorbing sites. Its northern terminus, Umm Qais — called Gadara in Biblical times — is home to Roman ruins and an Ottoman-era village. Continuing south, the trail visits Byzantine remains at Pella, Ajloun's hilltop bastion, canyons stretching down to the Dead Sea, Karak's Crusader stronghold and the otherworldly rock outcrops of Wadi Rum (location for countless movies, from *Lawrence of Arabia* to *The Martian*), ending at the resort of Aqaba on the Red Sea.

Few complete all 40 stages of that ambitious trek. For a rewarding taster taking under a week, tackle the Dana to Petra section, wild camping at scenic spots to absorb some of Jordan's untamed expanses, and ending at the archaeological world wonder. Though not hugely demanding in terms of terrain and distances, it's not to be taken lightly — an experienced guide is essential for safety and a more immersive experience. Timing is

START
Dana Village

FINISH
Petra

DISTANCE
80km (50 miles) approx.

DURATION
Four to six days

CHALLENGE LEVEL
★★★☆☆

WHEN TO WALK
February–April
& September–November

LEFT Atop Jebel Kharaz in Wadi Rum, along the Jordan Trail.

The Nabataeans

NOMADS FROM Arabia, Nabataeans settled Petra – then called Raqmu – by the late 4th century BCE; its population peaked at around 25,000 in the 1st century CE. The Nabataeans grew wealthy controlling passing trade, using those riches to create magnificent buildings blending Greek, Roman and local styles, and adorned with beautiful frescoes. The Romans took Petra, which was ravaged by earthquakes then fell into disuse, only 'rediscovered' by Swiss explorer Johann Burckhardt in 1812.

'HIKERS TRACE ANCIENT TRADE ROUTES AND BEDOUIN PATHS THROUGH ARID VALLEYS AND CANYONS, SKIRTING THE WADI ARABA DESERT AND PASSING BYZANTINE AND NABATAEAN RUINS.'

also important: spring's ideal for the northern stretches, after winter's bitter nights but before intense summer heat hits, and when wildflowers bloom on hillsides.

Pick up the trail in Dana, a modest village with intriguing Ottoman architecture, and descend from the mountain plateau into Dana Biosphere Reserve. Despite first impressions of an arid, scrubby, rocky expanse, this reserve encompasses Jordan's four biogeographical zones, home to hundreds of plants and animal species. Keep eyes peeled for Nubian ibex, griffon vulture, sand cat, lesser kestrel, spiny-tailed lizard and even Arabian wolf – though you'd be fortunate indeed to enjoy a sighting of that endangered subspecies.

What you will see are Bedouin camps, where you may be welcomed in for a glass of *shai* (tea) and the chance to learn about this nomadic culture. You'll also pass ancient copper

TOP Bedouin camp at Little Petra. **LEFT** The rock-carved wonders of Petra date back to the 3rd century BCE. **RIGHT** Navigating Petra's narrow Siq passage toward the Treasury (aka Al Khazneh).

ACCOMMODATION
Feynan Ecolodge near the start, otherwise wild campsites.

FOOD
Stock up before setting out. Purify water from springs and streams you pass.

GETTING THERE
Scheduled buses link Jordan's capital, Amman, with Wadi Musa for Petra, but nowhere closer to Dana. Minibuses serve nearby settlements like Al-Qadisiya and Tafila. Best arrange a package including guide and transport.

PLANNING
Hire an knowledgeable guide or join a tour. Entrance fees are payable for Dana Biosphere Reserve and Petra.

SAFETY
Conditions can be hot and arid, but flash floods can hit wadis and canyons. Carry ample water, wear suitable clothing and take local advice.

INFO
jordantrail.org

mines and waterfalls, and ascend to the plateau once more for spectacular views west across the Jordan River Valley.

The journey is more important than the destination, of course — but there's no denying that Petra makes an epic end to a trek. The historic marvels begin at the ancient service station now called Little Petra, where trade caravans stopped for refreshments in fresco-daubed caverns over 2000 years ago, and where you pick up tickets for the main site. Then it's on into Petra proper and its 500-plus ornately carved tombs, temples, palaces, baths, markets, even a theatre. Walk and wonder.

AUSTRALIA

NATURE / CAMPING

Scenic Rim Trail

QUEENSLAND, AUSTRALIA

APR

START
Thornton View Trailhead

FINISH
Cunninghams Gap

DISTANCE
47km (29 miles)

DURATION
Four days

CHALLENGE LEVEL
★★★★☆

WHEN TO WALK
April–September

Plunge into the world's largest subtropical rainforest on a trek through Gondwana's geological and biological history – a challenging hike for even the strongest legs.

In typically Aussie fashion, this hike does what it says on the tin: it's scenic, providing views across forests, valleys and forest-cloaked peaks from numerous lookouts; and it traces a rim – of ancient volcanoes, as it happens, adding geological spice to an already tasty recipe of diverse wildlife and challenging tramping.

True, it's not a long route – but it's also not an easy one. Paths are unmade, sometimes tricky to follow, often slippery and steep, with sheer ascents right from day one on the sweaty climb through Thornton View Nature Refuge to mount the first ridge. Best come when the weather's cooler and drier, bearing in mind that rainforest sometimes lives up to its moniker even during the 'Dry'. Mid-autumn is a sweet spot: greenery's lush after the end of the 'Wet', tourist numbers are yet to climb and camp bookings easier to snag.

And it's a two-tier affair. You can pay for eco-luxury accommodation, toothsome catering and an expert guide with the Spicers Scenic Rim Trail experience. But experienced backcountry hikers – confident at navigating, happy to carry kit and camp in the shade of gum trees and wattles – can enjoy this wilderness adventure for just a few bucks a night. You'll drink in the same cliff-top vistas, tackle the same climbs, encounter the same astonishing animals.

The walk traverses the biodiversity hotspot of Main Range National Park: you might encounter eastern grey kangaroos, quolls, bandicoots, rock and other wallabies, red-necked pademelons and the shrew-like yellow-footed antechinus, a small carnivorous marsupial – maybe even an echidna or platypus. You'll likely hear the croaks of endangered Fleay's barred frogs, along with the songs of black-breasted buttonquails and Albert's lyrebirds in cooler months.

ACCOMMODATION
Basic walkers' campsites, or eco-luxury guided experience (scenicrimtrail.com) in comfortable cabins.

FOOD
Bring all supplies and purify water from sources en route.

GETTING THERE
There's no public transport. Park at Thornton View Trailhead (not Cunninghams Gap), or arrange drop-off/pick-up with a transport provider.

PLANNING
Walk north to south. Book camp permits well in advance.

SAFETY
A topographic map is essential. Leeches, snakes and other biters are present — wear gaiters and bring insect repellent.

INFO
parks.desi.qld.gov.au

LEFT Camping in the shade of eucalypts, Main Range National Park. **TOP** Primo mountain views along the Scenic Rim Trail.

NATURE / CULTURE / COAST

South West Coast Path

SOUTHWEST ENGLAND

Trace a meandering, undulating trail around England's gnarled leg, past the winsome fishing villages, wild moors, clifftop castles, surf beaches, historic tin mines and fossil-dotted shores of Devon, Cornwall, Somerset and Dorset.

This route puts the roam into romance. It's the salt tang on the sea breeze. It's the boats bobbing at anchor in fishing villages. It's wind-bent trees, and high moors grazed by semi-wild horses and red deer; golden-sand beaches and seal-strewn rocks; foaming pots of ale and fresh crab sandwiches. It's the ineffable sense of walking to the end of the world and back.

Britain's longest waymarked National Trail (for now) snakes its way around the entire shorelines of Devon and Cornwall, plus hefty stretches of Somerset and Dorset. That's no cakewalk: its plentiful switchbacks notch up a calf-crunching 35,000m (114830ft) – four times the altitude of Everest.

Unlike the lofty Himalaya, in England's mild west you can walk in any month – though it's wise to dodge winter (closed facilities, short days and chillier, wetter weather) and summer, when temperatures and tourist numbers soar. Try April: days outstrip nights, wildflowers fleck clifftops, and sunny spells warm cockles and limbs alike.

The South West Coast Path has long been popular both for its beauty and because it offers plentiful and varied accommodation, relatively easy transport access and ample supply points. Walker numbers boomed further following the publication of Raynor Winn's memoir *The Salt Path*, painting a vivid – and now queried – picture of the experience (the movie, starring Gillian Anderson and Jason Isaacs, came out in 2025). So planning is key, whether you're aiming to complete all 1014km (630 miles) in one epic adventure, or break it up into shorter vacation-length chunks.

START
Minehead, Somerset

FINISH
South Haven Point, Dorset

DISTANCE
1014km (630 miles)

DURATION
30–52 days

CHALLENGE LEVEL
★★★★☆

WHEN TO WALK
Year-round, best April–October

LEFT Spring bluebells along the South West Coast Path near East Prawle, Devon.

UNITED KINGDOM

ACCOMMODATION
Campsites, B&Bs, pubs, hotels and self-catering. Wild camping isn't permitted, though many do it.

FOOD
Many shops and eateries. Some days have arid stretches – carry snacks and plenty of water. Pasties, available almost everywhere, make excellent hiking fuel.

GETTING THERE
Buses link Taunton Train Station with Minehead. South Haven Point is a short ferry ride from Sandbanks, from where buses run to Poole and Bournemouth train stations. Public transport serves many points along the length of the path.

PLANNING
Book accommodation well in advance. Check tide times and estuary ferry schedules, particularly for the section between Plymouth and Exmouth.

INFO
southwestcoastpath.org.uk
nationaltrail.co.uk

Each region has its own unique flavour. Walking anticlockwise, the first stretch from Minehead through Somerset and north Devon skirts the coastline of Exmoor National Park, traversing wild heath where yellow gorse flowers gleam, and shady woods harbour gems such as England's tiniest parish church at Culbone. Postcard-pretty villages include Porlock, Lynmouth and cobbled cutie Clovelly, while spectacular viewpoints include Great Hangman, the highest seacliff in England and Wales. Ten days to a fortnight should see you safely in Bude.

Across the border in Cornwall looms arguably the wildest and toughest stretch – a series of climbs and descents from Hartland Point to the dunes at Gwithian. But the two- to three-week epic from Bude to fortress-guarded Falmouth may also be the most enchanting – perhaps literally: in little Boscastle you can explore a fascinating Museum of Witchcraft and Magic. Then comes Tintagel, with its medieval castle ruins atop a crag legendarily

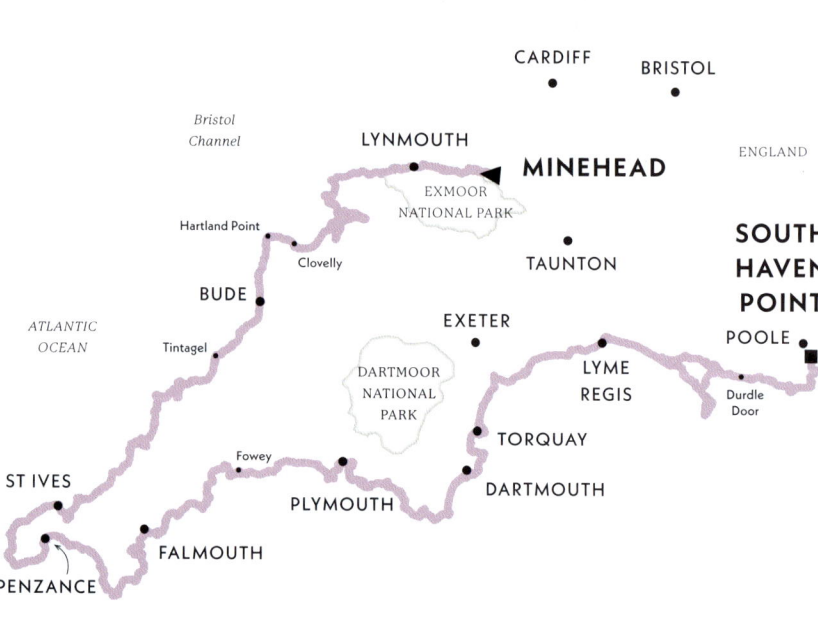

102

LEFT Hiking the South West Coast Path near Bude, north Cornwall. **BELOW** The harbour at Devon's chocolate-box Clovelly. **RIGHT** Heather in flower above Kynance Cove on Cornwall's Lizard Peninsula.

'THE FRESHLY MINTED KING CHARLES III ENGLAND COAST PATH, OPENED IN 2025, OFFERS SOME THRILLING ALTERNATIVE ROUTES TO SECTIONS OF THE EXISTING SOUTH WEST COAST PATH.'

home to King Arthur. Beyond, the artists' haven of St Ives marks the knuckle of England's toe, a land of megalithic quoits, dolmens and standing stones.

The going gets a little gentler along the shores of south Cornwall and Devon, with yachtie havens such as Fowey, Salcombe and Dartmouth, plus throwback bucket-and-spade resorts like Torquay and Teignmouth. Around fossil-hunting capital Lyme Regis, the trail again rears up on the craggy Jurassic Coast of east Devon and Dorset, punctuated by highlights including the photogenic rock arch of Durdle Door and ending with a traditional toe-dip in the sand and brine of Studland Bay, before signing off at South Haven Point.

Words on the west

THIS MAGICAL region is awash with literary connections. Exmoor's home to *Lorna Doone*, heroine of RD Blackmore's 1869 historical swashbuckler, and inspired Romantic poets William Wordsworth, Samuel Taylor Coleridge and Percy Shelley. Thomas Hardy fictionalised part of Cornwall (around Boscastle) and Dorset. Daphne du Maurier owned Menabilly near Fowey, body-double for Manderley in her 1938 masterpiece *Rebecca*. Lyme Regis' harbour wall, the Cobb, features in Jane Austen's *Persuasion* (1817) and John Fowles' *The French Lieutenant's Woman* (1969).

USA

NATURE / CULTURE / CAMPING

Rogue River Trail

OREGON, USA

START
Grave Creek

FINISH
Big Bend

DISTANCE
64km (40 miles)

DURATION
Four to five days

CHALLENGE LEVEL
★★★

WHEN TO WALK
April–June
& September–October

Follow in the footsteps of gold miners and Native Americans along the banks of this wild Oregon waterway – a walk into the wilderness and into the past.

The Rogue River Trail feels like a step back in time. The Native American Takelma lived alongside this waterway for thousands of years, till the discovery of gold brought an influx of Europeans. The ensuing Rogue River Wars (1855–56) saw the Takelma evicted and settlers move in. Visit today, and it seems as if those gold-digging incomers only just left: the trail passes ore-car tracks, homesteaders' graves, log cabins, historic ranches, pipes, flumes and stamp mills. The past is evoked in place names, too: Rainie Falls, coined for the old man who speared salmon here; Flora Dell Creek, after the wife of a local post carrier; China Gulch, where Chinese miners toiled during the late 19th century; Battle Bar, where the Rogue River Wars raged.

The wide, easily navigable trail was first blazed in the early 20th century, so miners and mule trains could gain better access to this wild, precipitous whitewater canyon. In places the route is hewn right into the cliffs, squeezing though ravines just a few metres wide; in others it cuts through thick, fern-frilled forest or groves of old oak and cedar. It's constantly crossing bubbling creeks and frothing waterfalls – keep an eye out for ducks and otters, plus bald and golden eagles gliding overhead and black bears foraging nearby.

Trail teams begin their annual maintenance in April, after the winter storms, so planning a trip from the middle of the month and into May is best, for clearer paths and warming weather; you'll also see a profusion of wildflowers and waterfalls raging, powered by snowmelt. The weather can still be unpredictable – expect some rain – but there will be far fewer hikers, making it easier to imagine the Rogue River as it was centuries ago.

ACCOMMODATION
Basic campsites along the trail, some with toilets/water.

FOOD
Carry all food. Pack out rubbish.

GETTING THERE
The trailhead in Rogue River-Siskiyou National Forest is accessible by car; book a shuttle to return to your vehicle.

PLANNING
Permits are required only by hikers being supported by boats.

SAFETY
Purify creek water. Store food in bear canisters (available to rent).

INFO
blm.gov

APR

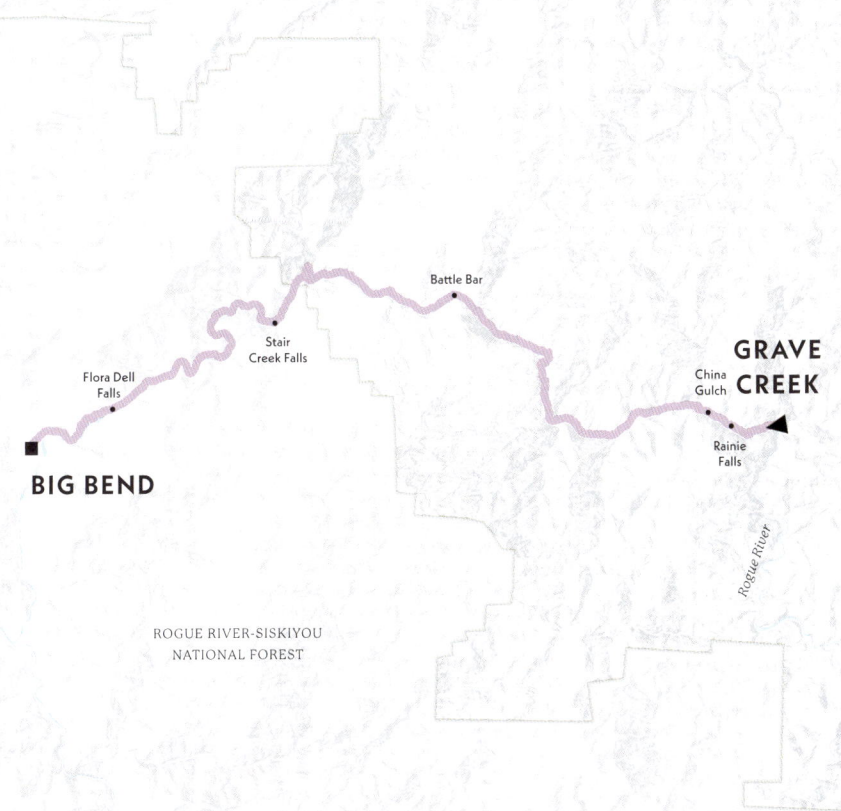

LEFT Ranch-style Rogue River lodgings at Paradise Bar. **TOP** Rafting the Rogue near Rainie Falls.

FOOD & DRINK / CULTURE

Moselsteig

MOSELLE VALLEY, GERMANY

Plot a grape escape along the meandering Moselle River among the vineyards, castles and Roman remains of this historic winemaking region.

What did the Romans ever do for us? Monty Python jokes aside, the ancient imperial power made quite the impact on swathes of Europe. Not just mighty amphitheatres, walls, gates and temples — though you'll find those along the Moselle Valley, snaking through far western Germany. Think drink: those inveterate invaders introduced winemaking to the region some two millennia ago. The results are visible almost everywhere. Vines stripe south-facing slopes, tendrils trained into heart shapes characteristic of the Moselle region, buds bursting into leaf as the mercury climbs in April — a fine but less-busy month to explore on foot. And signs advertise a *Weingut* (winery), *Weinprobe* (wine tasting) or *Weinverkauft* (wine for sale) around every corner.

Today, the Moselle is one of Germany's great wine regions — but its delicious Riesling, Elbling, Müller-Thurgau and Pinot Blanc are not the only reasons to take on its namesake trail. The waymarked walking route mostly follows the river from the three-way France–Luxembourg–Germany border at Perl to the confluence with the Rhine at Koblenz, with a fair few climbs to test your legs (and justify a cooling glass of white). It also offers a succession of treats for history buffs.

Not too long after setting out, beyond the limestone Nittel Cliffs, the trail arrives in Trier — or, as the Romans named it, Augusta Treverorum — once the largest city north of the Alps. Today it's a glorious confection of typically German facades, gables and market squares (with plenty of wine bars), and is studded with ancient remains. There are Roman baths, a Roman

START
Perl

FINISH
Koblenz

DISTANCE
365km (227 miles)

DURATION
14–24 days

CHALLENGE LEVEL
★★★☆☆

WHEN TO WALK
April–September

LEFT Marvel at the medieval in the Old Town of Bernkastel-Kues.

GERMANY

Decoding German wine

PRÄDIKATSWEIN IS the best-quality wine, with the highest level of natural grape sugar. Of this designation, Kabinett is light and often dry, Spätlese (late harvest) is richer and fuller-bodied, while Auslese is harvested later still and often sweet. Beerenauslese and Trockenbeerenauslese are dessert wines made from grapes with 'noble rot', while Eiswein is made from frozen grapes picked in winter. *Trocken* means very dry, *feinherb* off-dry and *lieblich* semi-sweet. *Prost!*

'RANGED AROUND A MOSEL LOOP NEAR BREMM LIKE A VAST, VERDANT AMPHITHEATRE, THE CALMONT VINEYARDS ARE REPUTEDLY THE WORLD'S STEEPEST, ANGLED AT UP TO 65 DEGREES.'

bridge, amphitheatre and the hulking Porta Nigra (Black Gate); even the core of the cathedral is Roman in origin.

Continue downstream and forward several centuries to Bernkastel-Kues, and discover the kind of romantic medieval Old Town you might expect to explore in a Brothers Grimm story: narrow cobbled alleys, timber-framed merchant houses, ruined Burg Landshut looming above.

That's a theme repeated along the way, reflecting the turbulent years of the 17th and 18th centuries, when French assaults left many castles in various states of often photogenic ruins. Around the next sweeping bend from Bernkastel, at Traben-Trarbach, the trail visits not one but two wrecked bastions, Grevenburg and Starkenburg.

And so it goes on: Burg Metternich peers down imperiously into the gorgeous 'Sleeping Beauty' village of Beilstein. Cochem's

TOP Grape vines stripe the riverbanks along the Moselsteig trail route. **LEFT** Village life at Ürzig, just a couple of Moselle bends from Traben-Trarbach. **RIGHT** Trier's Roman-era Porta Nigra (Black Gate).

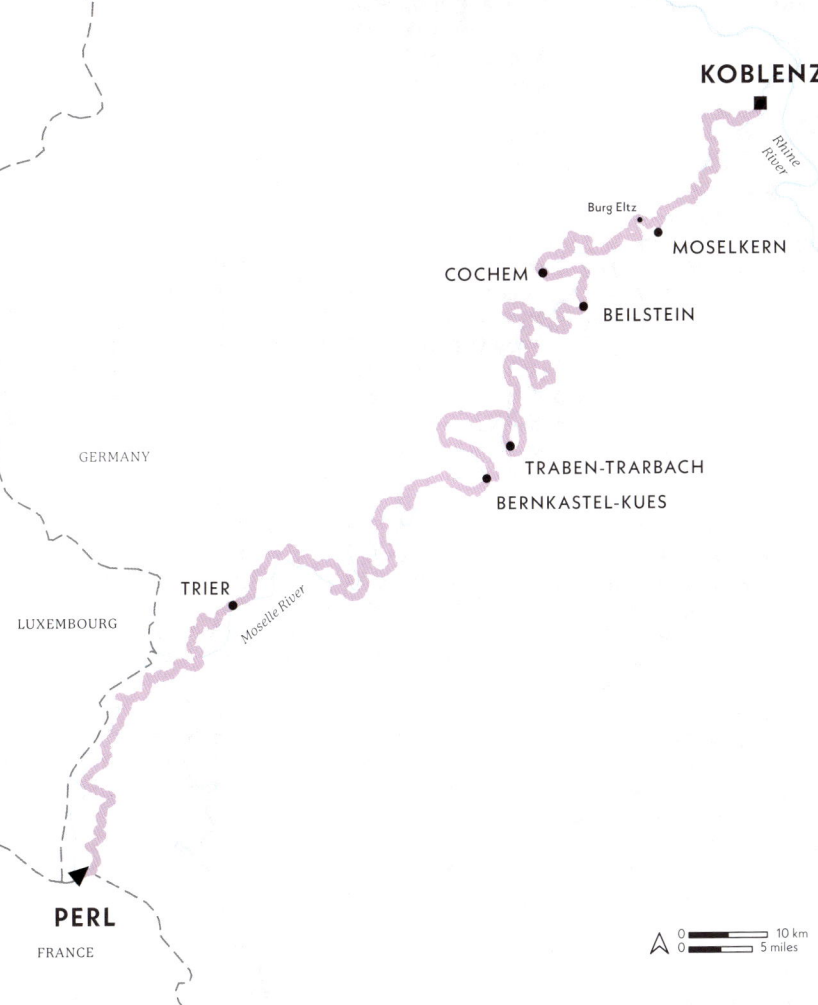

ACCOMMODATION
Guesthouses, B&Bs, hotels and campsites.

FOOD
Plentiful cafes, restaurants and *Weinguts* (wineries), plus local shops for picnic lunches.

GETTING THERE
Perl is a 40-minute bus ride from Luxembourg. Trains link Perl with Trier in an hour, and services continue on to Koblenz (1½ hours).

PLANNING
Navigation is straightforward. It's best to book accommodation in advance, though at this time of year you shouldn't have too much trouble.

SAFETY
Aside from sometimes muddy trails after rain, and any unsteadiness after wine tasting, this is a very safe route.

INFO
en.visitmosel.de/hiking

Reichsburg was whimsically reconstructed as a 19th-century romantic fantasy, all towers and turrets and tapestries; Burg Eltz near Moselkern vies with Bavaria's Neuschwanstein for most-fairy-tale-castle status.

You'll encounter any number of tempting places to refuel on local specialities, some being wine-related, of course: perhaps the best-known Moselle dish is *Tresterfleish*, pork marinated in grape pomace. There's fish, too, notably Mosel zander (pike-perch), and later in the year asparagus fills market stalls and menus. This being Germany, infrastructure makes cutting and pasting sections of the trail a breeze; if time is short, the Bernkastel to Cochem stretch would make a satisfying week's walking, with easy transport and plenty of cultural and culinary highlights along the path.

NATURE / CULTURE / MOUNTAINS

Singalila Ridge

WEST BENGAL, INDIA

START
Mane Bhanjang

FINISH
Rimbik

DISTANCE
83km (52 miles)

DURATION
Five to six days

CHALLENGE LEVEL
★★★

WHEN TO WALK
April–May
& October–November

Trace a dramatic mountain scarp flanking the Nepalese border for wildlife encounters, Buddhist monasteries and thrilling views of some of the highest Himalayan peaks.

Four of the planet's five highest summits form an intimidating phalanx along Nepal's northern border: Everest, Lhotse, Makalu and, far to the east, Kangchenjunga. Thankfully, to admire these 8000m-plus (26,247ft) behemoths you needn't don crampons and oxygen masks — just hike the Singalila Ridge.

This narrow range snakes north–south along Nepal's eastern border with the Indian states of West Bengal and Sikkim, rising to 3636m (11,930ft) and providing front-row seats to that show of starry summits. There are various possible hikes, but a rewarding option runs north along the West Bengal section over five or six days. Many walkers come in October or November, when days are typically clear and moderately warm, though April or May — when rhododendrons burst into frothy, gleaming bloom — is ideal.

From Darjeeling, take a jeep or shared taxi to the hiking hub of Mane Bhanjang; if you haven't already joined a group or met your (mandatory) guide, book one here. Then prepare to climb: it's a stiff haul of about 1000m (3280ft) on the first day alone, initially along a winding jeep track and passing the prayer-flag-flanked Buddhist monastery of Meghma Gompa. Bed down in a basic trekkers' hut or tent — tours typically offer a good level of camping comfort.

Soon the trail enters Singalila National Park, busy with sunbirds, orioles, minivets and other bird species, plus barking deer, wild boar, even leopard and elusive red panda. Day two continues ascending to Sandakphu, the ridge's highest point, delivering an extraordinary panorama of those loftiest peaks. Then it's on to Phalut on the Sikkim border for intimate views of Kangchenjunga, before descending east to lively Gorkhey and hike's-end Rimbik.

ACCOMMODATION
Simple trekkers' huts, private lodges or camping.

FOOD
Usually included in guided tours.

GETTING THERE
Shared jeeps and taxis run from Darjeeling to Mane Bhanjang, and Rimbik to Darjeeling, in about 1½ hours.

PLANNING
Permits required for Singalila National Park; you'll need a licensed guide (arrange in Darjeeling, Mane Bhanjang or via a tour company).

SAFETY
You'll feel the altitude at Sandakphu — walk slowly and drink plenty of (purified) water. Ensure travel vaccinations are up to date. Prepare for cold nights.

LEFT Meghma Gompa, on the taxing first leg of the Singalila Ridge trek from Mane Bhanjang. **TOP** Trekking through bamboo stands on the section from Phalut to Gorkhey.

MAY

Lagoonside camp in the shadow of Yerupajá on Peru's Cordillera Huayhuash Circuit (page 136).

I WANT A HIKE THAT'S A...

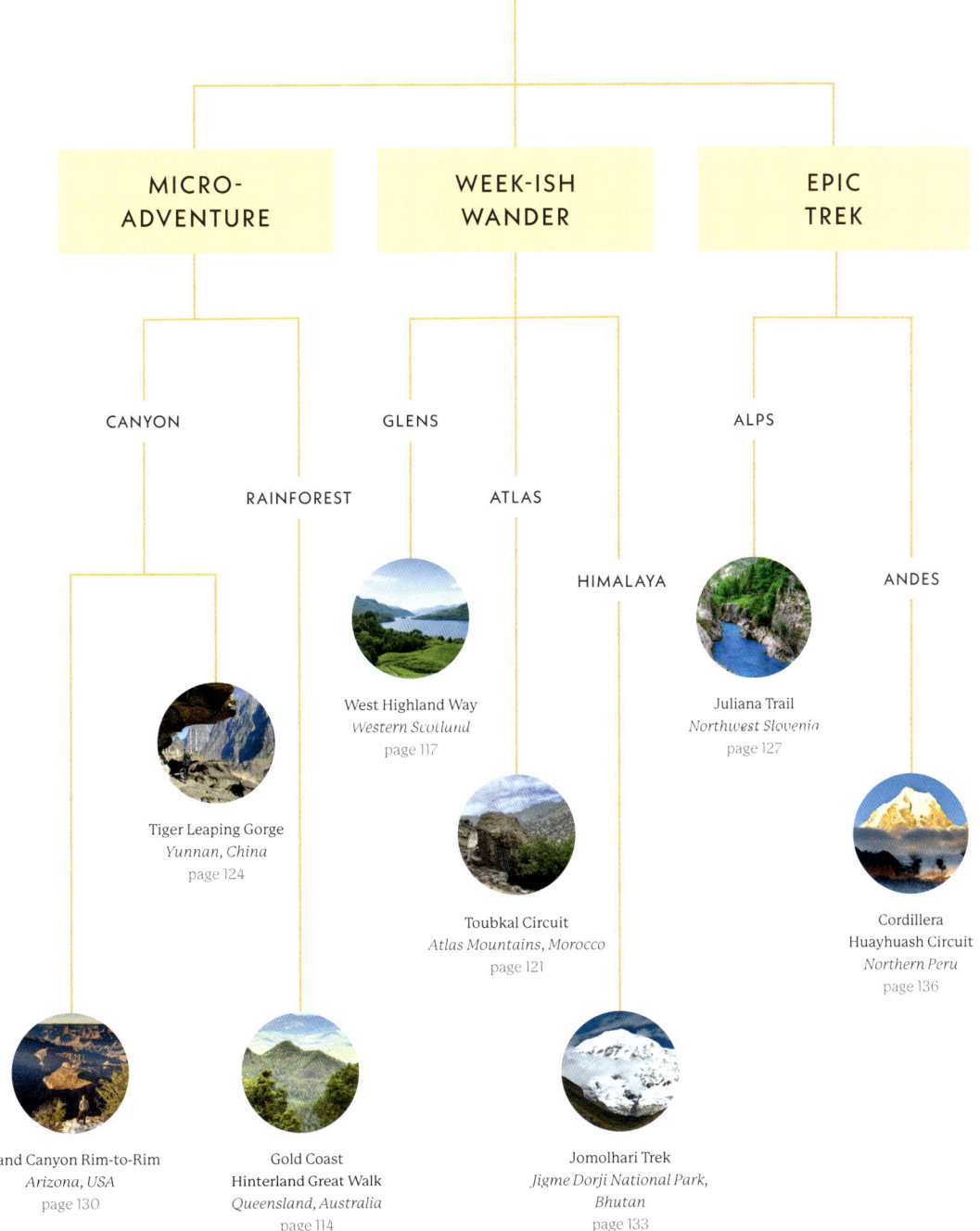

MICRO-ADVENTURE

CANYON
Grand Canyon Rim-to-Rim
Arizona, USA
page 130

RAINFOREST
Gold Coast Hinterland Great Walk
Queensland, Australia
page 114

Tiger Leaping Gorge
Yunnan, China
page 124

WEEK-ISH WANDER

GLENS
West Highland Way
Western Scotland
page 117

ATLAS
Toubkal Circuit
Atlas Mountains, Morocco
page 121

HIMALAYA
Jomolhari Trek
Jigme Dorji National Park, Bhutan
page 133

EPIC TREK

ALPS
Juliana Trail
Northwest Slovenia
page 127

ANDES
Cordillera Huayhuash Circuit
Northern Peru
page 136

AUSTRALIA

NATURE / CAMPING

Gold Coast Hinterland Great Walk

QUEENSLAND, AUSTRALIA

START
Green Mountains (O'Reilly), Lamington National Park

FINISH
Settlement Camping Area, Springbrook National Park

DISTANCE
54km (33.5 miles)

DURATION
Three days

CHALLENGE LEVEL

WHEN TO WALK
April–October

Immerse yourself in a tale of two parks on this S-shaped Great Walk through ecosystems that pre-date the dinosaurs.

Emerald, avocado, apple, jade, lime, lincoln, olive, pea, pistachio, turquoise: how many shades of green can you name? Ponder that during a hike through the chunk of Gondwana Rainforests straddling Lamington and Springbrook National Parks. This luxuriant swathe is an ocean of greens swimming with wildlife – and hikers, thanks to the three-day Gold Coast Hinterland tramp.

There's no guarantee you'll stay entirely dry in this patch of primeval rainforest, but avoiding wetter November–March is wise, to hike on trails a little less slippery. By May, conditions are that bit cooler, drier and more pleasant for walking. The track is accessible in both directions, though most begin at the western Green Mountains, from where more of the route is downhill. But you'll still start with the (relatively gentle) climb along the Border Track, tickling Queensland's boundary with NSW and tracing the rim of a vast extinct shield volcano. A series of lookouts along the ridge deliver sweeping vistas south and east – and there are more to come.

Veering north to Binna Burra, you'll pass the heads of Rifle Bird and Bell Bird Creeks – reminders to listen out for the 200 bird species that throng these forests. And not only the cracks and tinkling chimes of riflebirds and bellbirds: you'll likely hear the piercing, metallic calls of scrubbirds and the diverse mimicked songs of lyrebirds. Pademelons, wallabies, quolls, possums, sugar gliders and even platypus inhabit the parks, too. From here, the trail descends into the Numinbah Valley to cross into Springbrook National Park before a final climb to end at roaring Purling Brook Falls.

ACCOMMODATION
Walkers' campsites (book.parks.qld.gov.au); private campsites and other options at O'Reilly's (oreillys.com.au) and Binna Burra (binnaburralodge.com.au).

FOOD
Restaurants and cafes at O'Reilly's, Binna Burra and Springbrook plateau.

GETTING THERE
Both trailheads are around two hours south of Brisbane; there's no public transport, but parking is available at both ends.

PLANNING
Book accommodation well in advance.

SAFETY
Avoid walking in high winds or extreme heat. Watch for venomous snakes, stinging trees (gympie-gympie) and leeches.

INFO
parks.desi.qld.gov.au

MAY

LEFT Hiking the Gold Coast Hinterland near Binna Burra. **TOP** Purling Brook Falls, at the route's end.

NATURE / CULTURE / FOOD & DRINK / MOUNTAINS

West Highland Way

WESTERN SCOTLAND

Walk from the edges of Glasgow to the foot of the country's highest mountain via an ever-more dramatic unfurling of classic Scottish scenery.

The West Highland Way is Scotland's most popular long-distance trail – for several good reasons. First, it's easily accessible, starting on the outskirts of Glasgow. Second, although there are stiff climbs and wild terrain, it presents a satisfyingly manageable challenge. Third, it ticks off headline sites, from dreamy Loch Lomond to gorgeous Glencoe. And it exudes a powerful sense of drama, building in grandeur with every northward footstep to finish at the foot of Ben Nevis, Scotland's highest peak.

It's also a route that offers craic and camaraderie. More than 45,000 people hike the trail each year, with May most popular. This month heralds long days, more sunshine and less rain; the gorse is in brilliant-yellow bloom, the woodlands are awash with bluebells – and it's before the maddening midges are out in force: the largest numbers of biting females don't tend to arrive until early June.

So, more fellow trekkers – and for many hikers, the social aspect adds to the experience. Everyone is writing their own story along the same theme, and there's a delight in swapping tales of bogs, bugs and blisters over a wee dram at a bar en route.

What can you expect? From Milngavie (pronounced 'mull-guy'), the trail makes a flat-ish start, running between the Campsie Fells and Blane Water to the village of Drymen; along the way you could detour to Dumgoyach standing stones and Glengoyne Distillery. Beyond Drymen there's an ascent of Conic Hill, which bestrides the Great Divide separating Scotland's Highlands and Lowlands. It provides a magnificent Loch Lomond lookout, too,

START
Milngavie

FINISH
Fort William

DISTANCE
155km (96 miles)

DURATION
Five to eight days

CHALLENGE LEVEL

WHEN TO WALK
April–May
& September–October

LEFT The West Highland Way passes close to Glencoe's Lagangarbh Hut, hunkered below Buachaille Etive Mòr.

SCOTLAND

ACCOMMODATION
Wild camping is legal (with some restrictions around Loch Lomond). There are lodges, guesthouses and bunkhouses on the way, plus two bothies (basic, free accommodation huts).

FOOD
Pubs, shops, cafes and restaurants at fairly regular intervals. Pack snacks, and allow time for distillery visits.

GETTING THERE
Trains run from central Glasgow to Milngavie in 20 minutes. It's a scenic four-hour ride back from Fort William to Glasgow.

PLANNING
Book in advance – accommodation is sparser in the route's middle section and fills quickly.

SAFETY
Weather can be changeable – pack for all seasons. Take Avon Skin So Soft or Smidge repellent to deter midges.

INFO
westhighlandway.org

before the path drops to lakeshore Balmaha, then wends through forest to Rowardennan. There are more lovely views of the loch, and towards the Arrochar Alps, on the way to Inversnaid, home to an RSPB reserve and a crashing cascade. The trail gets tougher ahead, traversing rugged terrain where you might spot wild goats, ospreys or golden eagles. At Inverarnan, the 300-year old Drovers Inn is a fine place to rest.

Leaving Lomond behind, the route changes character, following the River Falloch to Crianlarich, with easier glen walking amid rising mountains. More woodland and valley-floor paths lead to the village of Tyndrum and the wildest section of the Way: from here there are no shops until Kinlochleven, some 45km (28 miles) away. It's fast-going at first, on military roads to Bridge of Orchy, where a sharp climb rewards with breathtaking views. Then the trail edges Loch Tulla before crossing epically isolated Rannoch Moor – it's like another world. Stop off at the Kingshouse Hotel

LEFT The approach to a the Devil's Staircase section of the West Highland Way. **RIGHT** Hiking through blooming bluebells toward legendary Loch Lomond.

'NEAR INVERSNAID, THE WEST HIGHLAND WAY PASSES ROB ROY'S CAVE, WHERE THE JACOBITE OUTLAW (AND SCOTTISH FOLK HERO) IS SAID TO HAVE HIDDEN FROM GOVERNMENT FORCES.'

for the classic shot of much-photographed munro (a Scottish mountain over 914m/3000ft) Buachaille Etive Mòr.

Another old military road leads to Altnafeadh, to look down glorious Glencoe, the 'weeping glen' where 30 MacDonald clansfolk were massacred in 1692. Then comes the zigzagging climb up the Devil's Staircase to the trail's highest point (548m/1798ft); on a clear day, Ben Nevis looms ahead. Kinlochleven is the staging post for the final push, over the Lairigmor pass and into Glen Nevis, to finish by Fort William's walker statue – aptly named *Sore Feet*.

Midge madness

MIDGES – SPECIFICALLY *Culicoides impunctatus* – are the bane of the Highlands. Though they're only tiny, and don't transmit diseases, these biting insects can cause unpleasant reactions in sensitive people, and extreme irritation to everyone. They appear from May and last until September; midsummer is usually midge-iest, and Scotland's west is more affected than the east. They are worst at dusk and dawn, but can't cope with strong winds. Check the latest levels online (smidgeup.com/midge-forecast).

NATURE / FOOD & DRINK / CULTURE / MOUNTAINS

Toubkal Circuit

ATLAS MOUNTAINS, MOROCCO

Discover Indigenous Amazigh villages and spectacular High Atlas scenery as you approach the summit of the highest peak in North Africa.

You could, if time is tight and you simply want to bag another peak, conquer North Africa's loftiest summit in a weekend. At 4167m (13,671ft), Jebel Toubkal is a hefty mountain, high enough to risk altitude sickness, but it's not a technical climb. Anyone with a reasonable level of fitness and experience hiking on rough-ish, rocky terrain will find it an achievable challenge. Nor is this a long trek: it's possible — and several European tour operators offer this — to fly to the nearest hub, Marrakesh; drive to the refuge at 3200m (10,500ft) for a sleep; rise early for the 1000m (3280ft) or so of ascent to the top; then dash back down, scoot to Marrakesh, and home you go.

But why would you? Morocco as a whole has so much to offer, and deserves your time — if only a day or two extra in Marrakesh to browse the buzzing souqs (bazaars), admire the ornate carved decoration and *zellige* tilework on mosques and *medersas* (Islamic schools), and dive into the glorious mayhem of the Djemaa El Fna square. The colours of the textiles and tanneries, the aromas of *harira* soup and tajines wafting through the alleys, the sounds of the muezzin calling the faithful to prayer and the music of nocturnal performers — it's irresistible.

The High Atlas is another world altogether, though — and well worth exploring in a little more depth. Whereas Morocco's cities tend to be dominated by people of Arab origin, the mountains are the domain of the Amazigh, Indigenous people who lived here long before the migration of Islamic forces across the region of North Africa known as the Maghreb. Their rust-and-ochre-hued

START/FINISH
Imlil

DISTANCE
68km (42 miles)

DURATION
Six days

CHALLENGE LEVEL
★★☆☆☆

WHEN TO WALK
April–May
& September–October

MAY

LEFT The mountain village of Imlil, starting point for the Toubkal Circuit into the High Atlas.

Moroccan cuisine

MOROCCAN FOOD is perfect fuel for hungry hikers. The ubiquitous tajine is a delicious, hearty casserole-like dish slow-cooked in an earthenware vessel with a distinctive conical lid. It's often made with chicken or lamb, though veggie versions are common, all packed with potatoes, carrots, onions, courgettes (zucchini), olives and more, often served with couscous. Alcohol isn't widely available in the mountains, but you'll be poured endless glasses of 'Moroccan whiskey' – sugared mint tea.

'THE HIGH ATLAS ARE THE TRADITIONAL HEARTLAND OF THE AMAZIGH – 'FREE PEOPLE' – INDIGENOUS NORTH AFRICANS WHO MAINTAIN DISTINCTIVE CUSTOMS, LANGUAGE AND ARCHITECTURE.

villages cling to the hillsides, many with welcoming *gîtes d'étape* or refuges offering simple hikers' accommodation.

To meet these welcoming and strongly independent-minded folk, eschew the straight up-and-down trek and instead follow a six-day circuit through Toubkal National Park. Though trails are accessible year-round – and Toubkal is an increasingly popular winter climb – winter nights can be chilly, with snow on peaks and high paths, while summers are hot and dry, with the most popular routes clogged by hikers. Autumn and, particularly,

LEFT Mountain views on the second day of the Toukbal Circuit trek. **RIGHT** A dawn ascent rewards with superlative sunrise views from Toukbal's snowcapped summit.

MOROCCO

ACCOMMODATION
Camping or basic *gîtes d'étape* (local guesthouses, typically with shared rooms and facilities). Mountain hut on Toubkal for summit night.

FOOD
Stock up in Marrakesh; some supplies and cafes in villages en route. Purify drinking water.

GETTING THERE
Shared *grands taxis* run Marrakesh–Imlil in under 1½ hours.

PLANNING
Hiring a guide or joining a group is recommended; theoretically guides are mandatory for the Toubkal ascent.

SAFETY
Altitude sickness is possible; ascend slowly and watch for symptoms.

INFO
Cicerone (cicerone.co.uk) and Trailblazer (trailblazer-guides.com) publish excellent guidebooks. A 1:50,000 Jebel Toubkal map can be bought in Marrakesh.

spring are ideal. May's nigh-on perfect, in fact, with trails clear, rainfall minimal and poppies, scabious and gentians speckling the foothills red, pink and blue.

The obvious starting point for a trek is Imlil, base for most experienced mountain guides — highly advisable — and the spot to pick up supplies. Set out clockwise, heading first east and steeply up to the Amazigh village of Tacheddirt. Then veer south across scree, over the Tizi n'Likemt and through a narrow gorge to overnight in Amsouzert or Aït Igrane. Climbing west past lovely, limpid Lac d'Ifni, the testing haul over the Tizi n'Ouanoums (3650m/11,975ft) rewards with wonderful views. It's downhill to the base-camp refuge to prepare for your dawn ascent of Toubkal. The return route passes the sizeable village of Aroumd before arriving back in Imlil for transfers to Marrakesh — and a night of celebration, having completed the circuit.

NATURE / CULTURE / MOUNTAINS

Tiger Leaping Gorge

YUNNAN, CHINA

START
Hutiaoxia (Qiaotou)

FINISH
Hetaoyuan (Walnut Garden)

DISTANCE
25km (15.5 miles)

DURATION
Two days

CHALLENGE LEVEL

WHEN TO WALK
April–May
& September–October

Marvel at one of the world's deepest canyons on a hike beneath some of Yunnan's most picturesque mountains.

For a reminder of the raw power of water, head for Tiger Leaping Gorge. Carved by the implacable flow of the Jinsha River over millions of years, its sheer rock walls plunge nearly 3800m (12,470ft) from surrounding peaks sporting poetic names such as Jade Dragon Snow Mountain. As so often in China, the gorge enjoys a delightfully fanciful origin story of a striped big cat escaping a hunter with a mighty jump across the valley at its narrowest point – still around 30m (98ft) wide.

Today, as is also the way in China, a road snakes along the gorge around midway up. To best absorb the natural drama, hike the upper trail near the top of the cliffs, gazing at those snowcapped summits and down to the Jinsha surging along the canyon's floor.

Though not a long hike, it follows paths that can be very slippery after rain, and there are plenty of ups and downs, climbing to around 2600m (8530ft) in places; avoid both the icy depths of winter and rainy summer – spring or autumn are ideal. Starting from Hutiaoxia (sometimes called Qiaotou), where buses from Lijiang drop off, it's a fairly relentless ascent first to the gorge itself and then to the upper trail – though the infamous '28 Bends' section beyond Naxi village is far less daunting than often claimed.

The rewards are fantastic views of those rock ramparts – including Jade Dragon Snow Mountain, soaring to 5596m (18,360ft) – and to waterfalls striping the verdant flanks of the gorge. The rest of the trail is more gently undulating; overnighting at one of the guesthouses midway along allows time to absorb the scenery (and some well-deserved food) before ending at Hetaoyuan, famous for its walnuts, perhaps with a detour down the steps to Tiger Leaping Rock itself.

ACCOMMODATION
Hostels and guesthouses en route (notably Halfway Guesthouse) and at Hetaoyuan.

FOOD
Cafes and snack kiosks.

GETTING THERE
Early buses run between Lijiang and Hutiaoxia (two hours). Buses run to Lijiang and Shangri-La from Tina's Guest House (near the end). Check times locally.

PLANNING
Small trail fee, payable locally. Make sure you have some cash.

SAFETY
The path is slippery after rain, and very steep to the bottom of the gorge. Bring a hat, sunscreen and plenty of drinking water.

MAY

LEFT Sheer rock walls and water-carved ravines in Tiger Leaping Gorge. **TOP** Follow steps and boardwalks to the spot where the mythical tiger is said to have made its leap across the surging Jinsha.

MAY

NATURE / FOOD & DRINK / CULTURE / MOUNTAINS

Juliana Trail

NORTHWEST SLOVENIA

Trace a meandering loop around Slovenia's iconic three-headed peak to discover moving history, cascading waterfalls, clifftop castles and culinary delights.

Two heads are better than one, it's said. Three must be perfect, right? Meet Slovenia's loftiest mountain, 2864m-high (9396ft) Triglav — literally 'three heads'. This sky-scraping triple peak holds a special place in the national psyche: it appears on the flag and coat of arms, and tradition holds that every Slovenian should summit Triglav at least once.

For hikers it has another allure. Not only is Triglav the focal point of its namesake national park, a 840-sq-km (324-sq-mile) biosphere reserve encompassing the lion's share of the Julian Alps, it's also the pivot for the looping route of the long-distance Juliana Trail. Designed to minimise negative environmental impacts and maximise benefits to local communities, it showcases glorious scenic and wildlife wonders, historic and cultural gems, food and drink. Though a not-inconsiderable 270km (168 miles), the trail never climbs above 1500m (4921ft), and with clear waymarking and ample facilities in appealing towns and villages at the end of each stage, it can be completed by walkers of moderate fitness and experience levels.

Being a low-altitude route, the trail is open from spring to autumn — we say come in May, when days are lengthening and some 300 species of wildflowers bloom across Alpine meadows but before crowds intensify in honeypots like Bled.

The circuit can be joined at any point, and tackled clockwise or anticlockwise. The first of the 16 officially numbered stages begins in Kranjska Gora, though, which makes a sensible place to begin. That first stretch opens with a tramp across the wooded southern slopes of the Karavankas, a range defining the northern

START/FINISH
Kranjska Gora (or Bled, Bohinjska Bistrica or Tolmin)

DISTANCE
270km (168 miles)

DURATION
10–20 days

CHALLENGE LEVEL
★★★☆☆

WHEN TO WALK
April–October

LEFT Bled Island in the waters of its namesake lake, capped by the Church of the Assumption.

ACCOMMODATION
Hotels, guesthouses, B&Bs, apartments and campsites.

FOOD
Restaurants and food stores at the end of most stages. Carry lunch supplies.

GETTING THERE
Frequent buses from Slovenia's capital Ljubljana serve Bled (one hour), Kranjska Gora and Bohinjska Bistrica (both under two hours), and Tolmin (under 2½ hours).

PLANNING
Book accommodation well in advance, particularly in smaller villages where options are limited. No fees or permits are required, and guides aren't necessary, though tours are available.

SAFETY
Some sections are slippery after rain; snow lingers into June on higher paths. Bring sunscreen, and tick repellent/remover.

INFO
julian-alps.com

border with Austria, climbing to the lookout at Srednji Vrh for views south to Triglav and the jagged peak of Špik.

Continue east along the Sava Valley past crashing *slaps* (waterfalls), distinctive *kozolci* (wooden hayracks) and Carniolan beehives painted with folkloric and Biblical scenes. At Begunje, pause for thought at the moving Museum of Hostages and the home of Slavko Avsenik, pioneer of brassy polka genre Oberkrainer and arguably Slovenia's most famous musical export. Then veer south to watch gingerbread being traditionally decorated in Radovljica's medieval moated heart, and west to admire the clifftop castle and island church on gorgeous, glacial Lake Bled. (Be sure to fuel up on a slice of artery-clogging *kremšnita* cream cake.)

The trail then turns wilder, climbing into the national park and through high pastures where transhumance herders mind their charges from larch-shingled cabins. Descend through

LEFT The Julian Alps tower over verdant farmland near Kranska Gora. **BELOW** Mt Triglav, Slovenia's highest peak and the pivot for the Juliana Trail. **RIGHT** Rafting the Soča River in Triglav National Park.

'ACCORDING TO LEGEND, LOVELY LAKE BOHINJ WAS BESTOWED ON UNPUSHY LOCAL PEOPLE BY GOD (BOH), WHO REWARDED THEIR PATIENCE WITH THIS MOST BEAUTIFUL PART OF HIS CREATION.'

Barje Goreljek, Europe's highest swamp, to Lake Bohinj – more raw and dramatic (and less touristy) than Bled, with excellent cheeses and lake trout to boost hikers' energy levels. It's a testing ascent over the ridge to the Bača Valley and the confluence with the Soča River, its waters an almost unbelievable turquoise-teal hue as it tumbles through rocky gorges populated by fantastical black-and-yellow fire salamanders.

Now heading north, the route passes WWI emplacements and the outdoor activity hub of Bovec, hopping briefly over the Italian border to Tarvisio before returning to Kranjska Gora – completing an electrifying circuit.

Super side trips

TWO TEMPTING side-trips make worthy detours from the original circuit. The three-stage, 42km (26-mile) Breginjski kot climbs forested slopes from the Soča Valley at Kobarid to the village of Breginj beneath Stol Mountain, descending to little Podbela overlooking the crystal-clear Nadiža River before returning to Kobarid. The more-challenging option is a four-stage, 60km (37-mile) leg linking Tolmin with the medieval walled village of Šmartno (Brda), promising steep and rocky sections but also great views.

USA

NATURE / CAMPING

Grand Canyon Rim-to-Rim

ARIZONA, USA

START
South Rim

FINISH
North Rim

DISTANCE
34km (21 miles)

DURATION
One to two days

CHALLENGE LEVEL

WHEN TO WALK
May–June
& September–October

Descend into the big, bold, beautiful bowels of the Earth on a matchless Grand Canyon crossing.

As the crow flies it's about 16km (10 miles) between the Grand Canyon's North and South Rims. But to cover the distance on foot — to descend into this almighty gash in the Colorado Plateau and heft back up the other side — is twice as far. And it ranks as one of the finest short hikes in the world.

The 1.6km (1-mile) deep Grand Canyon is both a rapture of red-orange rock and a 3D geography textbook. Its geological strata chart aeons of planet-making, with the schist at the bottom almost two billion years old. Switchbacking down through these layers from the South Rim, via either the South Kaibab or Bright Angel Trails — routes used by the Ancestral Puebloans for centuries — is like going back in time. It's also tough on the knees (pack trekking poles).

Standing on the canyon's floor, where the rims loom out of sight, the cottonwoods grow and the Colorado River roars, will make you feel about as small as it's possible to feel — like a bug in the belly of the planet. Enjoy the sensation: some hike the trail in one long day, but try to overnight at Phantom Ranch or one of the in-canyon campgrounds, if you can bag a spot. Then climb out via the gentler, shadier North Kaibab Trail to reach the less-visited North Rim.

Timing your Rim-to-Rim is all-important if you want the best of all worlds. South Rim facilities stay open year-round, but North Rim access roads and accommodation are closed from late November to early/mid-May, and some water sources are turned off. Then, from mid-June to mid-September, temperatures rise to incendiary levels — too hot to hike. Late May is the sweet spot for an epic crossing.

ACCOMMODATION
Reservations for Phantom Ranch are allocated by lottery, which opens 13 months in advance. Backcountry permits are required for campsites below the rim.

FOOD
Phantom Ranch serves meals to guests. Pack all other supplies.

GETTING THERE
Buses run from Flagstaff to South Rim.

PLANNING
To return to your starting point, book the Trans-Canyon Shuttle, which connects North and South Rims in 4½ hours.

SAFETY
Carry plenty of water and identify sources in advance.

INFO
nps.gov/grca

LEFT Enter the reservation lottery well in advance to snag a coveted cabin at Phantom Ranch on the canyon floor. **TOP** The Colorado River carves its winding route through the Grand Canyon.

MAY

NATURE / CULTURE / CAMPING / MOUNTAINS

Jomolhari Trek

, BHUTAN

Trek through the monumental wilderness of Jigme Dorji National Park in this long-secluded Himalayan kingdom, watching for yaks and – if you're really lucky – an elusive snow leopard.

The 'Kingdom of the Thunder Dragon' surely tops every places-to-trek-before-you-die list. Until the 1970s, this compact, long-isolated Himalayan nation was off-limits to foreign visitors; since then, its focus on Gross National Happiness above wealth has kept tourism to a minimum. More recently, though the emphasis on maintaining traditions and respecting Bhutan's Buddhist culture remains strong, access has become easier and a little cheaper. Its epic mountain landscapes, burly *dzongs* (fortress-monasteries), unique costumes and customs remain as enthralling as ever.

Most visitors experience just a fraction of the country's natural beauty and monuments, sticking to the cultural hotspots around Paro, Thimphu and Punakha. Head onto the high trails, though, and you'll discover an untamed world of 7000m-plus (22,967ft) summits, remote villages and rare wildlife.

If time and money are no object, hit the 403km (250-mile) Trans-Bhutan Trail, a month-long challenge traversing the nation along ancient pathways. But for most mere mortals, the Jomolhari Trek provides an accessible way to encounter Bhutan's natural wonders. Come in spring to dodge winter's deep chill and summer rains.

Though the route can be completed in around a week, logistics – and common sense – mean you'll bookend your hike with at least a day or two experiencing the marvels of Paro and capital Thimphu, likely including a climb to the near-mythical, cliff-clinging Taktshang Goemba, the 'Tiger's Nest Monastery'. From

START
Shana

FINISH
Dolam Kencho

DISTANCE
85km (53 miles) or longer

DURATION
Six to eight days

CHALLENGE LEVEL
★★★★☆

WHEN TO WALK
March–May
& September–November

MAY

LEFT Spy grazing yak on the Jomolhari Trek through the mountains of Bhutan's Jigme Dorji National Park.

Festival fever

AS IF Bhutan's *dzongs* (fortresses) and *gompas* (monasteries) weren't spectacular enough, many host *tsechus*, major Buddhist festivals typically involving the unfurling of huge *thangkas* (religious paintings) and performances by masked dancers. Staged on difference dates at venues across the country, you'll need to plan well ahead to experience the most popular, including those in Paro and Thimphu. A different but equally captivating event is October's Jomolhari Mountain Festival, celebrating the region's culture and wildlife.

'BHUTAN'S *GOMPAS* (MONASTERIES), CITADELS AND SPECTACULAR *DZONGS* (FORTRESS-MONASTERIES) WERE CONSTRUCTED TO DEFEND AGAINST INVADERS FROM THE NORTH.'

there, a shortish drive takes you to the trailhead at Shana — start of a trek taking you ever further among the high peaks and remote communities. The route arcs through the wilds of Jigme Dorji National Park, home to bharal (blue sheep), eagles, Himalayan marmots, goat-like takins, and even tigers and snow leopards — though you'd be incredibly fortunate to see either of those elusive big cats.

The trek initially follows the Paro River upstream, climbing steadily through pine and rhododendron forest and between scattered farmsteads. But make no mistake: though the terrain isn't the toughest, you're already over 3000m (9842ft) altitude, and the air only gets thinner and colder over the days to come. Fortunately, you'll be joined by an experienced guide and staff to help carry baggage and make your camping experience more comfortable.

TOP Masked dancers perform at a Buddhist *tsechu* (festival). **LEFT** A mule train along the Jomilhari Trek route through Jigme Dorji National Park. **RIGHT** Lingzhi Dzong, a welcome sight after crossing Nyile La.

ACCOMMODATION
Tents on the trek route, hotels at either end.

FOOD
Trek staff cook all food. Expect hearty fare including *ema datshi*, chillies in cheese, Bhutan's most popular (and warming) dish.

GETTING THERE
Two Bhutanese airlines, Drukair and Bhutan Airlines, fly to the international airport at Paro from other Asian hubs. Tour operators can arrange transfers to and from the trailheads.

PLANNING
Treks must be booked with a registered tour company, which organises accommodation, food, guides and transport. A US$100/day sustainable development fee is levied.

SAFETY
Prepare for cold weather and altitudes close to 5000m (16,404ft). Climb slowly and allow yourself time to acclimatise.

A couple of days' walking brings you to Jangothang – base camp for Bhutan's second-highest mountain, 7326m (24,035ft) Jomolhari, a hulking, border-straddling mass of rock and snow. Spend a couple of nights here, acclimatising to the altitude – topping 4100m (13,451ft) already – and perhaps meeting the yak herders who tend livestock in the area. Then it's onwards and upwards over the windswept Nyile La, one of two high passes punctuating the route. Your reward is the chance to admire the mighty Lingzhi Dzong, built in the 17th century to guard the frontier.

Rest up, because the biggest test of the trek awaits: the Yele La (4930m/16,175ft) – breath-snatchingly lofty and scenic, with magnificent views of the eastern Himalaya. Then it's pretty much all downhill, following the Thimphu River to the trailhead and your pick-up back to the capital and a celebratory Red Panda beer.

NATURE / CAMPING / MOUNTAINS

Cordillera Huayhuash Circuit

NORTHERN PERU

START/FINISH
Llamac

DISTANCE
130km (81 miles) approx

DURATION
Eight to 14 days

CHALLENGE LEVEL:
★★★★★

WHEN TO WALK
May–September

The trek around this compact but colossal Andean range is a tough and humbling dalliance with Peru's mountain giants.

Breathtaking – quite literally. This loop walk around the compact Cordillera Huayhuash rarely dips below an altitude of 4000m (13,123ft) – in fact, it mostly meanders well above that, and negotiates passes over 5000m (16,404ft). A head for heights, strong legs and careful acclimatisation are required – but the payoff is just as heady. Entirely above the treeline, the trek is a glorious widescreen epic of open pampa, vivid lakes and massive peaks – including Siula Grande, the 6344m (20,814ft) giant made infamous by mountaineer Joe Simpson's book *Touching the Void*.

If you're going to brave this land of extremes, best do it in the fairest weather. That means the dry season (May–September), when rainfall is low and skies largely clear, blue and optimal for views. Days stay mild (18°C–22°C/64°F–72°F), though nights drop below freezing – expect to open your tent to a sparkle of frost. And in this wild, remote country, hiring donkeys and guides is advisable.

Walking clockwise, there's no easy way in: from the campsite at Quartelhuain, it's a haul up to the first high pass at Cacananpunta. That sets the tone for the basic route, which stretches around 130km (81 miles) but has numerous variants that change the distance; all immerse you in a majestic forest of snowy peaks. Highlights include gazing down on the impossibly turquoise waters of Laguna Mitucocha; standing at Mirador Tres Lagunas, where a spatter of lakes reflect surrounding summits; soaking weary limbs in Viconga thermal baths; and crossing Santa Rosa (5060m/16,601ft), the trek's official high point, with heavenly views to match.

ACCOMMODATION
Twelve official community operated campsites, with variable toilet facilities.

FOOD
Solo hikers must carry supplies for the whole trek. Agencies provide meals and snacks.

GETTING THERE
Buses run between Lima and Huaraz (seven hours); private shuttles and an infrequent bus run between Huaraz and Llamac.

PLANNING
Independent trekking is for experienced hikers only. Guided trips include donkeys, cooks and equipment. Read reviews before choosing an agency. Fees must be paid to communities en route.

SAFETY
Acclimatise well.

INFO
huayhuash.com

LEFT Trekking the Cordillera Huayhuash delivers spectacular views of brilliant lakes and spiky summits.
TOP A picture-perfect trailside camp near Laguna Jahuacocha.

JUNE

Mountain camping at Refuge de Petra Piana, along the GR20 across Corsica's rugged spine (page 141).

JUNE

I WANT A HIKE THAT'S A...

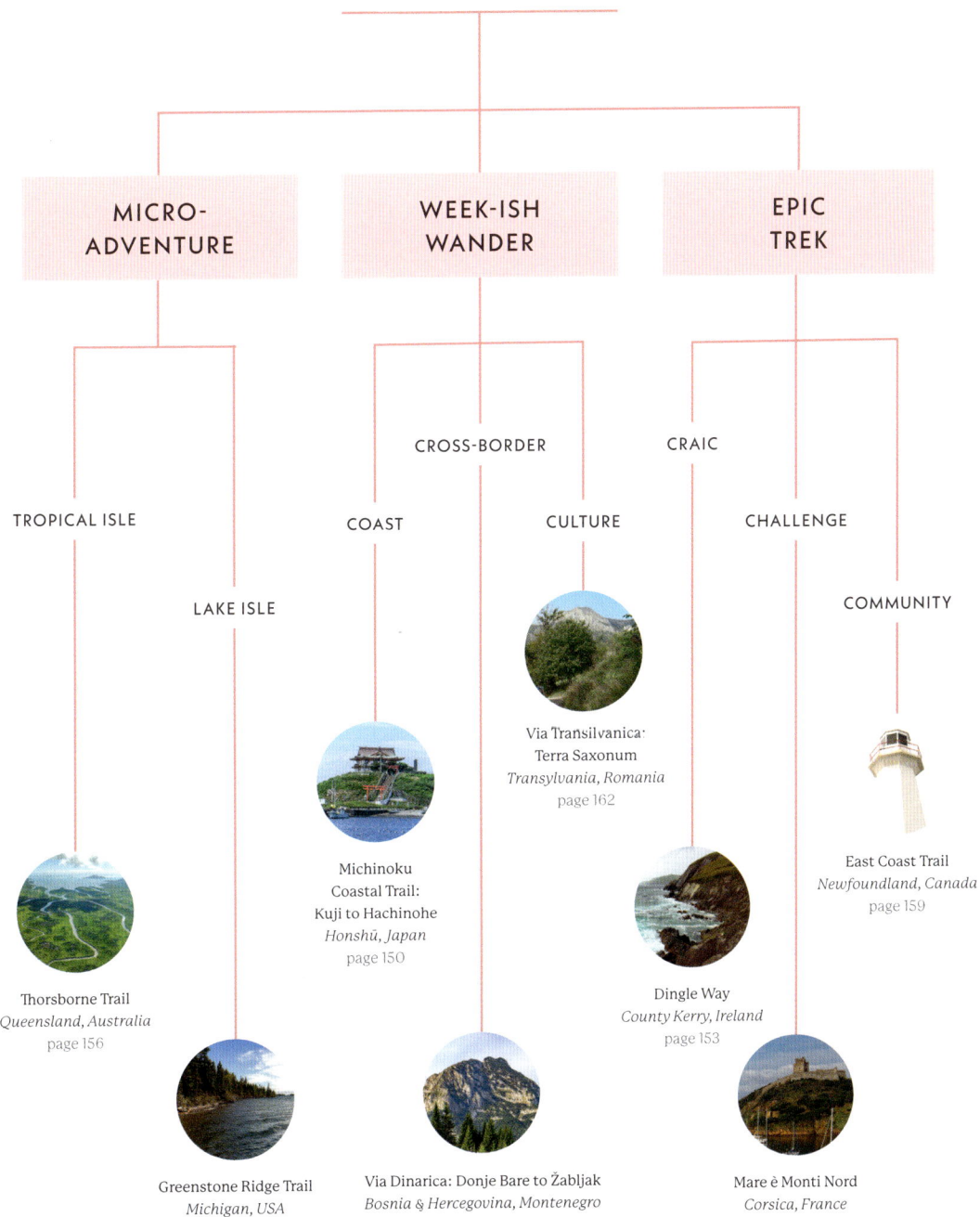

- MICRO-ADVENTURE
  - TROPICAL ISLE
    - Thorsborne Trail
      Queensland, Australia
      page 156
  - LAKE ISLE
    - Greenstone Ridge Trail
      Michigan, USA
      page 144
- WEEK-ISH WANDER
  - COAST
    - Michinoku Coastal Trail: Kuji to Hachinohe
      Honshū, Japan
      page 150
  - CROSS-BORDER
    - Via Dinarica: Donje Bare to Žabljak
      Bosnia & Hercegovina, Montenegro
      page 147
  - CULTURE
    - Via Transilvanica: Terra Saxonum
      Transylvania, Romania
      page 162
- EPIC TREK
  - CRAIC
    - CHALLENGE
      - Dingle Way
        County Kerry, Ireland
        page 153
    - COMMUNITY
      - East Coast Trail
        Newfoundland, Canada
        page 159
  - Mare è Monti Nord
    Corsica, France
    page 141

139

NATURE / CULTURE / MOUNTAINS / COAST

Mare è Monti Nord

CORSICA, FRANCE

With its rumpled interior and shimmering beaches, the l'Île de Beauté is a beautiful place for a walk, with the 'Sea and Mountains' route one of the best.

The apparent inaccessibility of much of mountainous Corsica has, strangely, long attracted people. There's a local phrase, '*prendre le maquis*', meaning to hide away in the shrub-cloaked interior of this rugged Mediterranean isle – which is exactly what Corsican guerrillas did in the 18th century when fighting the Genoese for independence. They gained their freedom in 1755, only to be conquered again, by the French, before the century was out. However, while the island has been part of France virtually ever since, it's never lost its sense of self. The Corsican dialect is similar to Tuscan, reflecting the proximity to Italy and those centuries of Genoese rule, while – particularly in the island's highlands – there's a strong sense of national pride and identity: they call it *l'âme Corse*, the 'Corsican Soul'.

To help preserve this, the Parc Naturel Régional de Corse was inaugurated in 1972. Covering almost 40% of the island, its founding mission was to promote ecotourism and combat the depopulation of the mountains; old huts were renovated, new refuges were built and trails were blazed to link isolated villages and encourage hikers to visit them. These trails have become the best way for outsiders to delve into the unreachable-seeming hinterland and discover Corsica's soul for themselves.

One of these trails is the Mare è Monti Nord, which wiggles between the sea (*mare*) and mountains (*monti*) of the natural park's wild west. Corsica has tougher, better-known treks, but this one manages to tick a lot of boxes without being cripplingly hard. Charting a course that stays largely in sight of the Med but also ascends closer to the high summits, the Mare è Monti Nord

START
Calenzana

FINISH
Cargèse

DISTANCE
122km (76 miles)

DURATION
10 days

CHALLENGE LEVEL
★★★★☆

WHEN TO WALK
April–June
September–October

LEFT The mountain village of Évisa, along the Mare è Monti Nord route through Corsica's wild northwest.

FRANCE

ACCOMMODATION
Most local villages have *gîtes d'étapes* or places for camping; some have hotels. Wild camping isn't allowed.

FOOD
Some shops, restaurants and cafes available at the start/end of stages, varying by village size. Carry some supplies.

GETTING THERE
Calvi is the nearest airport to the northern trailhead, Calenzana; Calvi to Calenzana is around 30 minutes by bus. From Cargèse, buses run to the capital, Ajaccio.

PLANNING
Book accommodation in advance in the popular spring/autumn months; although the trail is passable year-round, some *gîtes* close out of season.

SAFETY
A decent level of fitness is required. Avoid high summer.

INFO
pnr.corsica

offers a dazzling diversity of scenery: swathes of coastal maquis, deep valleys and ravines, the plunging Gorges de Spelunca, atmospheric old-growth chestnut forest, cobbled mule tracks and shepherds' paths, abandoned hamlets, colourful sea cliffs.

Marked with orange flashes, the route is broken down into 10 stages, none of which are overly long – some hikers choose to cover the whole trail in fewer then 10 days. This is perfectly doable, as long as you're sure of foot and fit enough for frequent ups and downs, but it's a shame to rush. There are villages placed just about often enough that you can spend each night in a homely *gîte* and get a glimpse of rural Corsican life.

The Mare è Monti Nord could technically be walked year-round, but accommodation options often close outside the main season, and temperatures can soar in July and August, intensified by the hot sirocco winds blown from the Sahara – so spring and autumn are the optimum times to tackle the route. June,

LEFT Cool off mid-hike in the freshwater pools of Vallée du Fango. **BELOW** Coastal watchtower along the Sentier du Douanier trail, Cap Corse. **RIGHT** Mare è Monti Nord highlights include gorgeous Girolata, reachable only on foot or by boat.

'THE OLD TRANSHUMANCE ROUTE BETWEEN CARGÈSE AND THE VILLAGE OF MARIGNANA, FORMING TWO STAGES OF THE MARE È MONTI, BECAME A KEY ROUTE FOR THE AMERICAN-BACKED RESISTANCE MOVEMENT DURING WWII.'

with its long days, open facilities, warm sunshine and generally more settled weather, is a fine choice.

And if it does heat up, rest assured that there are plenty of opportunities for cooling off along the way: for instance, take sea dips at wild Plage de Tuara, sandy Galéria and gorgeous Girolata (a traditional village still only accessible on foot or by boat), or frolic in the Vallée du Fango's natural pools.

Alternative ambles

CORSICA HAS many other tempting trails. The five-day Mare è Monti Sud (South), from Porto-Vecchio to Propriano, is less demanding that the northern route, and is also walkable year-round; along the way it passes comely villages, prehistoric remains and comfortable *gites d'étapes*. There are also three Mare à Mare (Sea to Sea) itineraries, slicing east–west across the island. Or try the two-day Sentier des Douaniers (Custom Officers' Trail), which loops the wild Cap Corse.

USA

NATURE / CAMPING

Greenstone Ridge Trail

MICHIGAN, USA

START
Windigo

FINISH
Hidden Lake or Rock Harbor

DISTANCE
66km (41 miles), plus spurs to campsites

DURATION
Four to seven days

CHALLENGE LEVEL

WHEN TO WALK
Mid-May to mid-September

Enjoy truly remote backcountry hiking across the pristine wilderness of Lake Superior's lonely Isle Royale.

Love the idea of being completely isolated from the modern world — no cars, no running water, almost no other humans or phone service? For experienced backcountry hikers and campers seeking solitude and a digital detox, with the chance of communing with nature in a very primal sense, the Greenstone Ridge Trail is a compact gem.

This glorious wilderness walk runs pretty much the entire length of Isle Royale, the least-visited national park in the US's Lower 48 states. Lying adrift in the northwest of Lake Superior, it's a long, remote, glacier-scoured strip of volcanic rock — you might even come across some of that eponymous greenstone — patched with spruce and fir, birch and maple, swamp forest and pine stands. And in these varying habitats lives a menagerie of wildlife that you may or may not want to encounter: wolves (unlikely), moose (hunted by the wolves), beavers, otters, martens and squirrels. Oh, and a range of biting flies and mosquitoes that build in intensity from June — the earlier you come, the better, though ferries typically run only mid-May to mid-September. The trail is busiest — a relative term — in July and August, when campsites may fill up; June's a good all-round bet.

The trail, which can be walked in either direction, runs partly along the shore but largely along the ridge that forms the island's spine. Expect rock-hopping, rooty and pine-needle-springy forest tracks, boardwalks through swamps, stretches across exposed granite and scrub, paths around inland lakes. Early in the season you'll likely clamber over or under plenty of fallen trees, and there are numerous ups and downs — which means grand vistas from viewpoints such as Lookout Louise, near the Hidden Lake trailhead, and Mt Franklin. Prepared to be wowed by the wild.

ACCOMMODATION
Backcountry campsites.

FOOD
Carry all supplies, purify water. Store food in animal-resistant containers.

GETTING THERE
Ferries and seaplanes connect harbours in Michigan and Minnesota with Windigo and Rock Harbor. Water taxis link Rock Harbor and Hidden Lake.

PLANNING
Park entrance fee (currently $7 daily) applies.

SAFETY
Wear insect repellent, long sleeves and trousers; consider a headnet. Wolves and moose are present, though you're unlikely to see the former; show moose respect. Prepare for all weathers.

INFO
nps.gov/isro

LEFT Bull moose, Isle Royale National Park. **TOP** The pristine Lake Superior shoreline of Isle Royale.

NATURE / CULTURE / FOOD & DRINK / MOUNTAINS

Via Dinarica: Donje Bare to Žabljak

BOSNIA & HERCEGOVINA, MONTENEGRO

Walk right across the Balkans – or pick a smaller section – on a trail that's strengthening connections and opening up some of Europe's least-spoilt mountains.

It wasn't so long ago that a trek through the Balkans would have been unthinkable. Albania was all but closed to the rest of the world until the 1980s; then the 1990s saw war rage across the former Yugoslavia. But times have definitely a-changed. In the early 21st century, an idea was hatched to forge a trail – the Via Dinarica – linking these formerly troubled countries, to build bonds and encourage adventurous outsiders to visit. And what an adventure: the Dinaric Alps remain some of the least-explored and most untouched reaches on the continent where, for now at least, mountain life is still lived the way it has been for centuries.

The Via Dinarica traces the range north–south from Slovenia to Albania via Bosnia & Hercegovina, Kosovo, Croatia, Serbia and Montenegro, using shepherds' paths, military roads, old trade routes and new connections. Stretching over some 1930km (1200 miles), it takes in an incalculable number of valleys and peaks, Alpine lakes and thick beech forests, wildflower meadows, cow pastures and olive groves, monasteries, mosques, ancient forts and war memorials – plus cheesemakers, bread-bakers, goat-herders and country folk proffering glasses of potent *rakia* (brandy). Tackling it all is a mammoth task; picking one chunk offers a tantalising taster.

The route was launched in Bosnia & Hercegovina and Montenegro: in 2010, a trial trail was blazed to link the former's

START
Donje Bare, Bosnia & Hercegovina

FINISH
Žabljak, Montenegro

DISTANCE
92km (57 miles)

DURATION
Four to six days

CHALLENGE LEVEL
★★★★☆

WHEN TO WALK
June–September

LEFT Piva Canyon in Durmitor National Park, along the Montenegro section of the Via Dinarica.

BOSNIA & HERCEGOVINA, MONTENEGRO

Different Dinarica

FOR ALTERNATIVE taster routes, consider more northerly stages in Bosnia & Hercegovina, hiking around the country's highest village, 1469m (4820ft) Lukomir, through Rakitnica Canyon, below Mt Drinača and past the Hajdučka Vrata rock arch. Or try the testing Kosovo section, doable in a week, which traverses Bjeshkët e Nemuna National Park in the Accursed Mountains, reaches 2656m (8714ft) Mt Gjeravica – Kosovo's highest peak – and climbs to Jelenka Pass on the Montenegro border.

'THESE HILLS ARE ALIVE – WITH FRAGRANT HERBS, EDELWEISS AND MOUNTAIN PINE; URAL OWLS AND GOLDEN EAGLES; GOAT-LIKE CHAMOIS, BROWN BEARS, WILD HORSES, WOLVES AND LYNX.'

Sutjeska National Park to the latter's Durmitor National Park. So this is as good a place to start as any – not least because the trail is fully marked on the ground only in these countries. Try sections 37, 38 and 39, totalling around 92km (57 miles). The official start of stage 37 is the lake of Donje Bare on Zelengora, Bosnia's 'Green Mountain'; stage 39 finishes, conveniently, at Montenegro's small but buzzing resort town of Žabljak.

Following this stretch means ticking off two countries. In Bosnia & Hercegovina you get to pass right below 2386m (7828ft) Maglić, the nation's highest peak, climbable on a detour. You'll also explore its oldest national park, Sutjeska, home to one of Europe's last primeval forests and site of the critical Battle of Sutjeska, fought in 1943 against the Axis powers and won by Tito's Partisans – it's memorialised in Tjentište, the main village.

TOP The summit of Maglić, Bosnia & Hercegovina's highest peak. **LEFT** Skakavac Waterfall, Sutjeska National Park. **RIGHT** Campers at route's end in Žabljak, Montenegro.

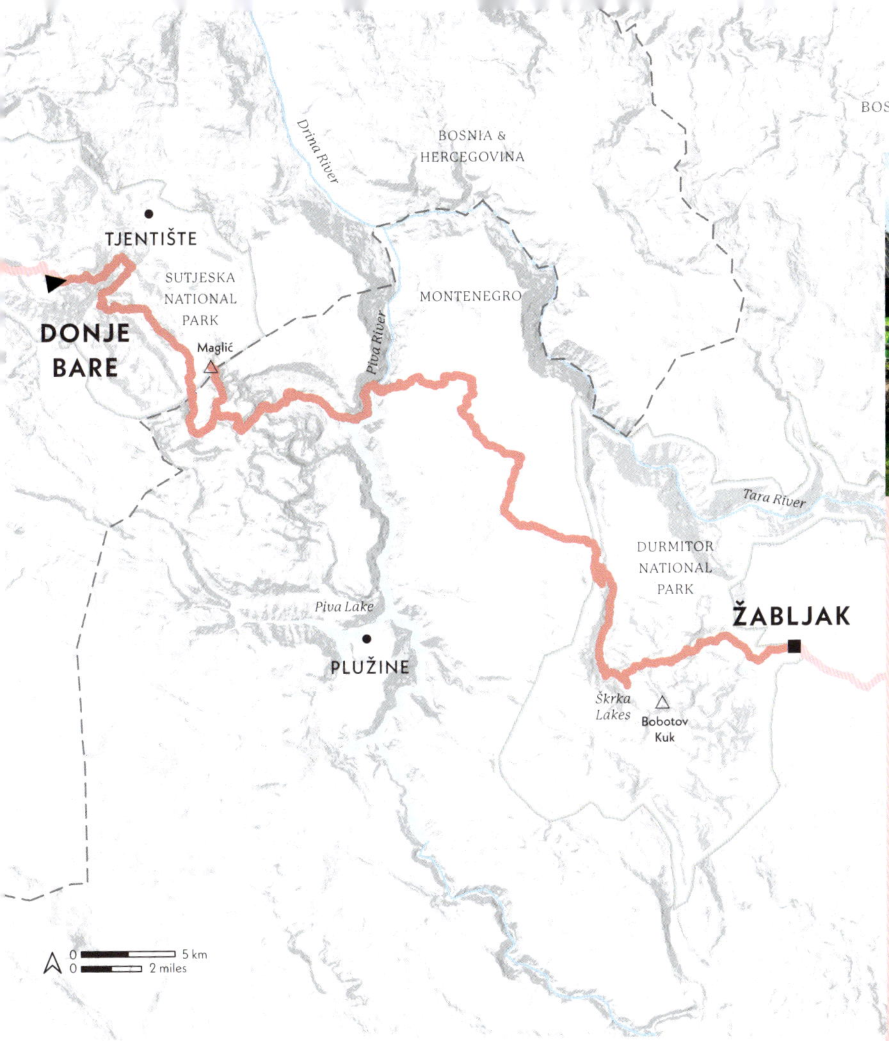

BOSNIA & HERCEGOVINA, MONTENEGRO

ACCOMMODATION
Mountain huts, shelters and homestays are fairly well spaced. Camping offers greater flexibility.

FOOD
Fresh, homemade food is a highlight. Cuisine is meat-heavy – vegetarians may be limited to bread and cheese. Expect effusive hospitality.

GETTING THERE
Buses from Sarajevo to Tjentište take around 2½ hours.

PLANNING
Download GPX files and take maps – markers aren't always easy to follow. Technically, permits are required to cross borders. Check the website for itinerary inspiration from past hikers. Tour operators offer guided and self-guided itineraries on stages of the Via Dinarica.

SAFETY
Carry some cash, and make sure you have plenty of water.

INFO
viadinarica.com
via-dinarica.org

In Montenegro, you'll be striding through Durmitor National Park's UNESCO World Heritage–listed landscapes, which encompass crashing waterfalls and sharp, toothy peaks, plunging Piva Canyon and the glittering, glacial Škrka Lakes – ideal for an icy dip. The whole place is an outdoor playground where many hikers take time out to raft the Tara River through the continent's deepest canyon. More experienced trekkers might add on an ascent of Bobotov Kuk (2523m/8278ft), the highest peak in the Durmitor massif.

The best time to walk in these mountains is June to September, when the weather is warm, the snow gone from the high passes and rainfall minimal; June tends to be a little quieter than the high-summer months. But at any time, come expecting peace and a hearty welcome.

NATURE / CULTURE / MOUNTAINS / COAST

Michinoku Coastal Trail: Kuji to Hachinohe

HONSHŪ, JAPAN

START
Kuji

FINISH
Hachinohe

DISTANCE
93km (58 miles)

DURATION
Five to seven days

CHALLENGE LEVEL
★★★☆☆

WHEN TO WALK
April–June
& September–November

Take a surf-crashed hike through the little-visited Tōhoku region, rich in ancient heritage and natural beauty.

Hiking can't quite cure all ills – but it can contribute to the revival of disaster-hit communities. In the Tōhoku region, that calamity was the 2011 earthquake – the most powerful ever recorded in Japan – and tsunami that claimed thousands of lives and devastated many more across northeast Honshū. As part of efforts to restore hope and livelihoods, the Michinoku Coastal Trail was created, running some 1000km (620 miles) between Soma in Fukushima Prefecture and Hashinohe in Aomori.

The route follows the rocky, wave-bashed coast and dips inland to explore rugged highlands, forested hills and far-flung settlements; the whole thing takes about six weeks. But it's easy to select one or more sections for a taster of this delightful, less-touristed region (Tōhoku means 'end of the road'). Spring promises ideal conditions before summer brings rain and high humidity.

The leg from the small city of Kuji to the endpoint near Hachinohe offers a fine scenic and cultural sampler. In Kuji, learn about the *ama* (sea women), female free-divers who collect seafood and seaweed from the ocean floor. Stride north past the *torii* gates of Itsukushima Shrine and through a series of small fishing harbours, drinking in spectacular vistas from Yokonuma viewpoint. Ford the Koge River and sink toes into the sand on Uge Beach, then from Kofunato veer inland along the ridge to summit Mt Hashikami (740m/2428ft), for views to the Kitakami Mountains. Descend forest trails to the shore and trace the boulder-studded Tanesashi Coast, ending at Hachinohe's Kabushima Shrine.

ACCOMMODATION
Camping, hostels, hotels and upmarket *ryokan* (traditional guesthouses).

FOOD
Easily accessible en route.

GETTING THERE
Kuji and Hachinohe have rail links to Tokyo and other cities. Same Station, close to Kabushima Shrine, is a 20-minute ride from Hachinohe.

PLANNING
Book accommodation at least a few days in advance; local booking companies can help non-Japanese speakers.

SAFETY
You may encounter leeches, ticks or even bears on some stretches — take local advice and heed precautions.

INFO
michinokutrail.com

LEFT The *torii* gate at Itsukushima, spectacularly set in the bay in front of the shrine. **TOP** Rugged Tōhoku coastline in Sanriku Fukkō National Park, south of Hachinohe.

NATURE / FOOD & DRINK / CULTURE / COAST

Dingle Way

COUNTY KERRY, IRELAND

Thrusting out into the crashing Atlantic waves, the Dingle Peninsula is home to some of Ireland's finest scenery – and one of its greatest walks.

Corca Dhuibhne — the Dingle Peninsula — is Ireland's wildest west, a rugged finger poking out into the Atlantic at the extreme edge of Europe. It feels remote, elemental and tinged with not a little magic thanks to its ephemeral light, ancient relics and the lilting voices of the Gaeltacht (Gaelic-speaking) community. '*Fáilte romhat isteach*', they say: 'You're most welcome here'.

Walkers are especially welcome. The well-marked Dingle Way circuits the peninsula, offering a sort of Ireland in miniature: it passes lively towns, archaeological sites, emerald meadows, relatively formidable peaks, ocean-smacked cliffs, restaurants serving succulent seafood and wonderful old pubs thrumming with Irish tunes.

The trail itself is a mix of well-maintained paths and country lanes that thread between hills, beaches, boulder fields and boggy bits. Rarely too taxing, the most challenging aspect is the changeable weather: it can feel pretty arduous being blasted by the elements. So a visit in late spring or early summer is best for drier, warmer conditions. June in particular offers near-endless days – over 18 hours of daylight on the summer solstice – but sits just before the very peak season, making it easier to secure accommodation and walk without hordes of other people. It's also a great time for cetacean-spotting, from both boat and land. Gaze out from clifftop vantage points like Slea Head and Clogher Head and you might spy common dolphins, minke whales or even humpbacks. And from March to July, puffins are burrowing nests on the Blasket Islands, too.

START/FINISH
Tralee

DISTANCE
179km (111 miles)

DURATION
Six to 10 days

CHALLENGE LEVEL
★★☆☆☆

WHEN TO WALK
April–October

LEFT Dingle Peninsula coastline at Dunquin, jumping-off point for boat trips to the Blasket Islands.

IRELAND

The Dingle Way starts and finishes in lively Tralee, capital of Kerry and home to the Kerry County Museum – good for some local background before hiking out. Most walk clockwise, heading first to the village of Camp via canal paths, Blennerville Windmill, open moorland and the sides of the Slieve Mish Mountains. The next overnight stop, beyond enormous Inch Beach, is Annascaul, birthplace of polar explorer Tom Crean and now home to the convivial South Pole Inn. Rural roads then wend via 16th-century Minard Castle to Dingle, where there's a wealth of drinking holes in which to recuperate and catch a trad music session.

Beyond, the trail soon reaches the peninsula's westernmost limits, where waves pound and the land is pocked with relics – the remains of over 500 Celtic *clocháin* (dry-stone beehive huts) dot the region, including around the fort of Dún Beag near Slea Head. There are fine views to the Blasket Islands – visit by ferry from Dunquin if time allows.

ACCOMMODATION
The peninsula has ample B&Bs and hotels, as well as glamping and camping options.

FOOD
Villages, where food and drink are plentiful, are never more than a few hours apart. Local specialities include seafood chowder, lamb and Dingle's delicious ice cream.

GETTING THERE
The nearest airport is Kerry. Tralee is served by trains and buses; trains from Dublin to Tralee, via Mallow, take around four hours.

PLANNING
The route is well waymarked. Book accommodation far in advance during high season.

SAFETY
Pack for changeable weather. There is a fair amount of walking on tarmac, with a few sections on busier roads – beware traffic.

INFO
thedingleway.ie

LEFT Rainbow meets rain clouds on the ever-emerald Dingle Peninsula.
RIGHT The cliffside ruins of Minard Castle, on the Dingle Way route between Annascaul and Dingle.

'DUNQUIN'S SCENICALLY SITED BLASKET CENTRE EXPLORES THE HERITAGE OF THE SUBSISTENCE FARMERS AND FISHERS WHO LIVED ON THE BLASKET ISLANDS UNTIL THEIR EVACUATION IN 1953.'

Soon, Mt Brandon starts to loom. The loftiest summit in Ireland outside of the MacGillycuddy's Reeks, 952m (3123ft) Brandon augurs the route's highest, hardest section: crossing the mountain's shoulder, rounding a saddle, passing an ancient ogham stone. It's a steep descent via blanket bog and boulders to the sleepy village of An Clochán.

The next day, to Castlegregory, is easier, including a stride along Ireland's longest beach, Fermoyle Strand. All that remains is a longish tramp via the seashore and rural roads back to Tralee – your wild west loop complete.

A saintly stroll

MT BRANDON is named after Brendan the Navigator, patron saint of sailors and travellers, born in County Kerry in 484 CE. It's thought he received a vision atop his now-namesake mountain, telling him of a great land to the west; he set off on his legendary voyages from Brandon Creek, just below. According to the Irish epic *Navigatio Sancti Brendani Abbatis*, Brendan and his followers sailed the Atlantic, encountering mythical creatures and discovering enchanted lands.

AUSTRALIA

NATURE / CAMPING / MOUNTAINS / COAST

Thorsborne Trail

QUEENSLAND, AUSTRALIA

START
Ramsay Bay

FINISH
George Point

DISTANCE
32km (20 miles)

DURATION
Three to five days

CHALLENGE LEVEL

WHEN TO WALK
April–September

JUN

Play Robinson Crusoe on the isolated tropical wilderness of Hinchinbrook, Australia's largest island national park

Being cast away on a tropical isle is mostly as you'd anticipate. You'll collect water from streams, shower under waterfalls, wallow in balmy lagoons. You'll trek humid forest and empty coconut-palm-shaded beaches, and summit peaks for superlative views. Known to the Indigenous Bandjin people as Munamudanamy, Hinchinbrook lies off the Queensland coast between Cairns and Townsville. Most of this pristine island of some 400 sq km (154 sq miles) is strictly off-limits – to humans, that is. Its volcanic peaks, eucalypt stands, rainforest, mangroves, seagrass beds and near-shore waters host animals ranging from flying foxes and sunbirds to bright blue Ulysses butterflies and green turtles.

To experience this wilderness, hike the Thorsborne Trail along the east coast. Though relatively short, it's deceptively challenging: entirely self-supported, you'll need to wade or rock-hop across rivers, tackle sandy and swampy ground, and carry all supplies and camping gear, bedding down in basic campsites. Winter's best – avoid the wettest months (the trail closes January and February).

The rewards are as rich as facilities sparse. Watch for dugongs on the crossing from Cardwell to Ramsay Bay, from where you'll pass an ancient shell midden – one of few reminders of Aboriginal occupation – then stroll along Blacksand Beach before climbing Nina Peak (312m/1024ft) for lookouts to inland mountains. Over three or four days, you'll explore rainforests, paperbark swamps and Australia's most diverse mangroves. Look for turtles and fish in pools at the bases of Zoe and Mulligan Falls. And see the sand come alive with countless tiny soldier crabs scuttling out of your way as you tramp along Zoe Beach and around the palm-fringed sands to George Point and your boat pick-up, to return to the modern world.

ACCOMMODATION
Basic campsites.

FOOD
Bring all supplies, purify water from streams.

GETTING THERE
Boats ferry walkers from Cardwell to Ramsay Bay and George Point to Lucinda; booking details on Queensland National Parks website.

PLANNING
Book campsite spots well in advance – places are limited to 40 daily.

SAFETY
Crocodiles, mosquitoes, sandflies and jellyfish are all concerns, as are slippery rocks and high rivers after rain – take all relevant precautions.

INFO
parks.desi.qld.gov.au

LEFT Spy turtles and fish in pools at the base of Hinchinbrook's Mulligan Falls. **TOP** Island views from atop Zoe Falls on the Thorsborne Trail.

JUN

NATURE / FOOD & DRINK

East Coast Trail

NEWFOUNDLAND, CANADA

Explore some of Canada's wildest Atlantic shores, where whales blow, icebergs drift, fishing communities thrive and traditional music fills the air.

The East Coast Trail, which wraps around Newfoundland and Labrador's rugged Avalon Peninsula, isn't really one walk – it's 25 of them, and growing. There's currently a quarter-century of wilderness-wandering stages, ranging from 4km to 20km (2.5 miles to 12 miles) in length; these are linked by shorter 'community walks' that lead through settlements en route, offering a chance to bed down, eat up, resupply and learn about the people who live on this incredible coast. You could thru-hike the lot, but many choose to dip in and out.

There's logic in breaking it up. Ocean-facing Newfoundland is subject to the whims of the North Atlantic; it gets a lot of wind, fog and rain, which can put a literal dampener on things. You might not fancy consecutive weeks of that. On the plus side, the region is gifted with some magical marine spectacles: from May to June, icebergs from Greenland can be seen drifting by; from June to August, you could catch the tell-tale spray of a migrating whale. Hence June, with its warming weather (average highs of 17°C/62°F), long days and pre-peak crowds, offers a good window for a shore-hugging walk.

What of the East Coast Trail itself? It's a registered charity, largely run by volunteers, with the aim of developing a wonderful hiking route, minimising its environmental impact and ensuring it remains open for future generations. As well as maintaining the existing trail, there are plans to extend it further around the Avalon coast.

Beginning at Topsail Beach on Conception Bay, and heading northward to Cape Francis, the trail almost immediately hits

START
Topsail Beach

FINISH
Cappahayden

DISTANCE
336km (209 miles)

DURATION
15–25 days

CHALLENGE LEVEL
★★★☆☆

WHEN TO WALK
June–September

LEFT Sea views from Signal Hill National Historic Site, on the East Coast Trail near St John's.

Left in suspense

SETTLED IN 1840, La Manche was a small fishing community tucked into an inlet on the Avalon coast, between Cape Broyle and Tors Cove. By the 1960s, the population had dwindled to just 25; after a winter storm demolished the village bridge, the settlement was abandoned. However, in 2000 the East Coast Trail rebuilt a 50m-long (164ft) suspension bridge: hikers following the 6.4km (4 mile) La Manche Village Path (Stage 17) can cross to visit the ruined houses.

'THE TRAIL IS FREE TO USE BUT EXPENSIVE TO MAINTAIN. IF YOU CAN, BUY A TRAIL MEMBERSHIP (FROM C$25 PER YEAR); PROFITS ARE USED TO HELP FUND REPAIRS AND PROTECT THE ROUTE.'

some of its most strenuous sections, with steep climbs, brook crossings and peat bog – but also big views, dramatic cliffs, waterfalls tumbling to the waves and the odd starrigan, a wonderful Newfoundland word for a weather-blasted tree standing solo on a hilltop.

From the cape, the trail heads southward, eventually reaching artsy Quidi Vidi village and provincial capital St John's, with its jelly-bean-row houses and cool live-music scene. A little beyond lies Cape Spear, where a dazzling lighthouse – designated a National Historic Site – marks Canada's easternmost point.

LEFT Berry Head Arch, on the East Coast Trail near the endpoint at Cappahayden. **RIGHT** Shoreline homes at artsy Quidi Vidi.

CANADA

ACCOMMODATION
B&Bs, cottages and other accommodation options in communities along the trail. There are six designated, non-serviced campsites; otherwise, ask permission from landowners before wild camping.

FOOD
Stores and cafes in many communities. Refuel on *toutons*, a sort of pancake/doughnut cross.

GETTING THERE
St John's International is the closest airport. It's a 20-minute taxi journey to Topsail Beach.

PLANNING
Public transport is limited. Use local taxis to access trailheads. On weekends from April to November, volunteers lead open-to-all guided hikes.

SAFETY
Weather is changeable – check forecasts and plan an exit strategy in case of storm conditions.

INFO
eastcoasttrail.com

The trail now traces the Southern Shore, an area settled by a significant number of Irish immigrants – you might still catch their brogue in accents here. The walking continues to be wild, passing plunging fjords, looming cliffs, wave-bashed sea stacks and wildlife hangouts – two sections, Mickeleens Path and Beaches Path, skirt the Witless Bay Ecological Reserve, where puffins and other seabirds nest on the rocks.

Later, there's more human interest, as the route leads to Ferryland Lighthouse and the Colony of Avalon archaeological site – home to the remains of the oldest continuously occupied British settlement in North America, established in 1621.

The trail finishes in Cappahayden, a little fishing town with a history of pirates and shipwrecks, a setting of wild waves and jagged rocks, and a sense – as with all of this trail – of a place that is at one with Mother Nature.

ROMANIA

NATURE / FOOD & DRINK / CULTURE / MOUNTAINS

Via Transilvanica: Terra Saxonum

TRANSYLVANIA, ROMANIA

START
Archita

FINISH
Micăsasa

DISTANCE
200km (124 miles)

DURATION
Eight to 11 days

CHALLENGE LEVEL

WHEN TO WALK
May–October

Trek Transylvania for a deep dive into a region of medieval villages, fortified churches and centuries-old traditions.

Transylvania: the name conjures images of mountain-perched castles, howling wolf packs, mist-swathed forests and, naturally, vampires. The truth, of course, is a little different. This ancient region of central Romania remains rich in rural traditions and historic sites. No vampires prowl its wooded valleys and peaks (as far as we know), but wolves and bears roam its wilder reaches. And yes, Vlad III, the 15th-century Wallachian prince whose cruelty partly inspired Bram Stoker's *Dracula*, was born in Sighișoara.

But Transylvania is looking to its future – or, at least, to introduce hikers to its beautiful hinterland while supporting rural communities via the Via Transilvanica. Snaking for 1400km (870 miles) from Putna to Drobeta-Turnu Severin, and divided into seven major regional sections, it's a full immersion into 2000 years of history, diverse landscapes and wildlife. With some legs traversing high mountains, it's best tackled in warmer months – June, on the cusp of summer, is ideal for walking among wildflowers.

Our pick for an accessible adventure is the Terra Saxonum section, meandering east–west through a landscape settled by Saxons since at least the 12th century. These incomers, invited by the Hungarian kings who ruled Transylvania, introduced aspects of their culture, food and architecture. The route runs through forests and pastures, visiting key cultural and historic marvels: pastel-hued Saxon villages; Sighișoara's walled, cobbled Old Town; medieval castles like Renaissance Bethlen at Criș and Micăsasa's Brukenthal; and fortified churches in Roadeș, Cloașterf, Daia and Biertan.

ACCOMMODATION
Mostly guesthouses and pensions, some hostels and hotels.

FOOD
Many guesthouses offer meals. Try Saxon-style specialities like *palukes* (polenta, *mămăligă* in Romanian) and *sarmale* (stuffed cabbage leaves).

GETTING THERE
Trains link Braşov–Archita and Micăsasa–Sibiu (around three hours). Braşov and Sibiu have international airports.

PLANNING
The trail website has a downloadable guide, and the route is waymarked with orange arrows and VT signs.

SAFETY
Bear encounters are rare, but make noise if walking at dawn or dusk. Give shepherds' dogs a wide berth. Bring insect repellent to ward off ticks, mosquitoes and biting flies.

INFO
viatransilvanica.com

LEFT Wonderful Cernei Mountains wilderness along the Via Transilvanica. **TOP** Biertan, one of many Saxon-era villages on the route's Terra Saxonum section.

JULY

The Zanskar River in Hemis National Park, site of India's Markha Valley Trek (page 172).

I WANT A HIKE THAT'S A...

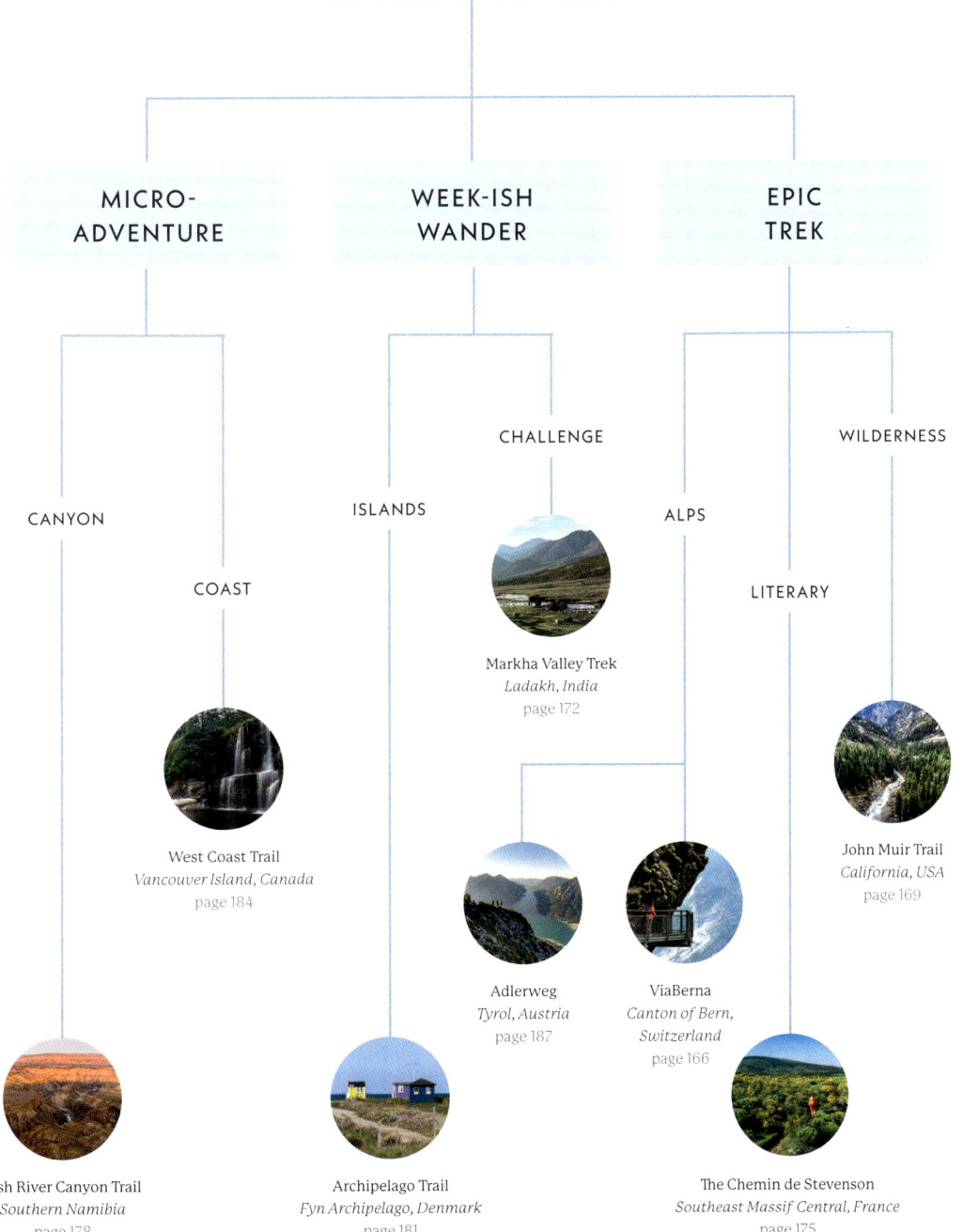

MICRO-ADVENTURE

CANYON

COAST

West Coast Trail
Vancouver Island, Canada
page 184

Fish River Canyon Trail
Southern Namibia
page 178

WEEK-ISH WANDER

ISLANDS

CHALLENGE

Markha Valley Trek
Ladakh, India
page 172

Adlerweg
Tyrol, Austria
page 187

Archipelago Trail
Fyn Archipelago, Denmark
page 181

EPIC TREK

ALPS

LITERARY

WILDERNESS

ViaBerna
Canton of Bern, Switzerland
page 166

John Muir Trail
California, USA
page 169

The Chemin de Stevenson
Southeast Massif Central, France
page 175

NATURE / FOOD & DRINK / CULTURE / MOUNTAINS

ViaBerna

CANTON OF BERN, SWITZERLAND

START
Bellelay

FINISH
Susten Pass

DISTANCE
304km (189 miles)

DURATION
14–20 days

CHALLENGE LEVEL

WHEN TO WALK
Mid-June to September

Hike across Switzerland's pin-up canton between the Jura Mountains and the Alps, via airy ridges and azure lakes.

Switzerland is famed for many things. Chocolate. Cheese. Cuckoo clocks and punctual trains. Alpenhorns and edelweiss. Mountains and democracy. That last point's important for understanding the pride locals take in their cantons, the semi-autonomous states that make up the Swiss Confederation.

And Bern has good reason to be proud. The second-largest canton encompasses two major ranges, the Jura and the Alps, featuring picture-postcard peaks like the Mönch, Eiger and Jungfrau. It's home to Swiss capital Bern, with its lovely medieval core, and a string of jewel-like lakes — Biel, Brienz, Thun — in gorgeous hues of blue. Chocolate-box villages stud slopes ringing with the clanks of cowbells and the roar of cascades — including mighty Reichenbach Falls, where Sherlock Holmes plunged to his death (or did he?).

Snaking southeast from Bellelay in the Jura to the Susten Pass on the border with Uri canton, the 20-stage ViaBerna provides a taster of all that's great about Bern. Though not generally as lofty as other Alpine trails, it's fully accessible only in summer — July's an ideal time, when snow's less common on the highest stretches and meadows are speckled with flowers. This being Switzerland, there are ample places to stay and eat, and trail markers aplenty (follow SchweizMobil Route 38). The ViaBerna is designed to tick off the region's greatest hits. So there are dramatic Jura gorges like the narrow, eerie Taubenlochschlucht; Bern's historic Old Town, with its Zytglogge tower showcasing a 15th-century astronomical clock; the fairy-tale castle at Thun. And there are paths following the meanders of rivers or yielding unparalleled panoramic vistas of those lakes and peaks — the Faulhornweg section between Schynige Platte and First being perhaps the finest 16km (10 miles) of walking in Europe.

ACCOMMODATION
Hotels, B&Bs and mountain inns; listings with contacts on ViaBerna website.

FOOD
There are plenty of restaurants and shops. Stock up on excellent cheese, bread and chocolate for picnics.

GETTING THERE
Switzerland's efficient, integrated public transport system (sbb.ch) links trailheads to major cities (with airports) at Bern, Basel, Geneva and Zürich in under three hours.

PLANNING
Book accommodation in advance. Luggage transfer services are available.

SAFETY
Prepare for all weather conditions, and bring appropriate gear.

INFO
viaberna.ch
schweizmobil.ch

LEFT Wildflowers at Susten Pass, along the ViaBerna. **TOP** Superlative views from Schynige Platte, on the ViaBerna's Faulhornweg section.

NATURE / CULTURE / CAMPING / MOUNTAINS

John Muir Trail

CALIFORNIA, USA

Wander mindfully via the majestic meadows, lakes and mountains of the Sierra Nevada, to explore the beloved playground of the godfather of national parks.

'I only went out for a walk and finally concluded to stay out until sundown, for going out I found, was really going in.' So wrote John Muir (1838–1914), author, naturalist, nomad, philosopher and patron saint of the national park. Muir, who was born in Scotland but emigrated to the USA with his family aged 11, adored the wilderness. He spent years walking across backcountry America, living at one with its great outdoors, and loved Yosemite – the 'grandest of all the special temples of Nature' – most of all. He became a passionate advocate, personally petitioning presidents about landscape preservation, and finally achieved his dream when, in 1890, Yosemite became one of the world's first national parks.

So it's fitting that the wilderness thru-hike now bearing his name should begin in his most beloved valley. The official start is the Happy Isles trailhead, from where the route undulates (a lot) southwards into the Sierra Nevada to finish on top of Mt Whitney – at 4421m (14,505ft), the highest point in the contiguous United States. The route can be walked in either direction, but most hikers choose southbound, to better acclimatise to the rising altitude, and for that triumphal finish atop Whitney's mighty summit.

The trail was championed by the Sierra Club, the grassroots environmental organisation founded by Muir in 1892; it was finally completed in 1938, the 100th anniversary of Muir's birth. With some 14,325m (47,000ft) of elevation gain and very little contact with the outside world, the hike is a serious undertaking. Phone service is nonexistent, there are no hotels and only

STAR
Happy Isles trailhead, Yosemite Valley

FINISH
Mt Whitney, near Whitney Portal

DISTANCE
340km (211 miles)

DURATION
20–24 days

CHALLENGE LEVEL
★★★★

WHEN TO WALK
July–September

LEFT Mt Whitney, climax of the John Muir Trail through the wild wilderness of the Sierra Nevada.

USA

ACCOMMODATION
There are a few designated locations where camping isn't allowed; otherwise, pitch wherever you choose.

FOOD
Trekkers must be self-sufficient. Organise resupply drops in advance. Water sources are plentiful – take a filter or other purification system.

GETTING THERE
Public transport is limited. The easiest option is to park at the exit trailhead and take a private shuttle to the start.

PLANNING
Permits are required. Enter the lottery six months from your desired start date; if unsuccessful, check back for unclaimed/cancelled permits, or try to bag a walk-up permit.

SAFETY
Bear canisters are mandatory. Test all kit. Learn basic first aid.

INFO
pcta.org

a few places to resupply en route – trekkers must carry all their kit and most of their provisions, and carefully organise food drops in advance.

You must also secure a precious permit – one of the toughest tests of all: numbers are limited and the trail is open only for a short period, usually June–September. Optimal months are July and August, when competition for permits is highest but conditions are best: the snow has usually melted, rivers aren't running so high – so are easier to ford – wildfires are less likely, nights aren't so cold and there are fewer mosquitoes.

In short, the John Muir Trail is both physically and logistically challenging – but it sure is magnificent. This is wilderness hiking in a pristine mountain environment, every step revealing an even more exquisite experience or vista. There are the soul-lifting sunrises over Thousand Island Lake, with Banner Peak and the Minarets reflected in its mirror sheen; and the strange sight

LEFT Hiking the Sierra Nevada on the John Muir Trail. **RIGHT** Highlights of the trail include Thousand Island Lake, its limpid waters reflecting Banner Peak and other surrounding summits.

'"THOUSANDS OF TIRED, NERVE-SHAKEN, OVER-CIVILIZED PEOPLE ARE BEGINNING TO FIND OUT THAT GOING TO THE MOUNTAINS IS GOING HOME; THAT WILDNESS IS A NECESSITY" – JOHN MUIR, OUR NATIONAL PARKS.'

of the Devils Postpile's columnar basalt cliffs. There's camping in utter isolation on the shores of a different lake each night, and the invigoration of frigid dips. There's the brilliant bounty of lupins, paintbrush, coyote mint and mariposa lilies; or the chance glimpses of mule deer, marmots, racoons, maybe black bears. There are the views from 4009m (13,153ft) Forester, the trail's highest pass. And at the end, there's the contentment of standing on Mt Whitney, having received all nature's gifts.

Further on foot?

FOR MOST of its length, the John Muir Trail follows the same paths as a section of the Pacific Crest Trail. This gargantuan 4265km (2650-mile) country-crossing adventure snakes between Campo, on the Mexican border, and Manning Park, Canada, through California, Oregon and Washington, avoiding civilisation and sticking to protected wildernesses. Most thru-hikers walk south–north, start in April/May and take around five months. It requires a Pacific Crest Trail Association permit but not an additional Yosemite permit.

NATURE / CULTURE / CAMPING / MOUNTAINS

Markha Valley Trek

LADAKH, INDIA

START
Chilling

FINISH
Shang Sumdo

DISTANCE
71km (44 miles)

DURATION
Five to seven days

CHALLENGE LEVEL

WHEN TO WALK
July–August

Traverse the remote, rugged Zanskar region, an elevated swathe of 'Little Tibet' beneath Himalayan peaks.

With its Tibetan Buddhist monasteries, lunar landscapes and distinctive traditions and wildlife, Zanskar stands scenically and culturally apart from the rest of the country. A place of high, rocky terrain north of the main Himalayan range, it's accessible to hikers only in July and August, when passes are fairly snow-free.

This relatively short but epic trek follows the Markha River, a tributary of the mighty Zanskar, past Buddhist *gompas* (monasteries, ruined forts and palaces, soaring outcrops and cliffs. The valley runs through Hemis National Park — home to reputedly the world's highest density of snow leopards (though you'd be lucky to spot one), plus the argali and bharal sheep they predate, and Tibetan wolf, brown bear, Himalayan marmot and birds of prey.

Treks start from various villages south of regional hub Leh; for gentle acclimatisation, begin in Chilling (itself at around 3200m/ 10,500ft), ascending gradually southeast to reduce the risks of altitude sickness. You'll crisscross the milky-blue river on creaking wooden footbridges. You'll visit villages shaded by willows, poplars and apricot trees, and pass stupas and *gompas* where prayer flags snap in the mountain breeze. You'll hike beneath curiously shaped pinnacles, folded rock formations and lichen-oranged boulders, and watch golden eagles and griffon vultures soaring overhead. Eventually you'll climb above the treeline to the high plateau at Nimaling, where yak herders ward their shaggy charges beneath imposing 6400m (21,000ft) Kang Yatse. Here you rest and prepare for the big challenge: crossing the 5260m (17,257ft) pass of Kongmaru La and descending sharply into the Indus Valley. It's only been a week — but it feels like you've crossed another world.

ACCOMMODATION
Camping or homestays.

FOOD
Meals available from homestays; on guided treks, staff provide food. Purify water.

GETTING THERE
Leh, the nearest airport and major transport hub, is an hour's drive from Chilling and Shang Sumdo. If not on an organised trek, hire a jeep.

PLANNING
Joining a guided trek is wise, and simplifies logistics.

SAFETY
Prepare for rugged terrain and hike slowly, allowing time to acclimatise to high altitudes.

LEFT Mountain dwelling in Chilling, start point of the Markha Valley Trek. **TOP** Hiking the trail through the Zanskar region, beneath a cradle of Himalayan peaks.

NATURE / CULTURE / MOUNTAINS

Chemin de Stevenson

SOUTHEAST MASSIF CENTRAL, FRANCE

Follow in the footsteps (and hoofprints) of Robert Louis Stevenson and his donkey through the forested, volcanic Cévennes Mountains of southern France.

Choosing the ideal attributes for a hiking companion can be a conundrum. When Scottish writer Robert Louis Stevenson was plotting his journey through the Cévennes in 1878, he looked for carrying power rather than conversation. So he plumped for Modestine the donkey, who proved to be irritatingly obstinate but hugely entertaining for onlooking locals — and for readers of the book that resulted from their journey.

Published the following year, *Travels with a Donkey in the Cévennes* introduced not only that colourful creature but also the formerly little-known region through which they trekked. Stevenson would surely have been astonished to learn that, 150 years later, a version of their route has found favour with long-distance walkers. Today, the red-and-white waymarked Chemin de Stevenson is one of France's legendary Grande Randonnée paths.

Though the Cévennes aren't lofty in the mould of, say, the Alps, sections over 1000m (3280ft) may be clad in snow during winter, with temperatures plummeting below freezing. In addition, much of the region's accommodation closes between late October and Easter. So it's only really possible to complete the route between April and October, with summer typically bringing the driest and sunniest days.

Though Stevenson and Modestine set out south from the then-remote village of Le Monastier-sur-Gazeille, today's Chemin de Stevenson starts in Le Puy-en-Velay. This characterful little

START
Le Puy-en-Velay

FINISH
Alès

DISTANCE
272km (169 miles)

DURATION
12 days

CHALLENGE LEVEL
★★

WHEN TO WALK
April–October

LEFT Le Puy-en-Velay, start point of the Chemin de Stevenson hike through the Cévennes Mountains.

FRANCE

Words on travel

BORN IN Edinburgh in 1850, Robert Louis Stevenson found fame with classics including *The Strange Case of Dr Jekyll and Mr Hyde*, but died aged just 44 in Samoa. He was also a pioneering travel writer; *Travels with a Donkey in the Cévennes* appeared four years before his first major literary success, *Treasure Island* (1883). His words resonate today: 'I travel not to go anywhere, but to go. I travel for travel's sake. The great affair is to move.'

'HIKE AMONG THE *PUYS* (VOLCANIC HILLS) AND FARMLANDS RENOWNED FOR GROWING THE REGION'S PEPPERY LENTILS, INTRODUCED BY THE ROMANS AND NOW A SAVOURED SPECIALITY.'

city has a fascinating medieval core capped with a distinctively striped hilltop cathedral. (It's also the starting point for one of the Camino de Santiago pilgrimage routes heading west to Spain.)

A day's walk brings hikers to Le Monastier, where a plaque commemorates Stevenson's departure. Though it has more mod cons than when the author visited, including places to stay and pick up provisions, it still has the air of a rural village. That sets the tone for the days to come, following trails through woods, rolling hills and fields, admiring medieval castles, crossing rivers – including the young Loire at Goudet, guarded by the ruined Château de Beaufort – and bedding down in stone-built *auberges* and *chambres d'hôtes*. Today this region seems blissfully bucolic; Stevenson found it rather backward, and was struck by an enduring fear of the Beast of Gévaudan, reputedly a wolf-man hybrid that terrorised villagers.

TOP Some hikers complete the Chemin de Stevenson with a donkey companion. **LEFT** Lac du Bouchet, on the route near Le Puy-en-Velay. **RIGHT** Approaching Mont Lozère, the hike's highest peak.

FRANCE

ACCOMMODATION
Camping, *gîtes d'étape* (walkers' hostels), *auberges* (inns), *chambres d'hôtes* (B&Bs) and hotels.

FOOD
Cafes and restaurants en route, plus some supermarkets, bakeries and village shops; plan ahead for a few lean stretches. Carry plenty of water.

GETTING THERE
Trains link Le Puy-en-Velay with St-Étienne-Châteaucreux in about 1½ hours, Paris in three hours. Alès is a 30-minute train ride from Nîmes, three hours from Paris.

PLANNING
Book accommodation well in advance, particularly for the trail's middle section where options are limited.

SAFETY
There are no significant risks beyond bad weather.

INFO
Trekking the Robert Louis Stevenson Trail (Cicerone, 2021).

Five days in, you'll reach La Bastide-Puylaurent, where Stevenson stayed at the Trappist monastery of Notre Dame des Neiges (Our Lady of the Snows); book ahead if you want to spend the night. If time is short, you could end the hike here (there's a train station) or even make it your start point: the southern seven-stage section enjoys dramatic views and summits the loftiest mountain on the route – 1699m-high (5574ft) Pic de Finiels on Mont Lozère, delivering a 360-degree panorama.

The path then weaves through ever-wilder terrain, along ridges and rocky trails, crossing boulder-strewn river valleys and passing prehistoric burial sites, shaded sometimes by chestnuts. Stevenson ended his journey in St-Jean-du-Gard; today's route continues east to Alès, an attractive town with a train station and plenty of places to toast your trek.

NAMIBIA

NATURE / CAMPING

Fish River Canyon Trail

SOUTHERN NAMIBIA

START
Hobas

FINISH
Ai-Ais Hot Springs Resort

DISTANCE
85km (53 miles)

DURATION
Four to five days

CHALLENGE LEVEL

WHEN TO WALK
May to mid-September

Descend into Africa's greatest, most glorious gorge to trek through its dramatic twists and turns and camp out under a gazillion stars.

The Fish River Canyon is the world's second-grandest gorge, behind *that* one in Arizona. With flat-topped buttes, flying buttresses, graceful horseshoe bends and raw, rugged rock, it was – according to the local Nama people – created by the writhing of great serpent-god Koutein Kooru as he slithered across the desert to escape pursuing hunters. The more prosaic explanation is that this 160km-long (100-mile), 550m-deep (1804ft) fissure is the work of the Fish River, which has scoured through the ancient gneiss – and in doing so defined one of Africa's greatest walking trails.

The route begins with a stiff, quad-burning descent from high on the canyon rim, then follows the winding river to the end at Ai-Ais Hot Springs Resort – a surprising jolt of civilisation after days of isolation and camp-stove cooking. It's simple in theory, tough in practice. Though the walk is largely flat, it's slow going over soft sand and hard rock. There are no facilities. And the weather is hot. Indeed, for much of the year, the canyon is too inhospitable to enter – the trail is open only from May to mid-September, when the weather is bearable for hiking. June, in the middle of winter, is ideal: days average around 25°C/77°F (though nights are cold), and there's plenty of water in the river for cooling dips. Plus clear skies afford out-of-this-world stargazing – there's zero light pollution here.

The trail is a proper wilderness adventure. You must carry all you need, and there are no official campsites – simply sleep wherever takes your fancy. Watch fleeting, fiery sunsets before settling down on a sandy beach, listening to the calls of jackals or barks of baboons. You can also opt to take a handful of shortcuts that lead up rocky *kopjes* for great eagle-eye views.

ACCOMMODATION
Campsites and lodges near trailheads. Wild camping/bivvying en route.

FOOD
Self-sufficiency required. Take a filter/purification tablets to treat river water.

GETTING THERE
The canyon is 700km (435 miles) south of capital Windhoek. A shuttle bus connects Hobas and Ai-Ais.

PLANNING
Hiking permits are required; book in advance (nwrnamibia.com). Only 30 people are allowed to start the hike each day; checking in with Fish River Canyon National Park rangers at Hobas before setting out is mandatory.

SAFETY
Make sure you're fit and healthy; a signed doctor's certificate must be presented at the Hobas entrance gate before hiking.

LEFT A lonely aloe tree stands sentry in the harsh terrain of Fish River Canyon National Park. **TOP** The canyon from above, carved out over millennia by the snaking Fish River.

NATURE / FOOD & DRINK / CULTURE / CAMPING / COAST

Archipelago Trail

FYN ARCHIPELAGO, DENMARK

Wend your way around under-sung but idyllic Fyn and its scatter of outlying islands, hopping over the Baltic Sea by boat, bridge and boot.

Sitting between Zealand and Jutland, the island of Fyn (sometimes anglicised as Funen) is part idyllic vision of Danish pastoral living, part out-and-out fairy tale. It's considered the country's kitchen garden, liberally spread with wheat fields, dairy farms and fruit trees. It's sprinkled with moated and turreted castles and manors. And it's fringed by golden sand and cute fishing villages, with an associated archipelago that's even golden-er and cuter. The only city here is Odense, birthplace of Hans Christian Andersen, writer of many a fairy tale – which perhaps explains the general vibe.

Fyn (pronounced 'foon') is particularly lovely during those long, lazy days of Scandi midsummer, when the Baltic Sea is still brisk but bearable for swimming, when the lane-side honesty boxes are brimful with fresh berries, when temperatures average around 20°C (68°F), and when the sun hardly seems to set. Sure, it's the busiest time, but busy on Fyn isn't hectic; life here still unfurls at a pretty relaxed pace.

To tune in to this laid-back vibe, explore via the Archipelago Trail, one of Denmark's longest hiking routes. It's not really one path but a series of seven interconnected trails that weave around Fyn's southern shores and islands, within the South Fyn Archipelago UNESCO Global Geopark. This is a 'drowned' landscape, created when water levels rose after the last Ice Age. Only the highest hills nose above the surface, forming the 55 islands and islets dotted hereabouts. Walking here offers not only sylvan scenes of wood cabins, green pastures and blonde beaches but interesting geology, too.

START
Faldsled, Fyn

FINISH
Søby, Ærø

DISTANCE
220km (137 miles)

DURATION
Seven to 14 days

CHALLENGE LEVEL
★

WHEN TO WALK
May–September

LEFT Hike Archipelago Trail 7 to immerse in the bucolic coastal scenery of Ærø Island.

DENMARK

ACCOMMODATION
Various options in Svendborg and along the way; Broholm Castle is now a characterful guesthouse. Denmark has a network of free/cheap shelters that campers can use (bookenshelter.dk).

FOOD
Fresh produce abounds – look for roadside honesty stalls selling whatever fruit and veg is in season. Baked goods and fresh fish are excellent.

GETTING THERE
Svendborg is 50 minutes by train from Odense, which is itself around 1½ hours by train from Copenhagen.

PLANNING
The route is marked with blue-white hiker pictograms. FynBus serves the region. Ferries and bridges connect the islands.

SAFETY
There are few dangers. Watch out for cyclists on rural lanes.

INFO
visitfyn.com

The hub of this hike is the port of Svendborg, Fyn's second-largest town – several of the trail's strands spider from here, as do bus and ferry routes. Wending west, Trail 1 (39km/24 miles) wiggles from Faldsled to Fjællebroen via Faaborg and the 'hills' and valleys of the so-called Funen Alps – a pleasing if not mighty amount of undulation. Trail 2 (30km/18.5 miles) continues from Fjællebroen into Svendborg, crossing the Ice Age moraine ridge of Egebjerg Bakker. Trail 3 (30km/18.5 miles) heads east of Svendborg to the pretty fishing village of Lundeborg, first tracing the Skårupøre Sound before veering inland to pass the rose-pink towers of Broholm Castle.

Trail 4 (20km/12.5 miles) runs south of Svendborg, crossing the 1220m-long (4000ft) bridge to Tåsinge, skirting the island's east coast (via Valdemars Slot) then crossing another sea bridge to reach Rudkøbing on Langeland. From there, choices: Trails 5 (29km/18 miles) and 6 (26km/16 miles) explore this long, lovely

LEFT Svendborg, Fyn's second-largest city and the start point for several Archipelago Trail sections. **BELOW** Broholm Castle, one-time stomping ground of Hans Christian Andersen. **RIGHT** Fairy-tale Egeskov Castle in southern Fyn.

'TO IMMERSE DEEPER IN DANISH SEAFARING LIFE, PACK A COPY OF *WE, THE DROWNED* BY CARSTEN JENSEN, A POWERFUL MULTIGENERATIONAL NOVEL SET IN THE PORT OF MARSTAL ON ÆRØ.'

isle, with its low hills, prehistoric dolmen, sea cliffs and wild horses. Or you might hop straight to Trail 7 (36km/22 miles): a ferry connects Rudkøbing to the island of Ærø, for the section from Marstal's harbour – unbelievably, once the second-biggest shipping hub in Denmark – across to tiny Søby. Meandering along the northern coast of this charming isle, via the candy-box medieval houses of Ærøskøbing and, in summer, verges flush with wildflowers and butterflies, this is the Archipelago Trail at its most fairy-tale.

Father of fairy tales

HANS CHRISTIAN Andersen was born in Odense in 1805, and the city celebrates its most famous son at the quirky HC Andersens Hus museum and a themed city walking trail. Andersen travelled around Fyn, spending time at many of its 123 stately manors and castles, including Valdemars and Broholm. He also stayed at the Den Voigtske Gaard residence in Faaborg – he was smitten with the household's eldest daughter, Riborg, but she turned down his proposal of marriage.

CANADA

NATURE / CULTURE / CAMPING / COAST

West Coast Trail

VANCOUVER ISLAND, CANADA

START
Pachena Bay, Bamfield

FINISH
Gordon River, Port Renfrew

DISTANCE
75km (47 miles)

DURATION
Five to seven days

CHALLENGE LEVEL

WHEN TO WALK
May–September

This wild walk along the edge of British Columbia's biggest island is strenuous stuff, but worth every dogged step.

Don't underestimate the West Coast Trail. It's only 75km (47 miles) long, with relatively low elevation gain, but it's challenging. Tracing some of Vancouver Island's most ravishing Pacific-smashed shores, it's properly remote, with no settlements, shelters, shops or eateries (save for Nitinaht's beloved Crabshack floating restaurant). There are also more than 100 ladders to climb and descend, angry rivers to ford, deep gullies to cross, fallen trees to hoist over, boulders to scramble, mud to slog through, bears to avoid. But the rewards include a wonderland of old-growth rainforest, untouched beaches, caves, coves, cliffs, superlative sunsets and chances to spot sea lions, otters and whales.

The coastline between Pachena Bay and Gordon River lies within the traditional territories of Huu-ay-aht, Ditidaht and Pacheedaht First Nations peoples, who travelled and traded here for millennia. Then, from the 19th century, foreign sailing ships started to arrive — and flounder in the region's treacherous currents, storms and fog, so earning the 'Graveyard of the Pacific' nickname. In response, lighthouses were built, a telegraph line constructed and the Dominion Lifesaving Trail forged to enable rescuers to aid those wrecked offshore. It fell out of use but, in 1973, was included in the newly minted Pacific Rim National Park Reserve, and became the West Coast Trail. The trail is open only from 1 May to 30 September, with just 75 hikers permitted to start each day.

July is one of the busiest months, with the warmest, driest, clearest weather (though it will probably still rain), and long hours of daylight. But trail camaraderie — pitching up at campsites tucked in the forest or right on the beach, sharing tales of the best pools and the suckiest mud — is part of the joy.

ACCOMMODATION
There are 13 campsites, most with composting toilets and bear lockers.

FOOD
Pack supplies. At Crabshack camp near the Indigenous village of Nitinaht, a floating outlet offers seafood and snacks.

GETTING THERE
The West Coast Trail Express bus runs daily to the trailheads between Victoria and Nanaimo.

PLANNING
Hikers require a trail permit; reservations for the upcoming season tend to open in January and sell out quickly. Attending a pre-hike briefing is mandatory.

SAFETY
Carry bear spray.

INFO
parks.canada.ca

LEFT Black bears on the wave-bashed Vancouver Island coast. **TOP** The West Coast Trail takes in old-growth forests, cliffs and pristine coves.

NATURE / FOOD & DRINK / CULTURE / MOUNTAINS

Adlerweg

TYROL, AUSTRIA

Spread your wings on the epic 'Eagle Trail' across the Austrian Tyrol, traversing a succession of mighty mountain ranges as you go.

Gaze at a map of the Austrian Tyrol, trace the meandering route of its greatest trek, and what creature springs to mind? This game's a little like guessing constellations – it calls for a bit of imagination – but, once you've seen it, the resemblance is obvious: a bird of prey, head ducked below Innsbruck, wings spread to span the region.

The Adlerweg (Eagle Trail) is designed to showcase the Tyrol's scenic splendour. It traverses the phalanx of mountain ranges standing shoulder to ranked shoulder along the northern rim of the Inn Valley: from east to west, the Wilder Kaiser, Brandenberg, Rofan, Karwendel, Wetterstein, Mieming and Lechtaler Alps. Reaching 2870m (9416ft), with challenging scree patches, lingering snow and fixed ropes, this lofty trek is doable only between late June and mid-September.

It does, though, frequently duck down to visit villages and towns. While that makes for plenty of ascent and descent – well over 23,000m (75,460ft) – it also provides ample opportunities for cultural and culinary discovery. That means exploring Innsbruck's old centre, with its gleaming Goldenes Dachl (Golden Roof), but also tucking into *Käsespätzle* (cheesy little noodles), *Knödel* (dumplings) and, most moreish of all, *Kaiserschmarrn* – a dessert delight of shredded, sugared pancakes best served with a fruit compote and *Schlagobers* (whipped cream).

If the entire trail seems too gargantuan an undertaking – or if you can't spare so much time – good public transport means it's straightforward to split the route into two satisfying chunks east and west of Innsbruck, or to tackle one or more of the 24 stages.

START
St Johann in Tirol

FINISH
Arlbergpass (St Anton am Arlberg)

DISTANCE
326km (203 miles)

DURATION
21 days

CHALLENGE LEVEL
★ ★ ★ ★

WHEN TO WALK
July–September

LEFT Taking in terrific Tyrolean views along the Adlerweg, from atop Bärenkopf in the Karwendel Range.

AUSTRIA

East Tyrol add-on

THE ADLERWEG has been augmented with a second, separate route through the East Tyrol's magnificent Hohe Tauern National Park: the Adlerweg durch Osttirol. This two-part, 95km (59-mile) trail makes a challenging five- to seven-day standalone hike. The first leg, climbing from the Virgen Valley, skirts the flanks of the 3658m (12,000ft) Grossvenediger; the second, starting above Matrei in Osttirol, snakes beneath Austria's highest peak, the 3798m-high (12,460ft) Grossglockner.

'CELEBRATE THE END OF EACH DAY ON THE TRAIL WITH OTHER HIKERS IN A CONVIVIAL MOUNTAIN HUT, CLINKING BEER GLASSES AS THE SUN SETS INTO THE HIGH ALPS. PROST!'

From the official start point at St Johann in Tirol, the Adlerweg climbs to a pair of natural marvels: the cave of Diebsöfen (Thief's Oven), and the Schleierwasserfall cascading down a 60m (197ft) rock face. Continue through forests and meadows, drinking in views of jagged Wilder Kaiser peaks and taking a dip in the Hintersteiner See mountain lake before descending to Kufstein, guarded by its hulking medieval fortress. The following stages switchback through the Brandenberg and Rofan ranges, alternating Alpine pastures and forests with testing ridges and peaks, notably the 1645m-high (5397ft) Köglhörndl, providing far-reaching views.

Arguably the most popular section, both spectacular and conveniently close to Innsbruck, comprises the five stages through the Karwendel Alps. This mightiest of the route's ranges is both demanding and exhilarating, with panoramic vistas north

TOP A marmot surveys Austria's Grossglockner. **LEFT** Summiting Scheffauer in the Wilder Kaiser, one of seven ranges on the Adlerweg route. **RIGHT** Riverside colour in culture-rich Innsbruck.

AUSTRIA

ACCOMMODATION
Hotels, guesthouses, inns, mountain huts.

FOOD
Cafes, restaurants and huts along the trail sell hearty local fare. Fountains and springs provide water; purify if collecting from natural sources.

GETTING THERE
Capital Innsbruck has an international airport; trains link to St Johann and St Anton (both around 1¼ hours).

PLANNING
No permits required. Book mountain huts several months or even a year in advance.

SAFETY
Most trails are wide and clear, but there are some steep, rocky sections. Prepare for changeable mountain weather.

INFO
tyrol.com

into Bavaria and south across the Inn Valley. Keep an eye out for chamois, mountain hares, fire salamanders and – aptly enough – golden eagles soaring over the crags.

A loop dips south of Innsbruck along the Zirbenweg (Stone Pine Trail), winding through pine forests and across the slopes of the Patscherkofel for views back to the Karwendel peaks. Then it's back to the main route west, using cable cars to link sheer climbs and plunges for views of Alpine tarns below.

You'll need a head for heights on the last seven stages, which trace the ridges of the Lechtal Alps, encompassing stretches alongside sheer drops before reaching the Arlbergpass and the border with neighbouring Vorarlberg. Congratulations: the eagle has landed.

AUGUST

Mt Rainier from Emerald Ridge, along the USA's aptly named Wonderland Trail (page 196).

AUGUST

I WANT A HIKE THAT'S A...

- **MICRO ADVENTURE**
  - GEOLOGY
    - Laugavegur
      Southern Iceland
      page 199
  - HISTORY
    - Lužnice Valley Trail
      Bohemia, Czechia
      page 202
    - Malmveien Historical Trail
      Trøndelag, Norway
      page 214

- **WEEK-ISH WANDER**
  - BALTIC
    - Baltic Coastal Hiking Trail: Nida to Šventoji
      Western Lithuania
      page 211
  - ARCTIC
    - Kungsleden: Abisko to Nikkaluokta
      Swedish Lapland
      page 193

- **EPIC TREK**
  - CHALLENGE
    - K2 Base Camp & Concordia
      Baltistan, Pakistan
      page 208
  - OUTBACK
    - Larapinta Trail
      Northern Territory, Australia
      page 205
  - BACKCOUNTRY
    - Wonderland Trail
      Washington, USA
      page 196

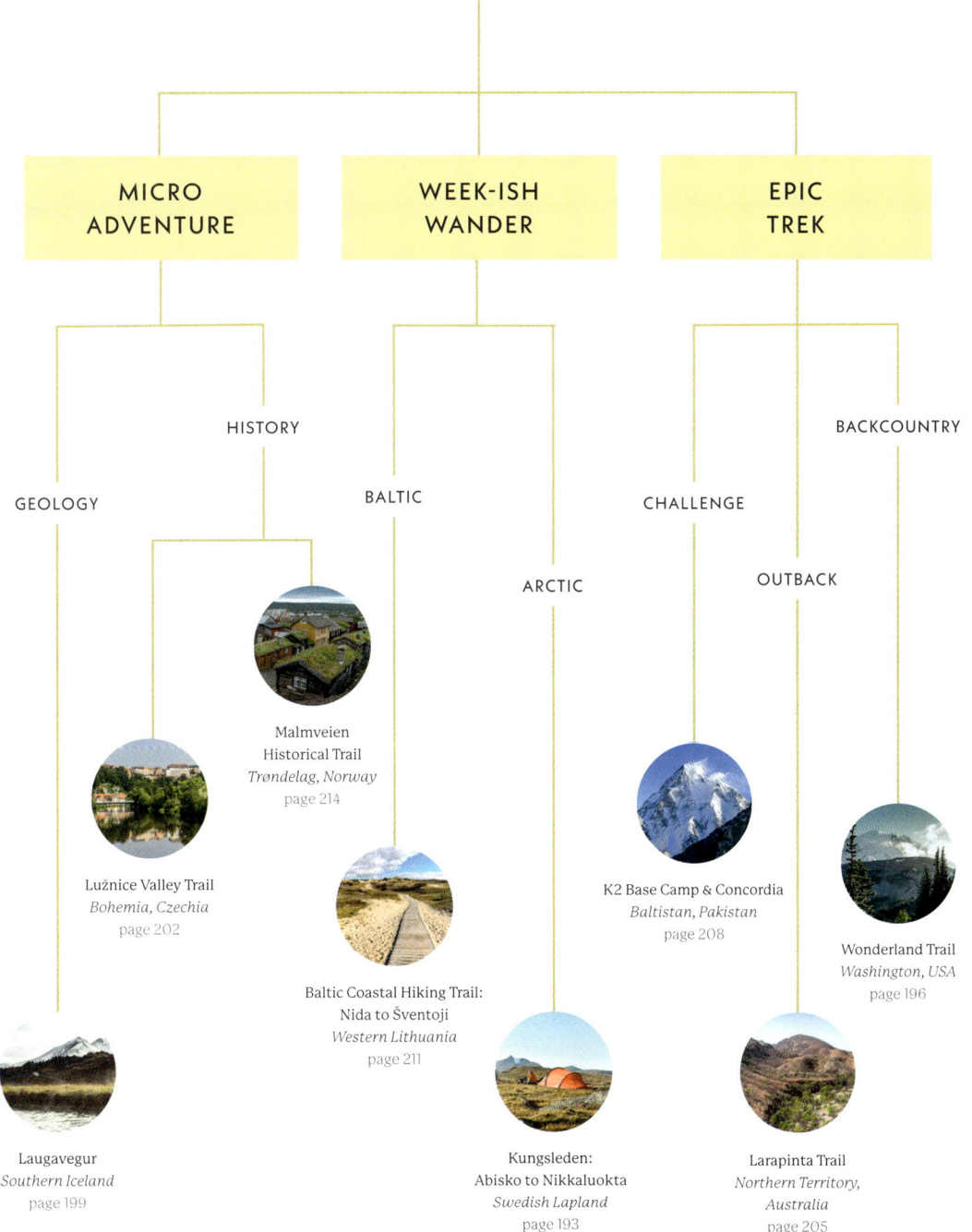

NATURE / CAMPING / MOUNTAINS

Kungsleden: Abisko to Nikkaluokta

SWEDISH LAPLAND

Stride out into untamed Arctic wilderness, hiking between remote cabins, across ancient bogs, past herds of reindeer and beneath Sweden's highest mountain.

Trust the Scandinavians. Create a 460km (286-mile) hiking trail through the big-sky expanses of Sweden's far north? Start high above the Arctic Circle in Lapland, where the mercury frequently plummets to -20°C (-4°F)? Waymark paths and build boardwalks across permafrost and bog, beneath jagged peaks and through birch forests, installing comfortable cabins and mountain stations for trekkers en route? No problem.

That's what the Svenska Turistföreningen (Swedish Tourist Association; STF) did in the early 20th century, linking together sections of historic paths. The majestic result was given a suitably regal name: Kungsleden, the King's Trail. In the decades since, it's become a byword for wilderness walking – one of the world's great long-distance hikes.

Snaking south from Abisko, near the Norwegian border, to the ski resort of Hemavan in Västerbotten County, the full route takes four or five weeks to complete. But it's easy enough to test-trek the first – some might say most dramatic (and popular) – stretch in a week or less, starting at its northernmost trailhead and finishing with a short diversion off the Kungsleden proper to hop off at Nikkaluokta, from where buses run to the nearest airport at Kiruna. Naturally, a hike through mountainous Arctic terrain isn't one for winter; come in the narrow window between snows, from late June to late September. And though this is definitely four-seasons-in-one-day territory – bring heavy-duty waterproofs

START
Abisko

FINISH
Nikkaluokta

DISTANCE
107km (66.5 miles)

DURATION
Five to seven days

CHALLENGE LEVEL
★★★☆☆

WHEN TO WALK
July–September

LEFT The Kungsleden route winds through the picture-perfect Arctic wilderness of Swedish Lapland.

ACCOMMODATION
STF cabins and mountain stations with beds and kitchens; some have restaurants, shops and saunas. Wild camping also permitted.

FOOD
Bring supplies and top up en route.

GETTING THERE
The nearest airport is at Kiruna. Kiruna–Abisko trains take under 1½ hours. Nikkaluokta–Kiruna buses run twice daily in summer (one hour).

PLANNING
Book beds in cabins/stations well in advance, particularly the small STF Tjäktja Mountain Cabin.

SAFETY
Bring good-quality waterproof layers, boots, gaiters and insect repellent. Take care when wading across streams.

INFO
swedishtouristassociation.com

— summer brings many delights. There's the chance to hike during the longest days, when the sun hardly sets. Sweet, golden-yellow cloudberries, nature's perfect trail food, fruit among the bogs. Alpine flowers bloom, young animals abound, and temperatures are (mostly) ideal.

From the northern trailhead, the route delves immediately into Abisko National Park, one of Sweden's oldest. Though bear, wolverine and lynx roam its expanses, sightings are very rare; one animal you are likely to encounter is reindeer, herded in the region by Sámi people for thousands of years. You might also spy birds of prey — eagles, buzzards, gyrfalcons — soaring overhead.

First traversing mountain birch forest, the trail emerges into open ground and climbs to a viewpoint over the surging Abiskojåkka River. At the day's end, bed down beside shimmering Lake Abiskojaure — ideal for a refreshing (read: chilly) dip. Continuing south, the route climbs above the treeline, heading up

LEFT Reindeer range free along the Kungsleden route. **RIGHT** Near the start of the hike in Abisko, the Abiskojåkka River surges through the ancient forests of its namesake national park.

'FROM ABISKO, ADMIRE VIEWS OF THE GLACIER-CARVED, U-SHAPED LAPPORTEN – ČUONJÁVÁGGI (GOOSE VALLEY) TO THE NORTHERN SÁMI – HANGING LIKE A SLACK ROPE BETWEEN PEAKS.'

Kieronbacken and across wild heathland dotted with lakes and guarded by hefty mountains. The next stage weaves across the delta of the Alesätno River before ascending to the 1150m-high (3773ft) Tjäktja Pass. Much of the next section runs through the alpine moorland of Tjäktjavagge, a broad, 30km-long (19-mile) valley lined by sheer-sided peaks and glaciers, eventually weaving upwards on rocky paths to Singi. Here, Sweden's loftiest mountain, 2097m (6880ft) Kebnekaise, looms to the east. Veer off the Kungsleden through the Laddjuvagge Valley to reach Kebnekaise Mountain Station (add a day to summit the icecapped south peak) before descending through more birch stands to Laukkujärvi Lake and Nikkaluokta – a cluster of cabins that makes a suitably laid-back end to an adventure far from the modern world.

Climbing the Cauldron

SWEDEN'S HIGHEST mountain, Kebnekaise – derived from the Sámi name, Giebmegáisi (Cauldron Peak) – looms over the penultimate night's stop on this Kungsleden section. In fact, it's two peaks: the northern, ice-free summit rises to 2097m (6879ft), while the elevation of the glacier-topped southern peak – the easier ascent – varies depending on conditions. The western approach can be tackled in a long full day (18km/11 miles round-trip) from STF Kebnekaise Mountain Station – a worthy climax to your Kungsleden adventure.

USA

NATURE / CAMPING / MOUNTAINS

Wonderland Trail

WASHINGTON, USA

START/FINISH
Longmire

DISTANCE
150km (93 miles)

DURATION
Nine to 14 days

CHALLENGE LEVEL
★★★★★

WHEN TO WALK
Mid-July to mid-October

Trace an undulating circuit around Mt Rainier on one of America's most aspirational backcountry hikes.

Here's a key fact about Mt Rainier: it's the most glaciated peak in the USA's Lower 48 states. Some 28 named ice-sheets clad this 4392m-high (14,410ft) active stratovolcano, plus numerous snowfields – grinding, crunching masses that have scoured deep gouges and sheer ridges into its flanks. All very dramatic and beautiful – but, more important is what it means for hikers tramping a full circuit around its slopes: when you're not climbing up, you're going down. There's not much flat on the Wonderland Trail – which makes this switchback circuit one of North America's most challenging routes; with over 7000m (23,000ft) of ascent and descent, it's for experienced backcountry hikers and campers only. It's also among the most spectacular trails, particularly in summer, when wildflowers festoon meadows, and paths and wilderness campsites are reliably snow-free and open to hikers.

There's road access at a few points around the circuit, and the route can be tackled in either direction, but most head out clockwise from Longmire, where you can pick up permits and trail information from the Mt Rainier National Park HQ, and perhaps enjoy a night in a real bed before heading out into the wilds.

And what wilds. You'll experience old-growth forests of cedar, fir, pine and hemlock, subalpine meadows and scrub with heather and huckleberry, and sheer upper slopes cut by gushing icemelt streams. You might encounter salamanders and snakes, eagles and owls, pikas and porcupines, and perhaps evidence of elusive cougars, bobcats and even wolverines, recently recorded in the park for the first time in a century. And each day you'll enjoy views of a different face of Mt Rainier, reflected in golden lakes or set aflame by the rising sun to the east. Wonderland: the name says it all.

ACCOMMODATION
Camping at 18 designated wilderness sites; National Park Inn at Longmire.

FOOD
Carry all supplies (or leave caches at trailheads); purify water.

GETTING THERE
Longmire is two hours' drive southeast of Seattle.

PLANNING
A Wilderness Permit is required for backcountry camping; book these well in advance through the early-access lottery system from February.

SAFETY
Carry rain gear, insect repellent and all kit for navigation and emergencies. Seeing black bears and cougars is rare but not impossible; research how to deal with encounters in advance.

INFO
nps.gov

LEFT Mowich Lake in Mt Rainier National Park, just one of the many wonders of the Wonderland Trail.
TOP Curtis Ridge reflected along the Wonderland Trail.

NATURE / CAMPING / MOUNTAINS

Laugavegur

SOUTHERN ICELAND

Find your feet in the Land of Fire and Ice on the classic 'Hot Spring Route', walking through some of the planet's weirdest wilderness.

Iceland is undeniably unusual – in all the best ways. Its geology is like nowhere else on Earth. Indeed, so relatively young and lively is this Arctic-edge isle that you can almost watch it being formed before your eyes. Fumaroles smoke, geysers spurt, fissures shift, volcanoes vomit and spill. It's a rather exciting place to go for a walk.

The most popular trail is the Laugavegur (the 'Hot Spring Route'), which runs from Landmannalaugar in the heart of the Southern Highlands to Þórsmörk – the 'Valley of Thor', named after the Norse god of thunder. It only takes a few days, but provides a crash course in the great Icelandic outdoors.

When to hike? The season is short, the trail usually opening mid/late June, depending on the harshness of the previous winter. This makes planning an early season hike risky. July has the best weather and long days – highs of 12°C (54°F), up to 20 hours of daylight – and is consequently busiest. In August the weather is still good but it tends to be a little quieter, especially towards the end of the month as things turn a touch cooler. Though of course, this is Iceland: the weather, or the volcanoes, could do something weird at any time.

There are six well-spaced huts along the route, offering heated dorms, bathrooms, kitchens and camaraderie but no electricity. These are bookable only for north-to-south walks starting at Landmannalaugar; however, if you're willing to pitch at the adjacent campsites instead, you can hike in either direction. Assuming you kick off the hike at Landmannalaugar, it's worth getting there the day before starting out, for the chance

START
Landmannalaugar

FINISH
Þórsmörk

DISTANCE
55km (34 miles)

DURATION
Three to five days

CHALLENGE LEVEL

WHEN TO WALK
Late June to early September

LEFT Admire Landmannalaugar's striped rhyolite mountains before setting out on the Laugavegur.

ICELAND

Onward!

KEEN HIKERS finishing the Laugavegur can continue on the Fimmvörðuháls Trail. This 25km (15.5 mile) route runs south from Þórsmörk to the showstopping waterfall of Skógafoss. Along the way, it passes freshly created lava fields and fizzing cascades, traces the Kattarhryggir (Cat's Spine) ridge and slips between the Eyjafjallajökull and Mýrdalsjökull glaciers. Tackle it in one long day, or break your journey at one of the two huts en route. Buses connect Skógar with Reykjavik.

'THE ICELANDIC HIGHLANDS ARE AWASH WITH MYTH AND FOLKLORE. YOU'LL HIKE PAST ROCK FORMATIONS THAT RESEMBLE GIANT TROLLS, AND PLACES ASSOCIATED WITH THE *HULDUFÓLK* (HIDDEN PEOPLE).'

to bathe in its hot springs and soak up the majesty of its many-hued rhyolite mountains, variously streaked with striking reds, purples, yellows and greens.

From here, the trail climbs steeply to a lava field and straight into a hotbed of geothermal activity, with mud burping in pots, vents puffing steam and vivid-green moss brightening the basalt. Gradually the rainbow rhyolite gives way to black volcanic slopes, and the waymarks lead to Hrafntinnusker Hut. Perched at 1110m (3642ft), amid a landscape of dark, ice-streaked peaks, it's the highest point on the trail.

The onward route to Álftavatn Hut hops across snow-filled ravines via slender snow bridges, eventually leading to the edge of Jökultungur, one of the Laugavegur's finest lookouts, with views of three glaciers: on a clear day you can admire the permanently icy Mýrdalsjökull, Eyjafjallajökull and Tindfjallajökull.

TOP Skógafoss Waterfall, a highlight of the Fimmvörðuháls Trail. **LEFT** Hrafntinnusker Hut, at the highest point on the Laugavegur trail. **RIGHT** The 'Rainbow Mountains' of Landmannalaugar.

ICELAND

ACCOMMODATION
There are six huts on the hike, which have heated dorms plus tent pitches outside. Wild camping isn't permitted.

FOOD
Huts sell basics such as dry camp meals and biscuits; it's best to bring supplies. Water is available at huts, and from streams (purify for safety).

GETTING THERE
Several companies offer bus services from Reykjavík to Landmannalaugar, and from Þórsmörk to Reykjavík.

PLANNING
Book huts online in advance (via fi.is). Both independent and guided trekking is possible.

SAFETY
Pack for changeable weather. Seek trail-condition advice from hut wardens. Fog and rain frequently impair visibility.

INFO
fi.is

Then a rocky descent dips to the Grashagakvisl River, which you may have to wade across.

After Álftavatn the trail fords a succession of rivers – you'll likely get wet feet at some point. There's a small hut at Hvanngil, but most press on to the black sands of Mælifelssandur – strange, exposed, elemental. Ahead lie deep canyons, moss-cloaked hills and, eventually, the welcoming hut at Emstrur, with its glacier views. Then all that's left is the trek to Þórsmörk, a diverse section blessed with craggy ravines and verdant greenery – Hallormsstaðaskógur is especially lush, with its stunted birch forest, herbs and wildflowers. At Langidalur Valley is journey's end, Þórsmörk – give yourself some thunderous applause.

NATURE / CULTURE

Lužnice Valley Trail

BOHEMIA, CZECHIA

START
Planá nad Lužnicí

FINISH
Týn nad Vltavou

DISTANCE
55km (34 miles)

DURATION
Four days

CHALLENGE LEVEL
★★☆☆☆

WHEN TO WALK
May–September

Stick to the river's edge for a splendid stroll through prime Czech walking country, with plenty of castles, woodland and medieval towns en route.

The clue's in the name. Toulava, the area through which the Lužnice Valley Trail passes, is derived from the Czech word *toulat* — meaning to roam unhurriedly through the countryside, imbibing its wonders. An excellent place, then, for a walk.

Toulava sits at the edge of Bohemia, a landscape of thick forests, rolling hills, attractive towns and the green, winding valley of the Lužnice River. The latter is the lodestar for this largely gentle hike that's rated one of the continent's best: it was the first Czech route to be awarded Leading Quality Trails certification by the European Ramblers Association. Unsurprisingly, it's well waymarked and a delight to walk. But when? Summer is busiest and hottest (expect temperatures from 20°C/68°F to 30°C/86°F), but comes with a lively buzz. Plus this heavily forested hike offers plenty of shade.

The trail is split into four stages. The first links the town of Planá nad Lužnicí with historic, castle-topped Tábor — founded in the 15th century by supporters of the Czech Hussite reform movement — and follows the wide, winding river; the best overview is from the lookout tower atop Hýlačka hill. Stage 2 continues through the valley, becoming steeper and rockier as it wends via old mills, rock tunnels and the ruins of Příběnice Castle. Stage 3 squeezes through an ever-narrowing gorge, first over the Stádlec Chain Bridge (built elsewhere in the mid-19th century and moved here in the 1970s), passing ruined Dobronice Castle and finally crossing the elegant Rainbow Bridge to reach the well-preserved old town of Bechyně.

The last leg begins with fine views before plunging into a deep canyon and finishing on the water's edge in Týn nad Vltavou, where the Lužnice meets the Vltava, Czechia's longest river.

ACCOMMODATION
There's at least one hotel, cabin or guesthouse at the end of each stage, and many more options in larger towns.

FOOD
Available in towns and villages along the way.

GETTING THERE
Planá nad Lužnicí is an hour and 20 minutes by train from Prague.

PLANNING
Book accommodation in advance. Some facilities close October–April. Luggage transfers can be arranged.

SAFETY
Phone coverage is limited on some sections. Paths can be slippery after rain.

INFO
toulava.cz

LEFT Dobronice Castle, on Stage 3 of the Lužnice Valley Trail. **TOP** The route crosses the Rainbow Bridge over the Lužnice as it winds its way toward Bechyně.

AUG

NATURE / CULTURE / CAMPING / MOUNTAINS

Larapinta Trail

NORTHERN TERRITORY, AUSTRALIA

Follow an ancient mountain range into the Red Centre on a trail that takes in sharp ridges, cool creeks and millennia of Indigenous Australian history.

The landscapes of central Australia look and feel their age – which is very old indeed. It was around 450 million years ago when the Alice Springs Orogeny – a significant tectonic episode – started sculpting the surrounding Outback, gradually squeezing the continent's edges into its middle and creating large mountain chains.

The Larapinta Trail follows the spine of one of those: the West MacDonnell Ranges – or Tjoritja, as it's known to the Arrernte, the land's Traditional Owners. The Arrernte chart their history back 40,000 years, and this region is imbued with their stories, sacred sites and Songlines – the Dreaming tracks that connect both ancestral lands and ancient mythologies. Now, the Arrernte allow walkers to explore here, too.

Linking the desert outpost of Alice Springs to 1380m-high (4528ft) Mt Sonder, Tjoritja's highest point, the Larapinta Trail is as challenging as you'd expect a multiday, off-grid, Red Centre bushwhack to be. The terrain is largely rough, rocky and loose underfoot, with some steep gradients and occasional scrambles over boulders and tossed-up debris. There are few facilities here, just simple campsites and a couple of kiosks where you can pick up basic supplies (and a few treats). And unless they choose to join an organised tour, hikers must be able to fully fend for themselves in the Outback.

There's also virtually no shade, which is why it would be verging on madness to try trekking the Larapinta outside the cooler winter months – walk it between May and August. Nights can be chilly, even dropping below freezing, but daytime

START
Alice Springs

FINISH
Mt Sonder

DISTANCE
223km (139 miles)

DURATION
12–20 days

CHALLENGE LEVEL

WHEN TO WALK
May–August

AUG

LEFT Ormiston Gorge, a highlight of the Larapinta Trail's Section 9.

AUSTRALIA

ACCOMMODATION
There are 26 designated campgrounds; most have shelters, toilets and water.

FOOD
Walkers must be self-sufficient. Food drops can be made/arranged at official storage points. There are water tanks en route.

GETTING THERE
Alice Springs is served by planes, buses and trains. Redbank Gorge (below Mt Sonder) is 2WD-accessible; transfers can be arranged.

PLANNING
Trail and camping fees must be paid in advance. There are 12 trailheads, including at Alice Springs and Redbank Gorge; shorter walks can be planned using alternative trailheads.

SAFETY
Phone reception is sparse and shade is limited.

INFO
larapintatrail.com.au
nt.gov.au

AUG

temperatures loiter around 23°C (73°F). That's warm enough for refreshing dips in waterholes en route (when appropriate – some are sacred, and the Arrernte ask you not to swim), but not as fierce as summer, when the mercury can push above 35°C (95°F). This is also the driest period, with August often most arid – a good time to see resurgent desert wildflowers.

So the Larapinta is hard. And dusty. And takes some organisation. But it's an absolute beaut. The trail can be walked in either direction, though most choose to hike east–west, beginning at Alice Springs Telegraph Station (dating back to 1872). Ahead lies a wilderness of witchetty bush, mulga scrub, ghost gums and eucalypt groves, of winding creeks and sinuous gorges, of rocky ridges and summits that overlook this primordial world.

The trail is well waymarked and broken into 12 stages. Standouts include Sections 4 and 5, from Standley Chasm to Hugh Gorge; this stretch leads over Reveal Saddle to Brinkley Bluff, an amazing spot to camp and look down the range's spine, before ascending Razorback Ridge for more immense views. Section 9

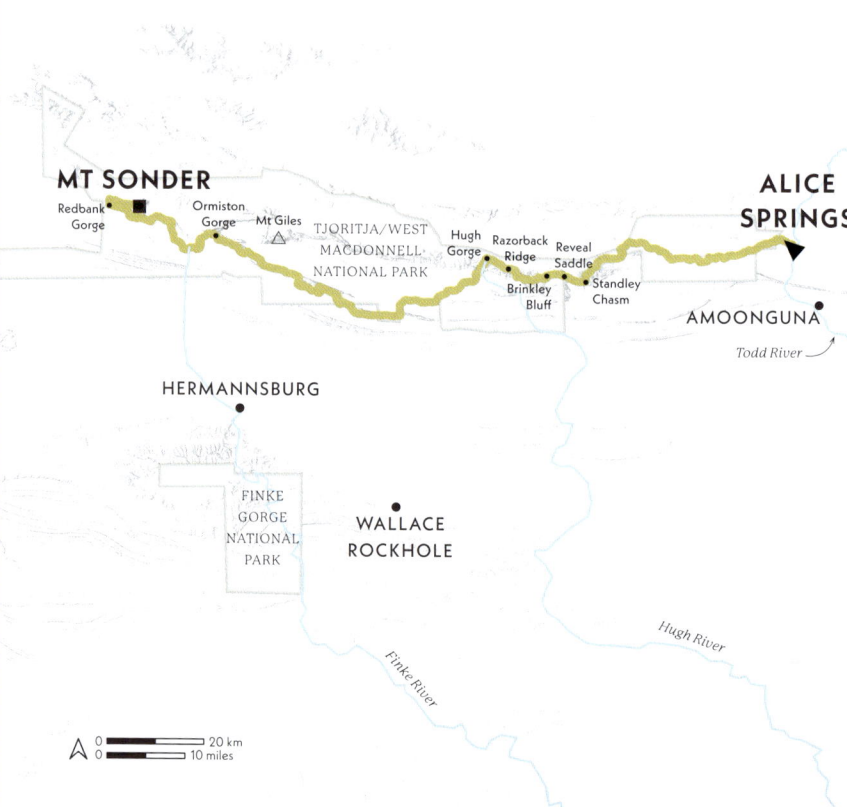

206

LEFT Rise early for the ascent of Mt Sonder, highpoint of the Tjoritja/West MacDonnell Range and a fitting end to the Larapinta. **RIGHT** Ormiston Gorge's waterhole attracts a wealth of wildlife, from red kangaroos to western bowerbirds.

'THE LARAPINTA ROUTE RUNS THROUGH WHAT THE ARRERNTE CALL TYURRENTYE, A LIVING, SPIRITUAL LANDSCAPE OF SACRED PLACES SUCH AS STANDLEY CHASM (ANGKERLE ATWATYE).'

is long but rewarding, with panoramas over the Alice Valley to massive Mt Giles, and a delightful campsite at Ormiston Gorge, complete with kiosk and showers. Then there's the grand finale: Mt Sonder. Rise early to climb in the cool morning air, take in all you've traversed, and give thanks to the Arrernte for sharing their land.

Side-strolls

IF THE Larapinta doesn't seem long enough, there are various side trips you can take along the way. From Ormiston Gorge, you could add on the 9km (5.5 mile) Ormiston Pound Circuit, considered one of the best day-walks in Tjoritja/West MacDonnell National Park. The 3km (2-mile) Dolomite Walk loops to the beguiling pool of Ellery Creek Big Hole. There are also short add-ons to Standley Chasm, Redbank Gorge, Glen Helen and Serpentine Gorge Lookout.

NATURE / CAMPING / MOUNTAINS

K2 Base Camp & Concordia

BALTISTAN, PAKISTAN

START/FINISH
Askole or Jhola

DISTANCE
170km (106 miles) approx

DURATION
14 days

CHALLENGE LEVEL

WHEN TO WALK
Mid-June to mid-September

Trek along a creaking glacier into the belly of the Karakoram to stand in awe before the planet's second-highest peak.

K2 is shorter than Everest — just — at 8611m (28,251ft) to Everest's 8849m (29,032ft). But it's a much more difficult and dangerous beast, with steeper slopes and a higher death rate: climbers have around a one in four chance of not making it back down alive. Its nickname is the 'Savage Mountain'. Rather than risk a summit attempt, far better to trek to its base camp. It's still a daunting challenge, and one that can be attempted only in the short summer trekking season — July and August are best, when passes are most likely to be snow-free and the weather more stable.

K2 stands on the Pakistan/China border, in the wild Karakoram Mountains. Reaching the trailhead at remote Askole is an experience, on roads susceptible to closure by landslides. From here — or Jhola, if your jeep has penetrated that far — the adventure begins. The out-and-back trail follows the Braldu River, then climbs onto the shifting ice of the Baltoro Glacier. It's a magnificent and challenging byway, threading deeper through an avenue of ever more dramatic peaks. Eventually, you'll arrive at the dazzling glacial confluence of Concordia. At an altitude of around 4500m (14,765ft), this frozen basin is embraced by many of the world's highest summits: the Gasherbrum group, Mitre Peak, Chogolisa and K2. Beyond, the Godwin-Austen Glacier runs to the foot of K2 — a distance of only 10km (6 miles), but encompassing some of the most technical terrain. The views are breath-stealing, both from the campsite below nearby Broad Peak and from K2 base camp, where the Gilkey Memorial commemorates those who've perished on K2's slopes.

ACCOMMODATION
Camping. On organised trips, porters will carry kit and erect tents for trekkers.

FOOD
Supplies must be packed in.

GETTING THERE
There's an airport in Skardu; from there it's a slow, winding jeep journey to Askole or Jhola, depending on road conditions. Landslides are frequent.

PLANNING
A trekking visa is required. Tour operators will organise permits and other logistics – research thoroughly before choosing a company.

SAFETY
Allow time for altitude acclimatisation. Check travel advisories.

LEFT K2 – the 'Savage Mountain' – from the Concordia campsite.
TOP Take in views of Mitre Peak and other super summits from the glacial confluence of Concordia.

NATURE / CAMPING / COAST

Baltic Coastal Hiking Trail: Nida to Šventoji

WESTERN LITHUANIA

This shore-hugging hike traces Lithuania's entire seaboard (almost), but it's just one part of an ambitious route along the coast of all three Baltic nations.

Welcome to the Jūrų takas, if you're rambling this in Lithuania. Or the Jūrtaka, if you're in Latvia. Or the Ranniku Matkarada, for those in Estonia. For English-speakers, it's the Baltic Coastal Hiking Trail. No matter: though this long-distance route may have multiple names, it has one goal: to stick to the shores of the Baltic Sea as closely as possible in the three countries it links.

This ambitious, enormous trail, launched in 2021, wends and wriggles from the Lithuanian town of Nida (bordering Russian enclave Kaliningrad) to the Estonian capital, Tallinn. Along the way it passes through dunes, bogs, bird-busy wetlands, forests, reed-fringed marsh, seaside spa towns and national parks. The full route stretches 1419km (882 miles), a hike of around 70 days. But it's designed in sections of 20km–30km (12–19 miles), most bookended by towns and villages with hotels, guesthouses, campgrounds and public transport. So if you're short on time, it's relatively simple to walk shorter stretches.

If that's you, you could do worse than starting at the beginning: set off from Nida, the trail's southernmost point, and cover the chunk that extends for most of the Lithuanian coast. It's a 107km (66.5-mile) hike along the Curonian Spit to Klaipėda and then onwards to the Latvian border at Šventoji; a loop of Rusnė, Lithuania's largest and only inhabited island, floating in the Nemunas Delta, is an extra 23km (14 miles) — a delightful

START
Nida

FINISH
Šventoji

DISTANCE
130km (81 miles)

DURATION
Five to six days

CHALLENGE LEVEL
★★☆☆☆

WHEN TO WALK:
April–October

LEFT Pine forest near Smiltynė on Lithuania's UNESCO-listed Curonian Spit peninsula.

LITHUANIA

Arboreal alternative

THE COASTAL route is one of two long-distance paths that make up the Baltic Trails network. The other is the even more ambitious Baltic Forest route, which runs 2141km (1330 miles) from the Lithuanian town of Lazdijai, on the Polish border, to Tallinn in Estonia via the Dubysa River valley, Gauja National Park (famed for its cliffs, caves and historic buildings) and Lahemaa National Park (renowned for its raised bogs). Allow upwards of 100 days.

'THE CURONIAN SPIT WAS FORMED BY WAVES AND WINDS 5000 YEARS AGO, BUT IS KEPT INTACT BY HUMANS: TREE-PLANTING STABILISES THE DUNES OF THIS FRAGILE ECOSYSTEM.'

addition, especially for birders. If birds are your passion, plan your hike to coincide with the spring and autumn migrations – in September and October three million birds can fly over each day. Otherwise, opt for summer. Though this is the busiest time on the Baltic Coast, it's also when things are less, well, Baltic: August is the warmest month, with temperatures reaching highs of 22°C (72°F) and the sea balmy enough for mid-walk swims. The downsides are higher prices and booked-up accommodation, but all the shops and bars are open, and resorts have a lively buzz. Ferries run more frequently, too – useful for getting to Nida and Rusnė the fun way.

The first stages run along the UNESCO-listed Curonian Spit – a slender, forested, sand-dune-bordered peninsula that separates the Curonian Lagoon from the Baltic Sea – hiking via the old, sleepy villages of Pervalka and Juodkrantė. From Smiltynė, at

TOP The country-spanning Baltic Forest Trail runs through Latvia's Lahemaa National Park. **LEFT** Hike the Baltic Coastal Trail to Lithuania's Dutchman's Cap viewpoint. **RIGHT** Curonian Spit dunes, Lithuania.

LITHUANIA

ACCOMMODATION
Hotels and guesthouses. Camping isn't permitted on beaches in Lithuania and Estonia, and only in certain areas in Latvia.

FOOD
The trail often passes shops and cafes, but some stretches are barren – plan ahead.

GETTING THERE
Nida can be reached by ferry and bus from Klaipėda; in summer, a boat also connects Nida with Uostadvaris on Rusnė.

PLANNING
Book accommodation in advance. Public transport serves many points on the trail – check timetables. The route is way-marked in both directions.

SAFETY
Storms may render some sections unsafe. Take appropriate footwear for sand, pebbles and pavements.

INFO
baltictrails.eu

the spit's end, it's a short ferry-hop to the historic port of Klaipėda, founded on 1 August 1252 – events are held annually to celebrate.

The trail continues north along the coast to the Latvian border, via sand and pebble beaches and through the Seaside Regional Park, where there's a good lookout from the bluff of Dutchman's Cap. But don't miss the Rusnė loop, accessible by train and bus from Klaipėda, or boat from Nida. Following quiet lanes and polder dykes, it takes in Rusnė 15th-century town, Uostadvaris Lighthouse and delta wetlands where you might spot waterfowl, waders, marsh harriers and even white storks (they fly south from mid-August).

NATURE / CULTURE

Malmveien Historical Trail

TRØNDELAG, NORWAY

START
Røros

FINISH
Langen

DISTANCE
50km (31 miles)

DURATION
Three days

CHALLENGE LEVEL
★★☆☆☆

WHEN TO WALK
June–September

Stroll the wild, lake-swathed Scandinavian borderlands and discover a fascinating mining past.

The Malmveien – 'Ore Road' – is a hike into both history and the wilderness. It starts from the UNESCO-listed town of Røros, founded following the discovery of copper in 1644; it became one of Norway's most important mining settlements, and its centre remains a huddle of 17th- and 18th-century wooden buildings. From here, the trail burrows southeast towards Femundsmarka National Park, a swathe of silver pines, lakes and waterways that, together with contiguous protected areas over the Swedish border, is one of southern Scandinavia's largest pristine regions.

The Malmveien follows the old transport route used to lug ore from the mines of the Storwartz Field (just outside Røros, now a visitor site) to the Femundshytta smelter on the shores of Femunden, Norway's third-biggest lake. Its route passes old charcoal furnaces, slag heaps and canal systems; there's also a Stone Age settlement at the mouth of the Feragselva River, and whispers of the region's Sámi people, who still herd their reindeer across its expanses. The national park itself is a primeval-looking landscape of rounded hills, low ridges and scattered boulders, alive with moose, beavers, loons and ospreys (which spend summers here), plus twisted pines, purple heather, vibrant-yellow wolf lichen and bushes bursting with raspberries, blueberries and cloudberries.

The hiking season runs from June to September; August – especially the second half – is ideal: days are still mild and long, but Norwegian schools go back mid-month, leaving the countryside even quieter. Plus all those delicious berries will be ripe for picking.

ACCOMMODATION
Den Norske Turistforening (Norwegian Trekking Association; DNT) operates two self-catering cabins on the route. Some beds can be booked in advance (hyttebestilling.dnt.no); some are reserved for drop-ins.

FOOD
Cabins have kitchens and are stocked with basic provisions and recipe suggestions. Berries can be foraged.

GETTING THERE
The Røros Railway connects Røros with Trondheim and Hamar. Buses connect Røros with Langen.

PLANNING
Pre-book accommodation in peak summer months.

SAFETY
Pack insect repellent. Check for ticks.

INFO
femundsmarkanasjonalpark.no
dnt.no/om-dnt/english

LEFT Forest cabin near Røros, at the start of the route. **TOP** The Malmveien laces through the pine forests of Femundsmarka National Park.

SEPTEMBER

The out-and-back Kalalau Trail traces the emerald cliffs of Kauaʻi's Nā Pali Coast, Hawaiʻi (page 230).

SEPTEMBER

I WANT A HIKE THAT'S A...

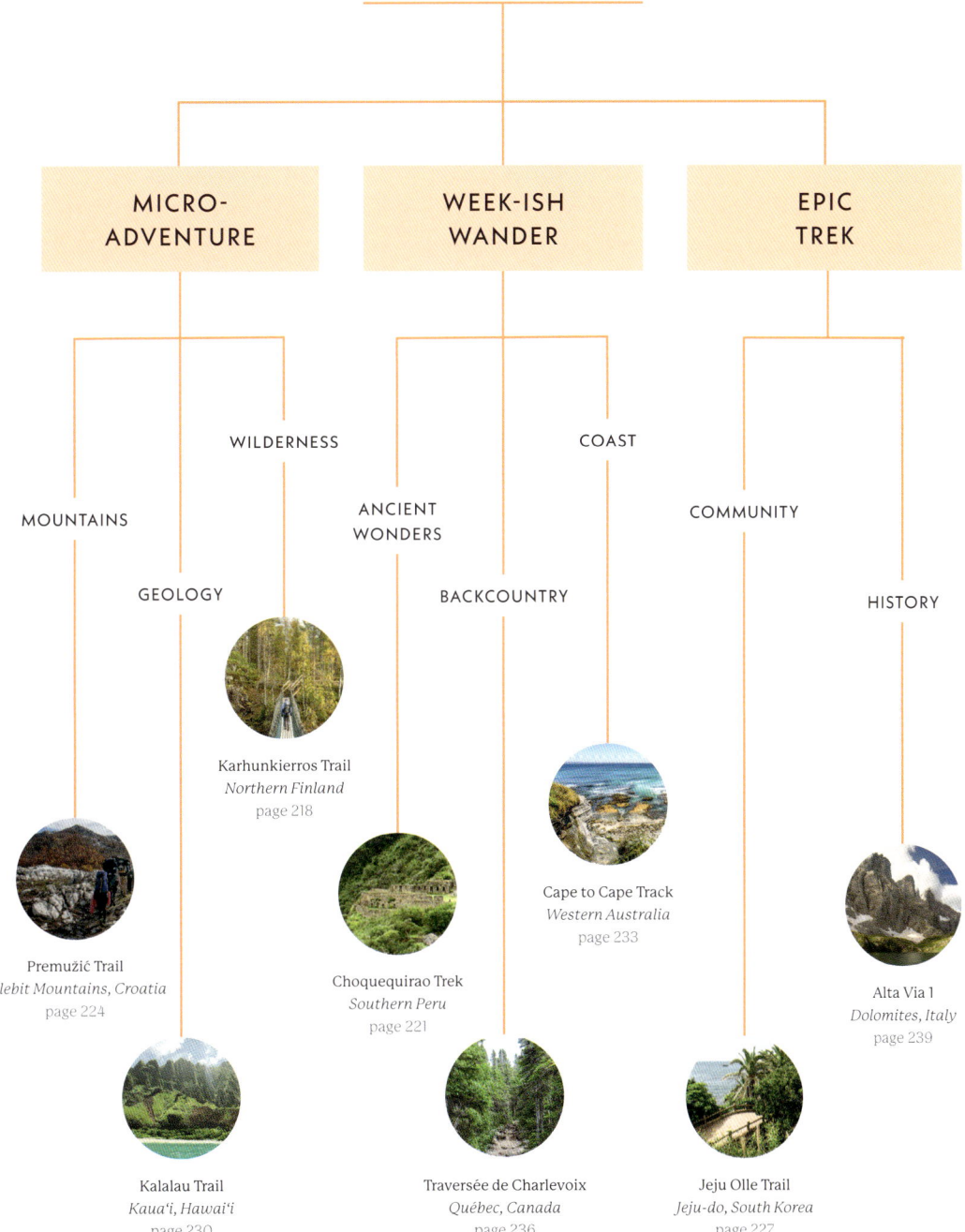

MICRO-ADVENTURE

- MOUNTAINS — Premužić Trail, *Velebit Mountains, Croatia*, page 224
- WILDERNESS — Karhunkierros Trail, *Northern Finland*, page 218
- GEOLOGY — Kalalau Trail, *Kaua'i, Hawai'i*, page 230

WEEK-ISH WANDER

- ANCIENT WONDERS — Choquequirao Trek, *Southern Peru*, page 221
- COAST — Cape to Cape Track, *Western Australia*, page 233
- BACKCOUNTRY — Traversée de Charlevoix, *Québec, Canada*, page 236

EPIC TREK

- COMMUNITY — Jeju Olle Trail, *Jeju-do, South Korea*, page 227
- HISTORY — Alta Via 1, *Dolomites, Italy*, page 239

FINLAND

NATURE / CAMPING

Karhunkierros Trail

NORTHERN FINLAND

START
Hautajärvi

FINISH
Ruka

DISTANCE
82km (51 miles)

DURATION
Three to five days

CHALLENGE LEVEL
★★★☆☆

WHEN TO WALK
June–October

Time your trek for the most special season to complete this classic hut-to-hut hike through Oulanka National Park.

The Finns call it *ruska* – the fleeting season when, for a few weeks in September and October, nature puts on a final flourish before winter descends. The trees and bushes flame in vibrant hues of purple, red and gold, the mosquitoes buzz off for the year, and bountiful fruits – blueberries, bilberries, cranberries, crowberries – are ripe for the plucking. It's certainly a tasty time to enjoy one of Finland's finest hut-to-hut hiking trails.

The Karhunkierros – 'Bear's Ring' – crosses Oulanka National Park, straddling Lapland and Northern Ostrobothnia regions. Until the 17th century, this was essentially the preserve of Sámi people. An important conservation area, the park is home to more than 400 protected animal and plant species, vital flood meadows, extensive boreal forest, craggy cliffs and canyons, crashing waterfalls, trickling rivers and raging rapids. It's not especially hilly – but there are challenges: negotiating sections of rocky, root-y ground, and planning a largely self-sufficient hike.

The trail can be followed in either direction, though most head south from Hautajärvi, a little village pretty much on the Arctic Circle, to reach Ruka. The trek takes three to five days, with numerous huts and camping places where you can break the journey. Clear trails stretch between the birch and pine, duckboards are laid over the cotton bog, steps are built into steeper climbs, suspension bridges span the crystal-clear rivers. In all, it's a breath of fresh, herb-scented air: the only sounds are the burble of water and the twig-crack of creatures roaming the forest – birds, moose or perhaps rutting reindeer. It's not entirely wild, though. Around a third of the way in, the trail passes Oulanka Visitor Centre – a fine place to make a very Finnish-style stop for coffee and a cinnamon bun.

SEP

ACCOMMODATION
Seven sleeping huts, plus day-use huts and shelters. Camping is permitted in designated areas.

FOOD
There are a few cafes so carry supplies and your own stove. Purify water, available from the plentiful sources.

GETTING THERE
Buses connect Hautajärvi and Ruka to Kuusamo Airport in hiking season.

PLANNING
Take a tent in case huts are full.

SAFETY
Write your name/plans in hut guest books. Download the emergency call app (via 112.fi).

INFO
luontoon.fi

LEFT Hiking the Karhunkierros Trail through Oulanka National Park. **TOP** Autumn colour in Oulanka.

NATURE / CULTURE / CAMPING / MOUNTAINS

Choquequirao Trek

SOUTHERN PERU

Avoid the crowds by accessing the famed Inca ruins of Machu Picchu via an alternative, backdoor trail passing another incredible 'lost city' along the way.

One way to hike to Machu Picchu is along the classic Inca Trail, the hugely popular 42km (26-mile) route requiring permits that sell out months in advance. But there's another way: via Choquequirao, a far-less-visited but still awe-inspiring Inca site. It's a longer, harder and more off-the-beaten-track approach, offering a greater sense of solitude — and the chance to explore a lost city that gives Peru's headline attraction a run for its money.

Choquequirao — Quechua for 'Cradle of Gold' — was built in the late 15th century at the peak of the Inca Empire. It's Machu Picchu's introverted little sister: both sites teeter on dizzying ridges, their stone buildings carefully arranged around plazas and along astronomical alignments. Choquequirao may have been a refuge for the last Sapa Inca (emperor) when the Spanish conquered this land in 1572.

It then lay largely forgotten until American explorer Hiram Bingham happened upon the ruins in 1909 (before revealing Machu Picchu to the wider world two years later). However, Choquequirao's size and awkward location delayed meaningful excavations until the 1970s; even now, most of the remains lie untouched and — until the long-mooted cable car is built — the only way to get here is on foot.

It's possible to visit on a three- or four-day out-and-back hike from the mountain village of Cachora (or from Capuliyoc, a little way into the trail). But it's more rewarding to extend the adventure by continuing through to Aguas Calientes in the Sacred Valley — the town of thermal springs and tourist buzz

START
Cachora (or Capuliyoc)

FINISH
Aguas Calientes (or Llactapata)

DISTANCE
100km (62 miles) approx

DURATION
Eight to nine days

CHALLENGE LEVEL

WHEN TO WALK
April–October

LEFT The Choquequirao Trek offers a less-trodden path to Aguas Calientes, gateway to Machu Picchu.

ACCOMMODATION
Camping, plus a few village guesthouses.

FOOD
Pack supplies and purify water. Organised tours provide meals and mules.

GETTING THERE
Cachora is a four-hour drive from Cuzco. Private transfers are easiest; alternatively, buses run to Abancay via the Ramal de Cachora stop – alight here for taxis to Cachora or Capuliyoc (13km/8 miles into the trek).

PLANNING
Guides aren't mandatory, unlike on the Inca Trail; however, organised trips simplify logistics and provide insight into archaeological sites. An entry fee applies for Choquequirao.

SAFETY
Acclimatise to the altitude. Trekking poles are recommended.

INFO
peru.travel

that's the gateway to Machu Picchu. Avoid the November–March wet season; rains peter out during April. September is one of the loveliest months: days are warm and largely clear and sunny, and it's just after peak season, so the trails – and Machu Picchu – will be less busy.

The hike is strenuous from the off, including a knee-jarring descent into the lush, flower-frilled Apurimac Canyon followed by a stiff, zigzagging ascent back up the other side. But the rewards are plentiful – particularly your arrival at Choquequirao, its ruins sprawled across slopes and ridges. From here, the trail leads over the Choquequirao Pass (3340m/10,958ft), past the Inca terraces at Pincha Unuyoc and down into the Río Blanco Valley before veering up through the cloud forest to the campground at Maizal (the 'cornfield').

This up-down pattern is repeated as you cross the San Juan Pass (4150m/13,615ft) and descend into the Río Yanama Valley,

LEFT A bird's-eye view of Inca settlement Choquequirao. **BELOW** Stone buildings at Choquequirao. **RIGHT** Campsite with a view on the Choquequirao Trek.

'CHOQUEQUIRAO REMAINS MYSTERIOUS BUT IS BELIEVED TO HAVE BEEN AN ADMINISTRATIVE CENTRE, A CHECKPOINT FOR THE FABLED INCA STRONGHOLD OF VILCABAMBA AND A KEY LINK BETWEEN CUZCO AND THE AMAZON.'

traverse the breath-stealing Totora Pass (4660m/15,289ft), then drop almost half that altitude to the Río Santa Teresa. The payoff is the phenomenal variety of experiences and sights, from butterfly-wafted semi-tropics to views of snowcapped behemoths like 6271m (20,574ft) Salkantay, the highest peak in the Vilcabamba range.

A final stretch leads to the Inca complex of Llactapata, from where you can see Machu Picchu spilling down a distant slope – a view few others experience. From Llactapata, walk along rail tracks (or catch a train) to Aguas Calientes, and prepare to explore wonder-of-the-world Machu Picchu.

What's at Choquequirao?

CHOQUEQUIRAO IS split into *hanan* (higher) and *hurin* (lower) sectors. A stone canal connects the two, carrying water from the Upper to the Lower Plaza. An array of stone structures is built into the slopes, including *collcas* (storehouses), long *lkallankas* (priests' houses) and ceremonial platforms. There are also temples, fountains, ritual baths, workshops, kitchens and holding pens for sacrificial llamas. White rock carvings of llamas are set into some of the terraces.

NATURE / MOUNTAINS / COAST

Premužić Trail

VELEBIT MOUNTAINS, CROATIA

START
Zavižan

FINISH
Baške Oštarije

DISTANCE
57km (35 miles)

DURATION
Three days

CHALLENGE LEVEL

WHEN TO WALK
June to early October

Stride along exquisitely made stone paths to explore a craggy karst range that offers awesome Adriatic Sea views.

It's appropriate that this hike through Croatia's North Velebit Mountains is named for its creator, Ante Premužić – because it's a masterpiece of trail-building. Nearly a century ago, a relatively easy path – with no big ascents or descents – was blazed through rugged, difficult, otherwise inaccessible karst terrain. To make it, forestry engineer and keen mountaineer Premužić employed the *suhozid* (dry-stone wall) technique, a skill bestowed with Intangible Cultural Heritage status by UNESCO. It took Premužić and his team four years to create the trail, which finally opened in 1933.

The route, much of which runs through the Northern Velebit National Park, has weathered the rigours of time and use to become a Croatian classic, packing a huge variety into its compact length. Intricate stone pathways weave between old shepherds' huts and mighty rock formations, cross wildflower meadows and enter forests of beech and fir, holly fern, saxifrage and speedwell. These mountains are rich in plant-life, home to more than 950 species and subspecies; day one passes the Velebit Botanical Garden, a great spot to see a host of endemics. And, this being a coastal mountain range, there are panoramic views across the sparkling Adriatic, too.

Most hikers spend their first night in Alan Hut, which offers simple dorms and warm welcomes – it's staffed mid-June to late October. The second stop was traditionally the simple Skorpovac Shelter but, at the time of writing, this had burned down, requiring an alternative hut stop or an off-trail diversion. The route finishes in the quiet mountain village of Baške Oštarije.

Late spring and autumn bring mild, pleasant hiking conditions. In September, expect temperatures ranging 15°C–25°C (59°F–77°F), plus snow-free trails, and balmy waters for post-walk soaks.

ACCOMMODATION
Mountain huts (some staffed) and free basic huts. Camping is not allowed within Northern Velebit National Park, but is permissible outside its boundaries.

FOOD
Carry supplies. Alan Hut offers some food.

GETTING THERE
Zavižan can be reached by car, taxi or hike (three to four hours) from Krasno.

PLANNING
Buy national park tickets at Babić Siča (the main entrance) or Alan Hut.

SAFETY
Check weather forecasts. Carry plenty of water.

INFO
np-sjeverni-velebit.hr

LEFT Limestone peaks in the Rožanski Kukovi region of Northern Velebit National Park. **TOP** Hike *suhozid* (dry-stone wall) pathways along the Premužić Trail.

NATURE / CULTURE / COAST

Jeju Olle Trail

JEJU-DO, SOUTH KOREA

Take a spin around this subtropical isle in the Korea Strait, where a network of trails introduces hikers to its distinctive culture and scenery.

Jeju-do sits apart from the rest of South Korea, literally and culturally. Lying some 80km (50 miles) off the south of the peninsula, this oval-shaped island was formed from the leftovers of an underwater volcanic eruption, and is dominated by 1947m (6388ft) Hallasan, the country's highest point. An independent country until the 10th century, Jeju is now South Korea's only self-governing province. It has its own (endangered) language and unique traditions, which include an abundance of mysterious *hareubang* (grandfather statues) and the UNESCO-recognised *haenyeo* (women of the sea) — freediving fisher-women, most of whom are 70-plus years old.

Jeju also has an impressive network of hiking routes that together form the Jeju Olle Trail — *olle* being local dialect for a narrow alley connecting a house to the road. There are 27 routes in total, 21 of which link up to loop the outer edges of the main island; the other six are extras, mostly rambling around smaller isles nearby.

The Jeju Olle Trail was inspired by the Camino de Santiago. After journalist Suh Myung-sook completed her Spanish pilgrimage, she decided to create something similar on her home island. The trail is now efficiently managed by the non-profit Jeju Olle Foundation, with the support of an army of volunteers. And it's very well managed indeed. Sections are clearly marked, with sign-stones at the start of every stage, distance posts telling you how far there is left to go, and ribbons and arrows pointing the way — blue for clockwise hikers (the most common direction), orange for anticlockwise. At junctions there are also blue

START/FINISH
Siheung

DISTANCE
437km (272 miles)

DURATION
27 days

CHALLENGE LEVEL
★★☆☆☆

WHEN TO WALK
March–May
& September–November

LEFT Bucolic Jeju-do coastline along Route 10 of the Jeju Olle Trail, near Songak-san peak.

Darkest hour

THE END OF WWII saw the departure of Japanese occupiers from Korea, but ultimately led to the division of the peninsula into north and south. The people of Jeju-do favoured a unified nation, and from April 1948 to May 1949 mounted an uprising in protest. South Korean authorities retaliated with brutal force, and an estimated 30,000 people – around 10% of Jeju's population – were killed. You'll pass numerous memorials and massacre sites as you hike the trail.

'LEGEND TELLS THAT THE DEMIGODS GO, RYANG AND BU EMERGED FROM HOLES IN THE GROUND AT SAMSEONGHYEOL – AN ARCHAEOLOGICAL SITE IN JEJU CITY – AND BECAME THE ISLAND'S FIRST PEOPLE.'

pony-shaped sculptures (the symbol of the trail called *ganse*; the name is derived from the local word for idling – a reminder that walkers should take it slow and enjoy the journey).

And it's quite the journey, wiggling between white-sand beaches, waved-smacked sea stacks, fishing villages (where you might watch *haenyeo* at work), ancient *batdam* (dry-stone walls), dense *gotjawal* forest, busy urban hubs and some of the island's 360-odd *oreum* (volcanic cinder cones). There are almost always views out to sea and up to Hallasan, glowering inland.

Autumn is a fine time to hike. From September the hot, sticky, monsoonal weather abates, summer crowds disappear and the

LEFT The Jeju Olle's Route 10 takes in the island's far southwest, from Hwasun to Moseulpo. **RIGHT** Route 8, from Wolpyeong to Daepyeong, delivers views of the hexagonal basalt cliffs at Jusangjeolli.

ACCOMMODATION
Plentiful guesthouses, hostels and *minbaks* (homestays).

FOOD
Routes pass villages, cafes and convenience stores – resupplying is easy.

GETTING THERE
Flights from Seoul to Jeju-do take just over an hour, sometimes more. Ferries cross to Jeju from various mainland ports, taking two to four hours. Siheung is accessible by bus.

PLANNING
Buy a Jeju Olle Passport to collect stamps and enjoy discounts on some services. Completer's certificates are issued from Olle HQ in Seogwipo (Route 7), so many thru-hikers start/end on this stage.

SAFETY
Don't hike during typhoons or heavy rain/snow. Be tick aware.

INFO
jejuolle.org

trees become increasingly fiery-hued; the water lapping those beautiful beaches is still sublime for swimming, too.

You can, of course, hike the whole thing: collect stamps in your Jeju Olle Passport along the way and you'll qualify for a completer's certificate. However, the beauty of this network is that it's simple to cut and paste individual sections, thanks to plentiful public transport and facilities.

Which stages to choose? Route 1, which starts at Siheung near the east coast, provides a classic introduction, with several *oreum* to climb. A leg stringing together Routes 6 to 10 offers a lot of variety, including second-largest city Seogwipo, the hexagonal basalt columns of Jusangjeolli, lush Andeok Valley and the mountain Songak-san. For a different vibe, Route 18 departs main city Jeju for country paths, dramatic coastal scenery and the mural village of Sinchon. All in all, island bliss.

NATURE / CULTURE / CAMPING / MOUNTAINS / COAST

Kalalau Trail

KAUA'I, HAWAI'I

START/FINISH
Ke'e Beach

DISTANCE
35km (22 miles)

DURATION
Two days

CHALLENGE LEVEL
★★★☆☆

WHEN TO WALK
May–September

This short but sweet trail packs a mighty geological punch, allowing privileged access to the formidable Nā Pali Coast.

Kaua'i formed around five million years ago, giving Mother Nature ample time to sculpt the oldest of the Hawaiian isles to perfection – and nowhere is her handiwork more impressive than along the Nā Pali Coast. Flanking the North Shore, this monstrous barricade of fluted volcanic cliffs rises up to some 1200m (3937ft), smacked by the deep-blue Pacific, tickled by waterfalls, incised by dizzying valleys and cloaked in luxuriant emerald fuzz. It looks impenetrable, yet the Polynesian navigators who first arrived here 800-odd years ago managed to put down roots in its seemingly inaccessible reaches.

Today, this inaccessibility is what draws hikers. The Kalalau Trail is the only way to explore Nā Pali's nooks and crannies. Day-hikers are permitted to walk the first two miles to Hanakāpī'ai Beach, which offers dramatic views. Permits, camping gear and greater fitness are required to trek the whole trail – best done in the drier season. This outrageously green outcrop is one of the rainiest places on the planet, but mid-April into October sees fewer downpours and more warm weather. September, when prices and visitor numbers start to fall after the summer peak, is a good choice.

This is an out-and-back route: onward progress beyond the long, sandy sweep of Kalalau Beach (the best place to camp) is thwarted by sheer cliffs, so you'll need to retrace your steps. Along the way, the trail crosses five valleys, visits spectacular beaches and sea caves, hops streams, gets splashed by waterfalls, flirts with native forest and passes overgrown farming terraces. Some sections, especially beyond the first campsite at Hanakoa (10km/6 miles in), are narrow, strenuous and vertiginous, with sheer drops to the ocean. But that's all part of this epic microadventure.

ACCOMMODATION
Camping areas at Hanakoa and Kalalau with composting toilets.

FOOD
Carry all supplies. Purify water from natural sources.

GETTING THERE
The trailhead is in Hā'ena State Park, around 1½ hours from Līhu'e Airport. Drive or book a shuttle. Book overnight parking in advance.

PLANNING
A camping permit is required, and can be bought up to 30 days in advance; numbers are limited.

SAFETY
Storms can make the trail unsafe. There's no phone reception.

INFO
kalalautrail.com

LEFT Hiking the short but superbly sweet Kalalau Trail. **TOP** The route traverses the lush valleys and and fabulously fluted cliffs of Kaua'i's Nā Pali Coast.

NATURE / FOOD & DRINK / CULTURE / COAST

Cape to Cape Track

WESTERN AUSTRALIA

Tramp the epic shoreline of Australia's far southwest, hiking between historic lighthouses as spring wildflowers bloom and whales cruise offshore.

You can't miss the start and end points of this hike. Gleaming white towers loom over both trailheads, like gargantuan pins stuck in the map by a helpful giant: the lighthouses at Cape Naturaliste in the north and, 93km (58 miles) south as the crow flies, Cape Leeuwin. Of course, you won't be following that hasty crow's route. Instead, the Cape to Cape Track plots a more meandering course through Leeuwin-Naturaliste National Park, alternating sandy shores and soaring cliffs with native forests and winsome villages.

This being Western Australia's temperate extremity – ending at the mainland's southwesternmost point – walking is possible year-round, though naturally hotter in summer (check for bushfire alerts), cooler and wetter in winter. But plot a Venn diagram of criteria for a dream hike, and September sits plum in the middle. It's warm but not scorching (important, given that many walkers use the basic campsites along the route), with modest tourist numbers; thousands of species of wildflowers are starting to bloom in profusion; and whales are still cruising past this month, along with pods of bottlenose dolphins. Not to mention surfers: there are up to 80 breaks along this stretch of coast, depending who you ask.

The scenic drama kicks in almost as soon as you set out from Cape Naturaliste, assuming you're walking north–south (though it's every bit as spectacular in the other direction). Just a few kilometres in, the trail reaches the lookout over Sugarloaf Rock, the distinctive outcrop on which red-tailed tropicbirds nest from September. Continue along the shore, the track at first raised

START
Cape Naturaliste

FINISH
Cape Leeuwin

DISTANCE
123km (76 miles)

DURATION
Five to eight days

CHALLENGE LEVEL
★★★☆☆

WHEN TO WALK
Year-round

LEFT The Indian and Southern Oceans meet at Cape Leeuwin, endpoint of the Cape to Cape Track.

ACCOMMODATION
Basic campsites en route, plus private campsites and holiday parks; there are also apartments and hotels nearby.

FOOD
Restaurants and food stores require short detours. Taste Margaret River's famous wines.

GETTING THERE
No public transport to either trailhead; use taxis – Dunsborough to Cape Naturaliste, Cape Leeuwin to Augusta.

PLANNING
No permits required. Book accommodation in advance.

SAFETY
From late spring through summer you might encounter snakes, including venomous (albeit shy) species; watch for them basking on the trail. In winter or after heavy rain, the mouth of Margaret River may be impassable; if so, detour inland.

INFO
trailswa.com.au

above the swells surging onto the break at Three Bears before descending to Kabbijgup Beach to pad softly across white sand, then climbing again to stroll through a sea of green to surfing hub Yallingup.

From here, a short but worthy detour leads to Ngilgi Cave – not just an astonishing subterranean gallery of huge stalactites and other formations, but a chance to learn about the mythology of the Wadandi, one of the region's Noongar Indigenous peoples, who've roamed these parts for at least 40,000 years.

Beyond Canal Rocks – watch for basking seals – pause for a cooling dip at the pool rather grandly dubbed Injidup Natural Spa. As the trail winds south, the highs become higher: Wilyabrup Cliffs are beloved of climbers and abseilers. The mouth of Margaret River marks the halfway point, more or less – a good excuse to sample the renowned wines produced in vineyards just inland. Increasingly now, impressive trees line the route:

LEFT Take time out from the trail to sample fine wines from locally grown vines. BELOW Scan the ocean from Cape Leeuwin for possible sightings of migrating humpbacks and other whales. RIGHT Cape to Cape Track coastline near Cape Naturaliste.

'COOL OFF MID-HIKE WITH A DIP AT GLORIOUS PROTECTED SWIMMING BEACHES AT HAMELIN BAY, FOUL BAY AND COSY CORNER; OR SIP WINE FROM MARGARET RIVER'S 200-PLUS VINEYARDS.'

jarrah and peppermint gums, melaleuca (Rottnest tea tree) and Australia's westernmost karri forest in Boranup, those arborial giants providing welcome shade.

There's a noisy welcome past Hamelin Bay at Cosy Corner Beach, where brine spurts through blowholes on lively days. It's a theatrical curtain-up for the craggy climax along Augusta Sea Cliffs — all limestone pinnacles atop granite heft — to Cape Leeuwin, the point where the Indian and Southern Oceans meet in a slap of surf: an apt high-five to congratulate triumphant hikers.

Whale tales

AUSTRALIA'S south-western corner flanks a key migration route for whales cruising between rich feeding grounds in the Southern Ocean and Antarctica, and warmer breeding areas to the north. Whale-watching boat tours depart daily from Augusta between June and September, but you might spot humpback, southern right or even mighty blue whales from the trail. Alternatively, climb to the top of Cape Leeuwin Lighthouse — mainland Australia's tallest, built in 1895 — for epic views of passing behemoths.

CANADA

NATURE / MOUNTAINS

Traversée de Charlevoix

QUÉBEC, CANADA

START
Zec des Martres

FINISH
Mont Grand-Fonds

DISTANCE
105km (65 miles)

DURATION
Six to seven days

CHALLENGE LEVEL
★★☆☆☆

WHEN TO WALK
June to late October

Take an autumnal hut-to-hut hike through Francophone Québec to see the trees turn and the stars shine.

Canada has a lot of wonderful wilderness, and a lot of wonderful wilderness trails. But you'll usually need to camp if you want to thru-hike for several days — there are few routes on which it's possible to trek from hut to hut. In this regard, the Traversée de Charlevoix is unique. The trail was first blazed by woodsman Eudore Fortin in 1978, as a ski-touring route; in the 1990s, a handful of Scandi-style log cabins were built. It's now managed by the Sentiers Québec-Charlevoix, which reinvests all profits into making the Traversée as good as it can be, and enabling more hikers to explore the region.

And it's well worth exploring. Charlevoix, just over an hour's drive northeast of Québec City, is a UNESCO-listed World Biosphere Reserve of mixed forest, taiga and tundra, fjords and bays, tidal flats and parts of the Laurentian Mountains. It's particularly spectacular in autumn, when trees are on the turn (usually peaking late September to early October), blueberries are ripe and juicy, weather is mild, tourists more sparse. Days are shorter than high summer — all the better for admiring inky, star-spangled skies.

The route, which cuts through the Charlevoix backcountry, is well-marked and generally not too tough, with a total elevation gain of 3336m (10,945ft). There are impressive panoramas from the hut atop Montagne de la Noyée, gorgeous views down the Hautes-Gorges Valley, swathes of trees (listen for woodpeckers), idyllic walking alongside the Malbaie River, and plenty of lakes and streams for refreshing dips. The trail steers clear of civilisation, only once crossing a tarmac road. But the cosy mountain huts — complete with mattresses, lighting, wood-burning stoves and even cafetières so you can make a decent brew — are civilised indeed.

SEP

ACCOMMODATION
Cabins and rustic campsites at the end of each stage.

FOOD
Pack supplies. Food drops can be organised.

GETTING THERE
Pick-ups can be arranged from Baie-Saint-Paul. Alternatively, book a car-shuttle service.

PLANNING
Advance booking is mandatory. Hikers must register at the visitor centre. The Deluxe Traverse package includes permits, accommodation, baggage and food transport, and vehicle transfer.

SAFETY
During hunting season (late September), orange bibs must be worn – available for sale/rent.

INFO
traverseedecharlevoix.qc.ca

LEFT Fiery fall colour around the hikers' cabin at Zec des Martres, near the Traversée de Charlevoix start point. **TOP** The Charlevoix trail traverses protected areas such as Parc National des Grands-Jardins.

NATURE / CULTURE / MOUNTAINS

Alta Via 1

DOLOMITES, ITALY

Follow in the footsteps of the WWI soldiers who fought in this breathtaking mountain range – and paved the way for today's hikers.

Alta Via 1 is very well named. It's an *alta via* – 'high road' – both literally and metaphorically, offering soul-lifting trekking through the dazzling Dolomites. It's also an appropriate 'number one' hike: rugged but not frighteningly tough, it's a good option for Alpine first-timers.

Over the course of ten or so days, the Alta Via 1 yields a bit of everything. There are dramatic ramparts of limestone and dolomitic rock, passes reaching up to 2752m (9029ft), meadows festooned with wildflowers, welcoming *rifugi* (mountain huts) dishing up hearty portions of fine food and bonhomie, and even thrilling (but not too scary) sections where metal handrails help you negotiate the wild terrain.

There's also a wealth of history. During WWI, the fortress-like Dolomites became a bloody if beautiful front line where Italian and Austro-Hungarian forces battled for four years, fighting both each other and the forces of Mother Nature. In the process, they constructed via ferrata (iron roads; networks of fixed lines, ladders and steps that enabled troops to clamber across rock faces); they also built gun emplacements and billets; dug long, dark tunnels; and burrowed miles of trenches. Movingly, the remains of these high-altitude skirmishes can still be seen along the trail. They make a chilling sight, even on a warm summer day.

And Alpine summer, from mid-June to late September, is really the only time to walk this classic route. It's when the trails are largely snow-free, when the *rifugios* are open, when the wildflowers are blooming and when the squeaking marmots are out

START
Lago di Bráies

FINISH
La Stanga, Belluno

DISTANCE
120km (75 miles)

DURATION
Eight to 12 days

CHALLENGE LEVEL
★★★☆☆

WHEN TO WALK
June–September

LEFT Lago di Bráies, start point of the Alta Via 1 through the dazzling heights of the Dolomites.

ITALY

Kaiserjäger Trail

NO TIME to hike whole Alta Via 1? The 9km (5.6 mile) Kaiserjäger (lagazuoi.it) offers a taster that's doable in around four hours. Looping from the Passo di Valparola, it's named for the Austro-Hungarian Alpine divisions once stationed on Mt Lagazuoi; the route they constructed to transport supplies has been repaired and is now a history-laden hiking path involving a nerve-jangling traverse of a steep, exposed ledge and a 10m-long (33ft) suspension bridge.

'THERE'S A MIX OF VOICES HERE. AS WELL AS ITALIAN AND GERMAN YOU'LL HEAR LADIN, AN ANCIENT ROMANCE LANGUAGE SPOKEN BY EARLY INHABITANTS OF THE DOLOMITES.'

of hibernation. July to August is the busiest period; September brings cooler temperatures but fewer crowds. Most hikers walk north to south, beginning by the turquoise waters of Lago di Bráies before climbing to the high plateau above. First stop is usually Rifugio Biella, a stern-looking stone hut at 2327m (7635ft), at the foot of Croda del Becco; once a military building, it's now a cosy cabin with shared dorms and fine home-cooked dishes.

Over the next few days, the Alta Via threads past the Fanes range toward Mt Lagazuoi and the route's highest point. The terrain around here is littered with military reminders, not least an optional detour into the Galleria Lagazuoi, a restored tunnel built by Italian troops – torches required.

LEFT Admiring serried Dolomites peaks along the Alta Via 1, close to Monte Civetta. **RIGHT** The route passes close to a string of gorgeous Alpine lakes.

ACCOMMODATION
Shared dorms in *rifugi* (mountain huts).

FOOD
Rifugi serve a hearty mix of Italian and Tyrolean dishes: pasta, polenta, stews, cured meats and cheeses. Pack trail snacks.

GETTING THERE
Trains and buses run to the town of Dobbiaco; a seasonal bus links Dobbiaco with Lago di Bráies. The closest airports are Bolzano, Innsbruck (in Austria) and Venice.

PLANNING
Book huts well in advance; or consider getting a tour operator to handle logistics.

SAFETY
The Alta Via 1 doesn't involve any via ferrata, but there are sections with cable handrails – you need a head for heights.

INFO
dolomiti.org

All the while, the Dolomites unfurl majestically. Many claim that these are Europe's best-looking peaks, and every footstep opens up another gorgeous view. There are the five iconic crags of the Cinque Torri; magnificently monstrous Monte Civetta, with Lago Coldai glittering below; the imposing spire of climbers' favourite Torre Trieste; and the route over the Forcella del Moschesin and up the rocky slopes of the Cima de Zita, which leads into Parco Nazionale delle Dolomiti Bellunesi – a good place to spot marmots and deer.

To top it off, days end not only with shots of grappa on convivial *rifugio* terraces but also with the famed *enrosadira* – that luminous phenomenon created when the late-afternoon light hits the grey peaks and sets them afire, glowing a rich rose-gold. Simply *bellissima!*

OCTOBER

Riverfront Stadt Wehlen, along the Malerweg hike through Germany's 'Saxon Switzerland' (page 267).

OCTOBER

I WANT A HIKE THAT'S A...

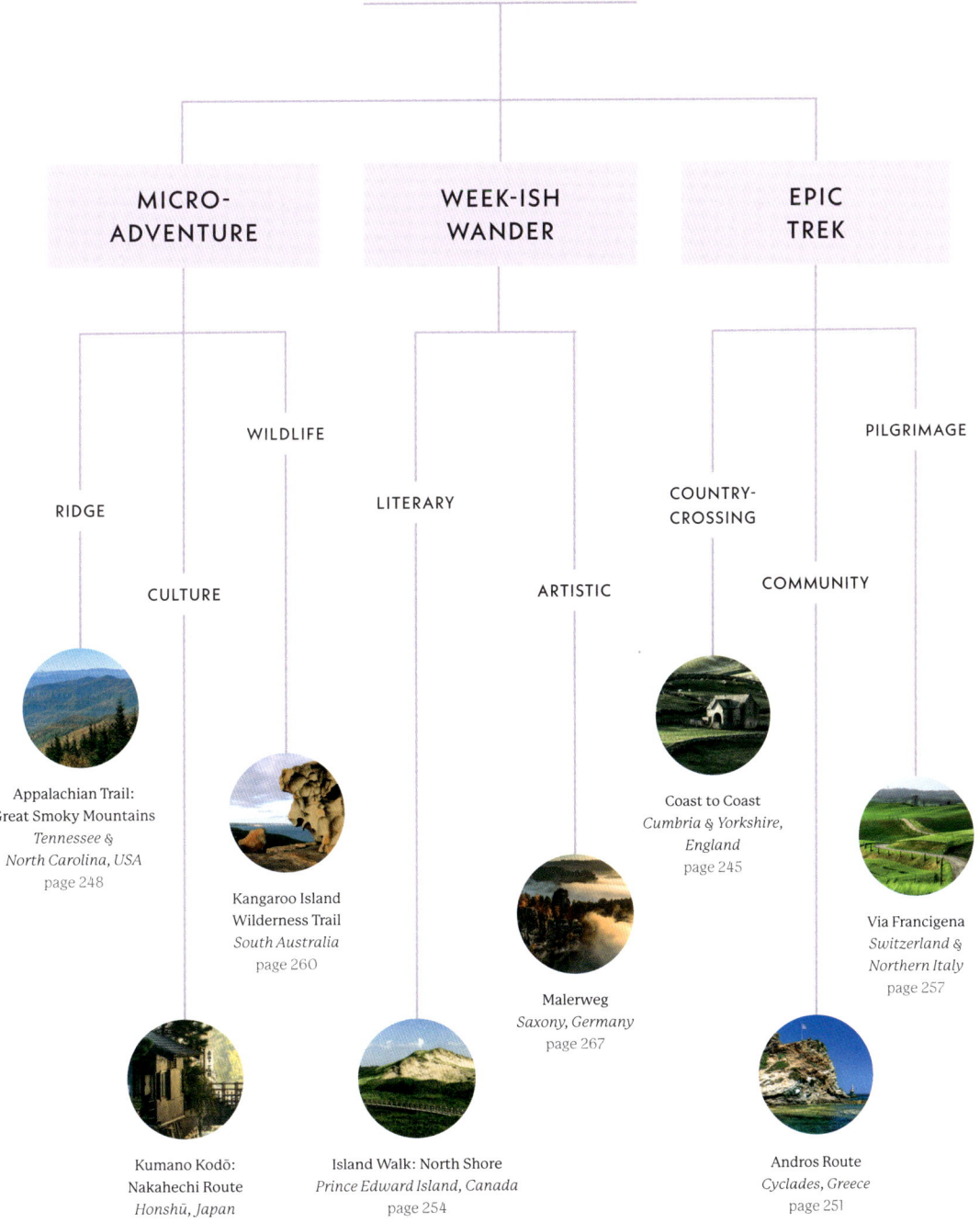

MICRO-ADVENTURE

- RIDGE — Appalachian Trail: Great Smoky Mountains, *Tennessee & North Carolina, USA*, page 248
- WILDLIFE — Kangaroo Island Wilderness Trail, *South Australia*, page 260
- CULTURE — Kumano Kodō: Nakahechi Route, *Honshū, Japan*, page 263

WEEK-ISH WANDER

- LITERARY — Island Walk: North Shore, *Prince Edward Island, Canada*, page 254
- ARTISTIC — Malerweg, *Saxony, Germany*, page 267

EPIC TREK

- COUNTRY-CROSSING — Coast to Coast, *Cumbria & Yorkshire, England*, page 245
- PILGRIMAGE — Via Francigena, *Switzerland & Northern Italy*, page 257
- COMMUNITY — Andros Route, *Cyclades, Greece*, page 251

243

OCT

NATURE / CULTURE / CAMPING / MOUNTAINS / COAST

Coast to Coast

CUMBRIA & YORKSHIRE, ENGLAND

Stride right across England from west to east, through three magnificent national parks, in the footsteps of fell-walking legend Alfred Wainwright.

When the Coast to Coast was conceived by pioneering rambler and writer Alfred Wainwright in the early 1970s, he was enthusiastic, claiming: 'Surely there cannot be a finer itinerary for a long-distance walk!' He had a point. Yet it's taken more than 50 years for one of Britain's most popular multiday hikes to finally become an official National Trail — a status it was given in 2025. As a result, the Coast to Coast now has proper signage and better accessibility, and is managed to higher environmental standards.

Wainwright certainly knew how to plot a great walk. His country-crossing trail runs between the Cumbrian village of St Bees, on England's west coast, and Robin Hood's Bay, North Yorkshire; between the two, the Coast to Coast up-downs via three of England's most magnificent national parks: the Lake District, the Yorkshire Dales and the North York Moors.

Most people walk west–east, which means beginning in Wainwright's beloved Lake District — setting off after a traditional dip of your toes in the Irish Sea. The trail climbs 352m-high (1155ft) Dent Fell, hugs wild Ennerdale Water and rises above Buttermere, which is flanked by some of Wainwright's favourite fells (his ashes are scattered on Haystacks). More mountains follow as the trail ascends Greenup Gill, descends to Grasmere, and climbs again for enormous views. Eventually, from the top of Kidsty Pike, the mood changes, morphing from rugged fells to limestone dales; the village of Shap, with its ruined 12th-century abbey, is tucked between the Lake District and Yorkshire Dales National Parks.

START
St Bees

FINISH
Robin Hood's Bay

DISTANCE
309km (192 miles)

DURATION
12–18 days

CHALLENGE LEVEL
★★★★☆

WHEN TO WALK
April–October

LEFT Buttermere and the Haystacks fell, in the Lake District section of the Coast to Coast hike.

ACCOMMODATION
Hotels, B&Bs, hostels and campsites on the trail and nearby — some places just off the route may be willing to pick up and drop off. Wild camping is technically illegal.

FOOD
There are plenty of pubs and shops accessible from the path.

GETTING THERE:
St Bees is on the Carlisle to Lancaster train line. Robin Hood's Bay is a 45-minute bus ride from Scarborough's train station. The nearest airports are Newcastle and Manchester.

PLANNING
Book accommodation in advance. Luggage transfer services are available.

SAFETY
Terrain can be muddy and boggy. Take walking poles. Know how to navigate in poor weather.

INFO
wainwright.org.uk
coasttocoast.uk

Next it's out onto wide, open, bird-twittered moorland to reach the market town of Kirkby Stephen and enter the Yorkshire Dales proper, studded with ancient cairns, tinkling waterfalls, stone-built villages (with accompanying tea shops) and the sweeping River Swale. Richmond (meaning 'strong hill') is a historic town with a Norman castle and plenty of places to rest and refuel.

Across the North York Moors National Park — the final stretch — lie the remains of Mt Grace Priory (England's best-preserved Carthusian monastery), the Bronze Age burial mound at Cringle Moor and swathes of windswept, heather-flecked uplands that, eventually, afford views to the sea. The finale is along the River Esk, past Grosmont's steam-pulled North Yorkshire Moors Railway and along the cliffs before dropping into the hill-clinging fishing village of Robin Hood's Bay — where, as custom dictates, a further toe-dunk in the North Sea bookends your hike.

LEFT Ullswater, one of many highlights on the Lake District leg. **BELOW** Tackling Greenup Gill on the Coast to Coast hike. **RIGHT** Dip your toes in the sea at route's end, Yorkshire's Robin Hood's Bay.

'"OH, HOW CAN I PUT INTO WORDS THE JOYS OF A WALK OVER COUNTRY SUCH AS THIS…THE SHEER EXUBERANCE WHICH FILLS YOUR SOUL" – ALFRED WAINWRIGHT, A PENNINE JOURNEY.'

Who was Wainwright?

ALFRED WAINWRIGHT (1907–91) was born in Blackburn, Lancashire, into relative poverty. He left school at 13, later qualifying as an accountant. But it was his first visit to the Lake District in 1930 that changed his life — he later noted that 'It was a moment of magic'. He moved to the Lakes in 1941 and, from the 1950s, began creating his *Pictorial Guides* — seven hand-written, hand-drawn volumes detailing routes and views from 214 Lakeland fells.

Wainwright divided his walk into 12 stages. Tackling one per day is doable but tough, especially over the challenging Lakeland section. Taking it slower makes for a more manageable adventure, as does walking before winter sets in, the moors become bleaker and the fells more treacherous. Summer enjoys the warmest temperatures, of course — but hiking in autumn means emptier trails, better accommodation availability, blackberries bursting from the hedgerows, and turning foliage setting the countryside aflame with a full Pantone chart of purples, reds and yellows.

OCT

USA

NATURE / CULTURE / CAMPING / MOUNTAIN

Appalachian Trail: Great Smoky Mountains

TENNESSEE & NORTH CAROLINA, USA

START
Fontana Dam

FINISH
Newfound Gap

DISTANCE
62km (38.5 miles)

DURATION
Three to six days

CHALLENGE LEVEL
★ ★ ★ ☆

WHEN TO WALK
April–May
& September–November

Tackle a taster of one of North America's great thru-hikes on a testing but rewarding trail through fiery fall foliage.

The stats for the Appalachian Trail (AT) are dizzying. Claimed to be the world's longest hiking-only footpath, it snakes for nearly 3540km (2200 miles) and passes through 14 states. Thru-hikers spend upwards of five months completing this largely tree-covered route, typically starting in spring from the southern trailhead in Georgia and reaching the endpoint in Maine by fall.

If spending half a year tramping the 'Green Tunnel' isn't an option, opt for one of the shorter stretches. Take the Great Smoky Mountains – and many people do: it's the USA's most-visited national park, but it's also perfect for a first AT outing. Largely tracing the ridge dividing Tennessee from North Carolina, this relatively modest section includes several stretches above the treeline – including the highest point on the entire trail, Kuwohi (formerly Clingmans Dome). This is one of several viewpoints where you can pause to enjoy vistas across the forested mountains – dreamy in October, when autumn foliage is at its blazing best, carpeting the slopes in gleaming golds, oranges and reds.

Hardy hikers could complete the striking stretch between trailheads at Fontana Dam and Newfound Gap in three days, though longer is better – both to enjoy the experience, and because it's pretty tough, with ascent totalling around 3200m (10,500ft). Though spotting wildlife in often dense forest can be hit and miss, there's plenty here: some 1900 black bears and more than 200 bird species inhabit the park, alongside spotted salamanders and white-tailed deer. All in all, an achievable autumn epic.

OCT

ACCOMMODATION
Backcountry campsites and simple shelters, some equipped with basic toilets.

FOOD
Carry supplies; purify water.

GETTING THERE
Car parks at both trailheads. Shuttle companies offer transfers from hubs like Gatlinburg.

PLANNING
Backcountry permits required – book in advance.

SAFETY
This is bear country: take precautions, and hang all food using the cable system in camps. Bring rain gear and prepare for all conditions. Trails can be rooty and slippery, particularly after rain. Check weather forecasts.

INFO
appalachiantrail.org

LEFT The Appalachian Trail through the Great Smoky Mountains includes the ascent of Kuwohi (aka Clingmans Dome). **TOP** Autumn colour along the AT route, at Newfound Gap in the Smoky Mountains.

OCT

NATURE / FOOD & DRINK / CULTURE / COAST

Andros Route

CYCLADES, GREECE

Amble across a laid-back and surprisingly lush Greek isle where ancient mule tracks and shepherds' paths have been lovingly restored for modern hikers.

Andros isn't like the other Cyclades. While hotspots like like Santorini or Mykonos heave, Andros has dodged overtourism: the island grew rich from shipbuilding, not holidaymaking, and it's still more frequented by weekending Athenians than by foreigners. Also, unlike many other Greek isles, it's an excellent place to take a hike.

Walking was always the norm here. This mountain-rucked, gully-gouged and unusually green island — the Ancient Greeks named it Ydrousa, the 'watery one' — is riddled with trails, from mule tracks to slabbed paths lined with distinctive dry-stone walls; these were once the only way for locals to travel between their farms and villages. But after WWII, when mass emigration saw many locals depart Andros — and other Greek islands — these timeworn ways were mostly abandoned.

Enter Andros Routes. This volunteer-run project was founded in 2010 in an effort to preserve the old footpaths and inject new life into some of the island's remotest places. The organisation has since created around 240km (150 miles) of marked, maintained hiking trails, including loops, day-hikes — and the Andros Route. This 10-stage, 100km (62-mile) continuous trail (with a fair amount of squiggling) enables thru-hikers to cover the island from north to south, and has been recognised by the European Ramblers Association as an official Leading Quality Trail.

The walking is occasionally rough and steep, but rarely too difficult. And, with so many additional paths mapped out, it's often possible to shortcut or divert from the main trail — buy a copy of the Andros Routes map (profits go toward maintaining the trails)

START
Frousei

FINISH
Dipotamata

DISTANCE
100km (62 miles)

DURATION
Five to 10 days

CHALLENGE LEVEL
★ ★ ★ ☆ ☆

WHEN TO WALK
April–June
& September–November

LEFT Hiking the island's green and hilly hinterland along the 10-stage Andros Route.

GREECE

Brilliant birds

THANKS TO its diverse topography and abundant greenery, Andros is a haven for avifauna. Almost half of the island is designated an Important Bird Area or wildlife sanctuary; the rocky coasts, offshore islets, woodlands and wetlands provide vital habitats. Special species to spot include Bonelli's eagle, Mediterranean shag and Eleonora's falcon — more than 85% of the global population of this species breeds on the Greek islands, before migrating to Madagascar from around mid-October.

'THE OLD PATHWAYS OF ANDROS NOD TO A CONTINUOUS HUMAN PRESENCE DATING BACK TO ANTIQUITY. MAINTAINING THEM IS VITAL TO PRESERVING THE ISLAND'S IDENTITY.'

and you can devise your own itinerary. Good planning is required, however: there is accommodation near the end of most, but not all, of the Andros Route's 10 stages, and public transport is limited. Also, be mindful of timing. This being Greece, hiking in the broiling summer months, when temperatures exceed 30°C (86°F), is not advised. Opt for spring, when the flowers are bright and bountiful or, better still, autumn — when the weather is mild, the light soft, the trees golden, the wind less boisterous and the sea temperature delicious for a mid-walk dip.

And Andros is a wonderful place to discover on foot. It's so geologically folded that it seems almost to be keeping secrets

LEFT The Andros Route traverses the island from north to south and takes in the comely capital of Andros Town. **RIGHT** The arched Kamara bridge and Venetian-built castle offshore of Andros Town.

GREECE

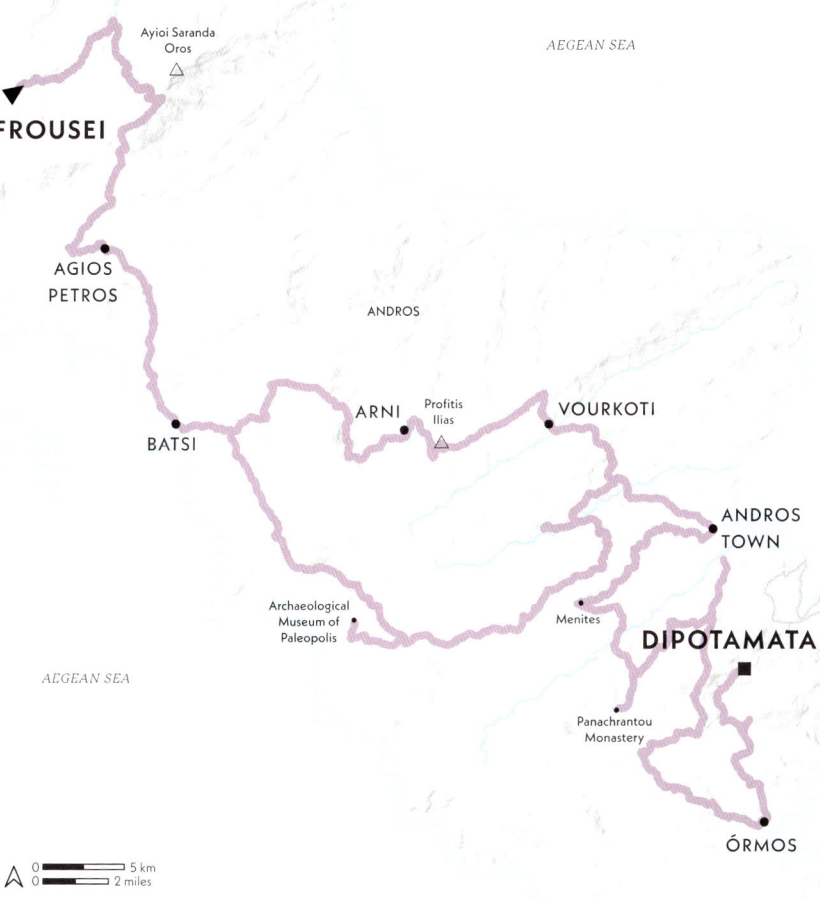

ACCOMMODATION
Small guesthouses and hotels – book in advance.

FOOD
Village stores and tavernas, though not on all stages. Carry supplies and plenty of water. Potable springs and rivers are marked by a pictogram of a droplet over a hand holding a cup.

GETTING THERE
The port of Rafina is a 20-minute taxi/40-minute bus from Athens' airport; ferries from Rafina to Andros take a little over an hour.

PLANNING
Getting to trailheads or accommodation at the end of stages may require a taxi.

SAFETY
Be prepared for the strong Meltemi (north wind) and hot temperatures in summer.

INFO
androsroutes.gr

– but walking is the ideal the way to explore its cracks, crevices and hidden heights, including the loftiest peak, Petalon, rising to 997m (3271ft). En route you'll encounter ruined castles, hillside monasteries, tiny chapels, oleander-pinked ravines, orchards, olive groves, clifftops fragrant with wild herbs, bushes buzzing with cicadas and bees, tavernas serving local *louzes* (smoked pork) and *petroti* cheese, and big views out to the blue-green sea.

You'll also happen upon some of the old watermills scattered across the island; there are ruins around Frousei, the route's northern trailhead, as well as in the spring-fresh hamlet of Menites. Look out for other ancient remains, such as those of Paleopolis, Andros' 7th-century BCE capital; the coastal site is partially excavated, with a small but fascinating archaeological museum. This is a trail that links past and present – but with one eye firmly on a sustainable future.

FOOD & DRINK / CULTURE / COAST

Island Walk: North Shore

PRINCE EDWARD ISLAND, CANADA

START
Kensington

FINISH
Elmira

DISTANCE
163km (101 miles)

DURATION
Seven days

CHALLENGE LEVEL
★★☆☆☆

WHEN TO WALK
May–October

Soak up some autumnal glory with a north-coast hike on the bucolic island that inspired *Anne of Green Gables*.

Prince Edward Island (PEI) may be Canada's smallest province, but it's big on character – or characters. Best known is that feisty redheaded orphan Anne Shirley, whose escapades at Green Gables were immortalised in LM Montgomery's early 20th-century novels. Another impactful local is Bryson Guptill, mastermind behind PEI's 707km (439-mile), 32-stage Island Walk.

Some legs of this round-island route weave inland to the rural heartland, but never stray far from the coast. Though it's open year-round, many facilities close from late October to April, and July and August are both busy and buggy. Early-ish autumn, when trees blaze with turning foliage, is the time to trek. The full circuit takes about a month, but a week's walking along the north shore, tackling sections 16 to 22, ticks off many of PEI's highlights.

From Kensington, roll through patchwork farmland to the village of New London, Montgomery's birthplace. Beyond lies Cavendish, where you'll find the author's former home, Green Gables (now a National Historic Site), and the throwback village of Avonlea. Beyond, you'll encounter history of a different kind: Rustico, the island's oldest Acadian settlement, dates from the second half of the 18th century. Then it's east into Prince Edward Island National Park, strolling the sandy shoreline past harbours and lakes, alongside marshes and through forests, pausing to savour fresh seafood in Morell or St Peter's. Watch for teal and ring-necked ducks as you pass Black Pond Migratory Bird Sanctuary before finishing at East Point Lighthouse – an illuminating end to a literary-flavoured hike.

ACCOMMODATION
Ample inns, B&Bs, guesthouses and hotels, not all near stage ends; transfers or detours are sometimes required. There are campsites near most sections.

FOOD
Cafes, restaurants, inns, take-aways and food stores; pack picnics for lean stretches.

GETTING THERE
Infrequent T3 buses link island capital Charlottetown with Kensington in an hour; plan carefully and book. Arrange a transfer from Elmira.

PLANNING
Book accommodation and transfers well in advance.

SAFETY
Weather can change rapidly in autumn; come prepared.

INFO
theislandwalk.ca

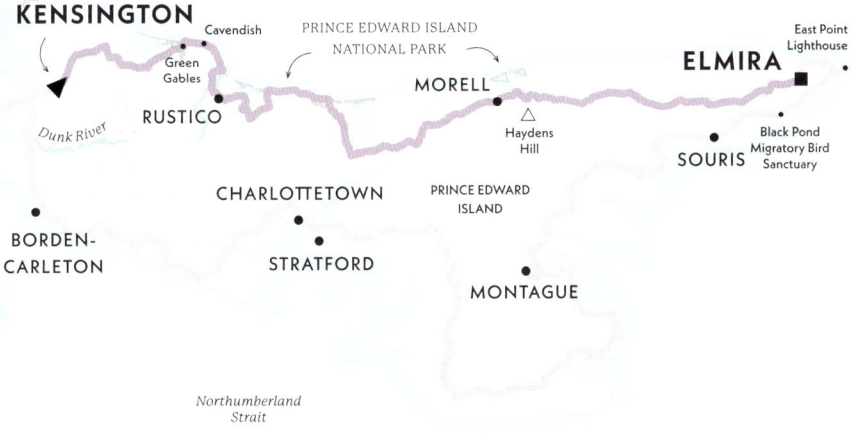

LEFT The Island Walk's north-shore sections take in the wetlands of Prince Edward Island National Park. **TOP** Covehead Harbour Lighthouse in PEI National Park.

NATURE / FOOD & DRINK / CULTURE

Via Francigena

SWISS ALPS & NORTHERN ITALY

Undertake all or part of a mighty pilgrimage, hiking in holy footsteps and savouring the cultural and culinary delights of Italy's diverse regions – plus a starter slice of the Alps.

Think walking from the Alps to Rome sounds like a long way? Well, the Via Francigena is an even bigger beast. Tracing a historic route taken – and recorded precisely – by Archbishop Sigeric in 990 CE, it's officially almost twice as long if (as Sigeric did) you start your pilgrimage to Rome in Canterbury, England. The Italian chunk of the trail is quite the adventure on its own, as well as being the best-signed, best-serviced and, arguably, best-looking section.

The Italian Francigena starts in Switzerland, in the Alpine village of Bourg-Saint-Pierre. The first day starts at 2473m (8114ft) altitude with a stiff trek over the border via the St Bernard Pass, a thoroughfare used for millennia and famed for its rescue dogs. In truth, October isn't optimal for this mountainous part of the route; the pass is only reliably open between June and late September – possibly into early October, depending on the year's snow. However, if you want to cross outside the season, there are options to borrow snowshoes in Bourg-Saint-Pierre (you can send them back with the postman), or take a bus through the year-round tunnel.

October is a good month to hike the rest of this deliciously varied route. Temperatures are mellow and walker-friendly (expect average highs of 18°C (64°F) in Ivrea, 21°C (70°F) in Lucca, 23°C (73°F) in Rome) and holiday crowds have thinned – though this pilgrimage is far, far less busy than the Spanish Camino routes, even in peak season. Autumn is also when the last grapes are being harvested and menus are full of seasonal goodness: wild mushrooms and chestnuts, bright squashes, all manner of game.

START
Bourg-Saint-Pierre, Switzerland

FINISH
Rome, Italy

DISTANCE
1010km (628 miles)

DURATION
35–50 days

CHALLENGE LEVEL
★★★☆☆

WHEN TO WALK
April–June
& September–November

LEFT The epic Via Francigena pilgrimage weaves through Italian regions such as the fertile Po Valley.

Come now and you'll taste the Francigena at its delicious best as you wend your way down Italy's western flank. You'll first traverse the Aosta Valley, passing the historic town walls of Aosta (Augusta Praetoria Salassorum to the ancient Romans) and a succession of castles – 14th-century Verrès, with its 2m-thick (7ft) walls, is especially imposing. Then plunge through Piedmont's vine-streaked slopes – stop to sip outstanding Nebbiolo wines – and continue through the bountiful low plains of the Po Valley, flush with lakes, rivers and rice paddies. Head on towards the foothills of the Apennines, finally crossing into dreamy Tuscany at Groppodalosio. Beyond stretches classic, idyllic Italy: gorgeous hilltop villages such as San Miniato and San Gimignano, handsome towns like Lucca and Siena, undulating countryside speared by cypress trees, glimpses of the Mediterranean Sea.

Many pilgrims skip the Alpine stages and just complete southern sections, perhaps setting off from the magnificent

ACCOMMODATION
Basic pilgrim accommodation at monasteries, churches, schools and *spedali* (pilgrim hostels), sometimes free/donation-based. B&Bs and hotels in some towns and villages.

FOOD
Good, plentiful food throughout. Some restaurants offer a special pilgrim's menu.

GETTING THERE
Direct trains run from Geneva to Martigny, from where buses connect to Bourg-Saint-Pierre.

PLANNING
Call ahead to book accommodation – essential in all seasons but especially outside peak months when some lodgings close. It's helpful to learn some basic Italian.

SAFETY
Check conditions before attempting to cross the St Bernard Pass. Consider diversions to avoid sections along busy roads.

INFO
viefrancigene.org

LEFT Hiking Stage 41 of the Francigena near Vetralla, in the Lazio region. **RIGHT** The Tuscany section of the route takes in perched hilltop villages such as San Miniato.

'THE FRANCIGENA ROUTE WAS REVIVED IN THE 1980S BY DEVOTEES WHO FOLLOWED ARCHBISHOP SIGERIC'S WAY AS CLOSELY AS POSSIBLE, MAKING CHANGES ONLY TO AVOID MODERN ROADS.'

Renaissance walls and elegant piazzas of Lucca. From here, it's some 400km (250 miles) to Rome, walkable in two or three weeks, and packed with Tuscan highlights.

Others choose to start from Viterbo, Lazio's best-preserved medieval town and the 13th-century residence of the popes, to complete the Francigena's final 100km (62 miles). This is the minimum distance required for any walker who's been collecting stamps in their *credential* (pilgrim passport) to obtain a *testimonium*, the official certificate of completion.

The northern Francigena

THE VIA FRANCIGENA officially starts at Canterbury's colossal cathedral and snakes across fertile Kent, the 'Garden of England'. At the White Cliffs of Dover, pilgrims must catch a ferry across the Channel. In France, the route heads south via Napoleonic and WWI battlefields and the bubbly vineyards of Champagne. It enters Switzerland at the Jura Mountains, veering around Lake Geneva to Lausanne and into the Valais, finally climbing to meet the Italian border.

NATURE / CAMPING / COAST

Kangaroo Island Wilderness Trail

SOUTH AUSTRALIA

START
Flinders Chase National Park Visitor Centre

FINISH
Kelly Hill Caves

DISTANCE
66km (41 miles)

DURATION
Five days

CHALLENGE LEVEL
★☆☆☆☆

WHEN TO WALK
March–November

Enjoy spring shoots and reviving bushland on an official Great Walk through this wildlife-rich island.

There's never a bad time to visit Kangaroo Island. Australia's third-largest isle is a haven for native wildlife, so there's always something to see: wallabies bounding, koalas mating, seals pupping, whales cruising by. But spring, with its budding orchids, bird-busy skies and mild temperatures, is lovely for a walk, as well as falling before peak bushfire season. The island was decimated by blazes in 2020 but, happily, is now bouncing back — and the now-reopened Kangaroo Island Wilderness Trail offers the perfect way to experience nature at its most resilient.

From the trailhead in the island's wild west, the path heads into the bush, first via Platypus Waterholes, then into eucalypt woodland and along the Rocky River to reach Cup Gum Campground. Day two heads to the crashing Southern Ocean — look for dolphins, seabirds and, between June and early October, southern right whales. The route passes close to Cape du Couedic Lighthouse before day's end at Hakea Campground, tucked behind a brilliant-white beach.

Beyond Hakea, the trail heads through mallee scrub towards the Dalí-esque Remarkable Rocks. Detour to see them up close before continuing to Banksia Campground, near Sanderson Bay. There's more wild coast-walking ahead, with an optional diversion to glorious Hanson Bay and a boat crossing of the South West River. A final yomp through pristine Cape Bouguer Wilderness Protection Area leads to Tea Tree, the final camp. From there, it's an easy amble via bird-flittered lagoons and sugar gums to Kelly Hill Caves — a wonderful end to a truly wild walk.

OCT

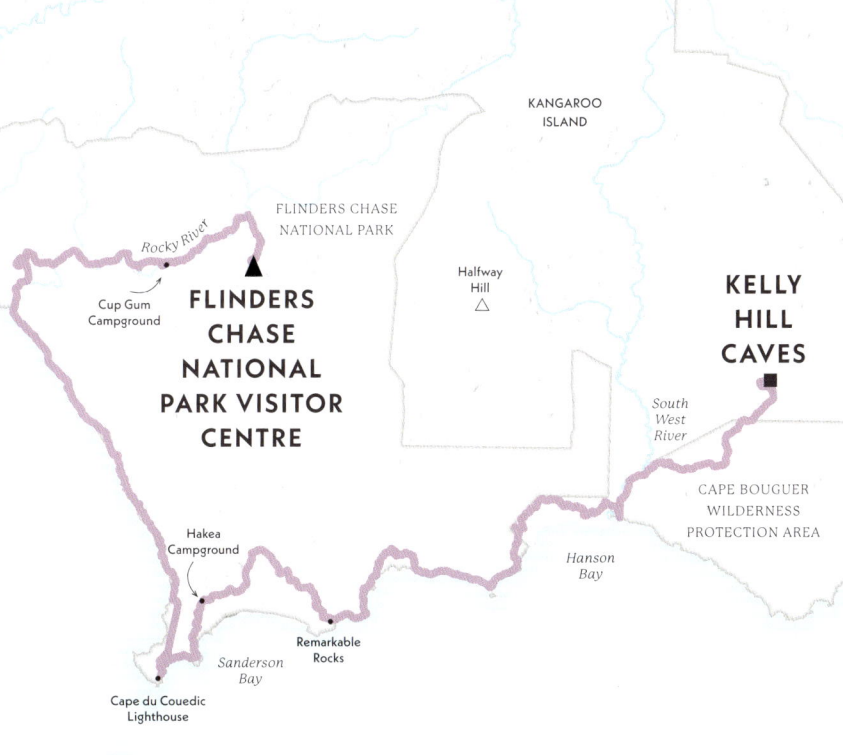

ACCOMMODATION
Well-maintained on-trail campgrounds with toilets and cooking shelters.

FOOD
Pack all supplies. Water is available at camps. Fire bans may be enforced — be prepared to make cold meals.

GETTING THERE
Kangaroo Island is 45 minutes by ferry from Cape Jervis. A car/taxi is required to reach the trailhead. A bus runs daily from Kelly Hill Caves back to Flinders Chase Visitor Centre; advance booking required.

PLANNING
Permits are mandatory. Only 48 people are allowed to start the trek each day.

SAFETY
Phone coverage is virtually nonexistent along the length of the trail.

INFO
parks.sa.gov.au

LEFT Keep eyes peeled for native wildlife along the Kangaroo Island Wilderness Trail, from wallabies and whales to koalas. **TOP** The Rocky River meets the sea in KI's Flinders Chase National Park.

NATURE / FOOD & DRINK / CULTURE / MOUNTAINS / COAST

Kumano Kodō: Nakahechi Route

HONSHŪ, JAPAN

Follow in the footsteps of countless Shinto and Buddhist pilgrims on an ancient trail through the forest-cloaked mountains of the Kii Peninsula.

Even emperors enjoy a good hike. OK, we're massaging the facts a little – but the point remains that over 1100 years ago it was Japanese Emperor Uda who travelled to the Buddhist shrines of Kumano on the mountainous Kii Peninsula, setting a trend that saw dozens more imperial pilgrimages here over the following four centuries. The region was sacred to Shinto before Buddhism took hold in Japan: *yamabushi* (ascetics) have trekked here from Yoshino since at least the late 7th century, and Kumano is believed to have had religious significance stretching back into prehistory, when it was thought to be inhabited by many deities.

Today, the objectives of the many who still tramp the Kumano Kodō – 'Old Roads to Kumano' – remain the three grand Kumano Sanzan shrines: Kumano Hayatama Taisha, Kumano Nachi Taisha and Kumano Hongū Taisha, that last devoted to Izanagi-Okami, a goddess said to have created Japan.

Rather like the Camino de Santiago in Spain, and also UNESCO World Heritage–listed, the Kumano Kodō isn't one route but several paths. Five interconnected pilgrimage trails evolved over the centuries after Uda's visit, spidering out from (or, rather, up to and connecting) the three shrines, and largely revived since the 1990s. Fewer emperors and aristocrats make the trek today, but many other hikers are following in those imperial footsteps. Some come to explore spiritual beliefs, but most simply walk to experience the glorious landscapes and traditional customs, to bathe in

START
Takijiri-ōji

FINISH
Nachi Taisha

DISTANCE
66km (41 miles)

DURATION
Four to five days

CHALLENGE LEVEL
★★★☆☆

WHEN TO WALK
March–May
& September–November

LEFT Hiking a tree-shaded section of the Kumano Kodō's Nakahechi route through Honshū's Kii Peninsula.

JAPAN

Kumano Kodō variants

THE MEDIEVAL Kohechi route winds 65km (40 miles) south from Kōya-san, sacred in Shingon Buddhism, through mountainous terrain; expect four challenging days. The 170km (105-mile) Iseji traces the Kii Peninsula's east coast between the Ise-jingū shrine and the Kumano Sanzan trio. The Ohechi route (120km/75 miles), skirting the peninsula's south, is renowned for its beautiful coastal scenery. A similar distance, but tougher, is the mountainous Ōmine Okugakemichi from Toshino.

'DISCOVER HOW THE ANCIENT SHINTO SHRINES AND BUDDHIST TEMPLES OF THE KII PENINSULA HAVE INFLUENCED JAPAN'S SPIRITUAL PRACTICES AND ARCHITECTURE OVER MANY CENTURIES.'

onsen (natural hot springs) and sample local cuisine – specialities include *shishi-nabe* (wild boar hotpot), river fish and *mehari* sushi (rice in *takana*, pickled mustard leaves).

Most popular of the trails is the Nakahechi, known as the Imperial Route. With its start a short bus ride from Kii-Tanabe Train Station, and its end even closer to Shingu's station, it's accessible, attractive and achievable for hikers with a moderate level of fitness and experience. Clearly waymarked and made up of mostly well-maintained paths (with plenty of steps), this stretch is open year-round – though both hot, humid, rainy summer and chilly winter are less than perfect times to trek. Autumn's ideal.

From the trailhead at the shrine of Takijiri-ōji, the path first climbs to Takahara village and continues to Chikatsuyu, home to the Kumanokodo Nakahechi Museum of Art. Beyond, tree-lined steps lead up to the Tsugizakura-ōji; nearby inns and guesthouses

TOP Views from Hyakken-gura Peak reward on the Nakahechi route's testing day four. **LEFT** Takijiri-ōji, where the Nakahechi begins. **RIGHT** Seiganto-ji Pagoda at Nachi Falls, endpoint of the Nakahechi hike.

ACCOMMODATION
Ryokan (traditional inns), *minshuku* (simpler guesthouses) and hostels near the trail, often in *onsen* (natural hot-spring resorts).

FOOD
Many pilgrims eat at their accommodation, which will likely also provide picnic lunches; there are some stores and teahouses near the route.

GETTING THERE
The start at Takijiri-ōji is a short bus ride from Kii-Tanabe Train Station, which is 2½ hours from Osaka. Buses run from the end at Nachi Taisha to Shingu Station, 3½ hours from Nagoya.

PLANNING
Book accommodation well in advance on this popular route.

SAFETY
Prepare for variable weather and steep climbs.

INFO
tb-kumano.jp

make this a convenient overnight stop. The following day switchbacks through wooded hills, sometimes emerging into fields or tea plantations, passing beneath wooden *torii* (gates) and visiting the prestigious Hosshinmon-ōji before reaching Kumano Hongū Taisha shrine in the valley. Many pilgrims stay at nearby Yunomine Onsen (hot-spring village) for a soothing soak.

Prepare for another testing climb the following day through cedar and cypress forest to Hyakken-gura Peak, offering amazing mountain vistas; then, it's a long descent to the village of Koguchi on the Akagi River.

The final day's route rises and then drops to the Kumano Nachi Taisha shrine, picturesquely perched before 133m-high (436ft) Nachi, Japan's tallest single-drop waterfall – its clear cascades a suitably cleansing end to a purifying pilgrimage.

NATURE / FOOD & DRINK / CULTURE

Malerweg

SAXONY, GERMANY

Put yourself in the picture on a photogenic trail in the footsteps of artists, hiking amid forested hills and other-worldly rock outcrops.

Not all mountains are made the same. The young but mighty Himalaya are metamorphic massifs, while billion-year-old chunks of continental crust underlie the Rockies. The volcanic Andes are quite different to the gleaming limestone shards of the Dolomites. Then there's the belt of pinkish outcrops straddling the border between the German state of Saxony and Czech Bohemia, sculpted into all manner of strange and mysterious forms: tabletops and pinnacles and pillars and crags and many more. These are the Elbe Sandstone Mountains — or, to give the landscape its more fanciful but enduring local name, Saxon Switzerland.

You need only spend a few minutes in this distinctive landscape to grasp what lured so many artists here, particularly from the 18th century when Romantic sensibilities came to the fore. It's impossibly picturesque, and quite unlike almost anywhere else — no wonder it inspired the likes of painter JMW Turner, composer Richard Wagner and writers Mary Shelley and Hans Christian Andersen. Two decades ago, a walking route was waymarked, linking old paths tramped by those luminaries into a spectacular near-circuit starting just southeast of stately Dresden, Saxony's historic capital.

The eight-stage Malerweg (Painters' Way) weaves between many of the best-known viewpoints — and that means plenty of climbs. This isn't a high-altitude range — the trail's loftiest point is about 550m (1805ft) — so it can be hiked year-round. That said, ascents and descents can be steep, with plenty of metal steps, handrails and fixed ladders, so winter can make the going

START
Liebethal

FINISH
Pirna

DISTANCE
116km (72 miles)

DURATION
Six to eight days

CHALLENGE LEVEL
★★★☆☆

WHEN TO WALK
April–October

LEFT Hike the Malerweg to marvel at Elbe Sandstone Mountain formations such as the bridge-spanned Bastei.

ACCOMMODATION
Inns, guesthouses, pensions and hotels en route.

FOOD
Cafes and restaurants are sparse on some sections – stock up on lunch supplies at bakeries and shops before setting out.

GETTING THERE
Trains run along the Elbe Valley, stopping at points along the Malerweg; Pirna is 22 minutes from Dresden. Veteran steamboats of the Sächsische Dampfschifffahrt (Saxon Steamship Company, saechsische-dampfschifffahrt.de) cruise this stretch, too.

PLANNING
No permits are required. Advance booking of accommodation and restaurants is advisable, though less important outside high summer.

SAFETY
Some sections include steep climbs and metal steps or ladders that can be slippery after rain.

INFO
saechsische-schweiz.de

slippery, and summer brings crowds and sweaty conditions in the humid forests that cloak much of the range. In autumn, forests glow with turning foliage and burgeon with fungi, while honeypot attractions like the extraordinary Bastei formation are more peaceful.

Much of the route is wonderfully accessible by public transport, with trains, trams and even vintage steamboats serving various points along the Elbe River, making it easy to plan shorter segments or even day-walks. But if your diary permits, you won't regret tackling the lot – if for no other reason than it's a great excuse to refuel on the region's many culinary delights, such as crisp white wines from Elbe vineyards and Saxon *Eierschecke*, a three-layered cheesecake custom-built for hungry hikers. You can savour these and more at Bergwirtschaft and Berggaststätte along the route – mountain cafes, often set atop high outcrops with amazing views, and perfect for mid-walk refreshment.

LEFT Trailside autumn colour in Germany's 'Saxon Switzerland'. **RIGHT** Hike the Malerweg in October to see the Elbe Sandstone Mountains' honeypot Bastei formation after summer crowds depart.

'PAUSE IN THE REVITALISED RIVERSIDE VILLAGE OF SCHMILKA, NEAR THE CZECH BORDER, TO SAMPLE ORGANIC BEERS AND BREAD BAKED USING FLOUR PRODUCED IN A 350-YEAR-OLD MILL.'

Walkers typically start at Liebethal and wind clockwise, visiting a lush gorge before descending to the fairy-tale riverfront town of Stadt Wehlen. Climbing once more, you reach the Bastei and the imposing castle at Hohnstein; then it's on to the iconic crags of the Schrammsteine, the diaphanous Lichtenhain Waterfall and the Kuhstall (Cow Stable) Cave. Head back to the river, and nursery-rhyme-cute Schmilka, crossing the Elbe to hike back west via the gnarled Pfaffenstein tabletop (beloved of rock-climbers) and hulking Königstein Fortress before finishing with the easy amble into Pirna, with its castle, atmospheric old town and ample bars in which to toast your trek. *Prost!*

Friedrich's vision

MANY PAINTERS drew inspiration from this near-mystical landscape, notably Caspar David Friedrich (1774–1840), figurehead of the German Romantic movement. Spending spells in the Elbe Sandstone Mountains, he wove various views into his dramatic imaginary landscapes. After hiking the Malerweg you might recognise Saxon Switzerland in works like *Feldstein near Rathen* (1828); the Zirkelstein is captured in a view from the Kaiserkrone in his most famous work, *Wanderer Above the Sea of Fog* (c 1818).

NOVEMBER

Trailside waterfall on the Routeburn Track through New Zealand/Aotearoa's South Island (page 273).

NOVEMBER

I WANT A HIKE THAT'S A...

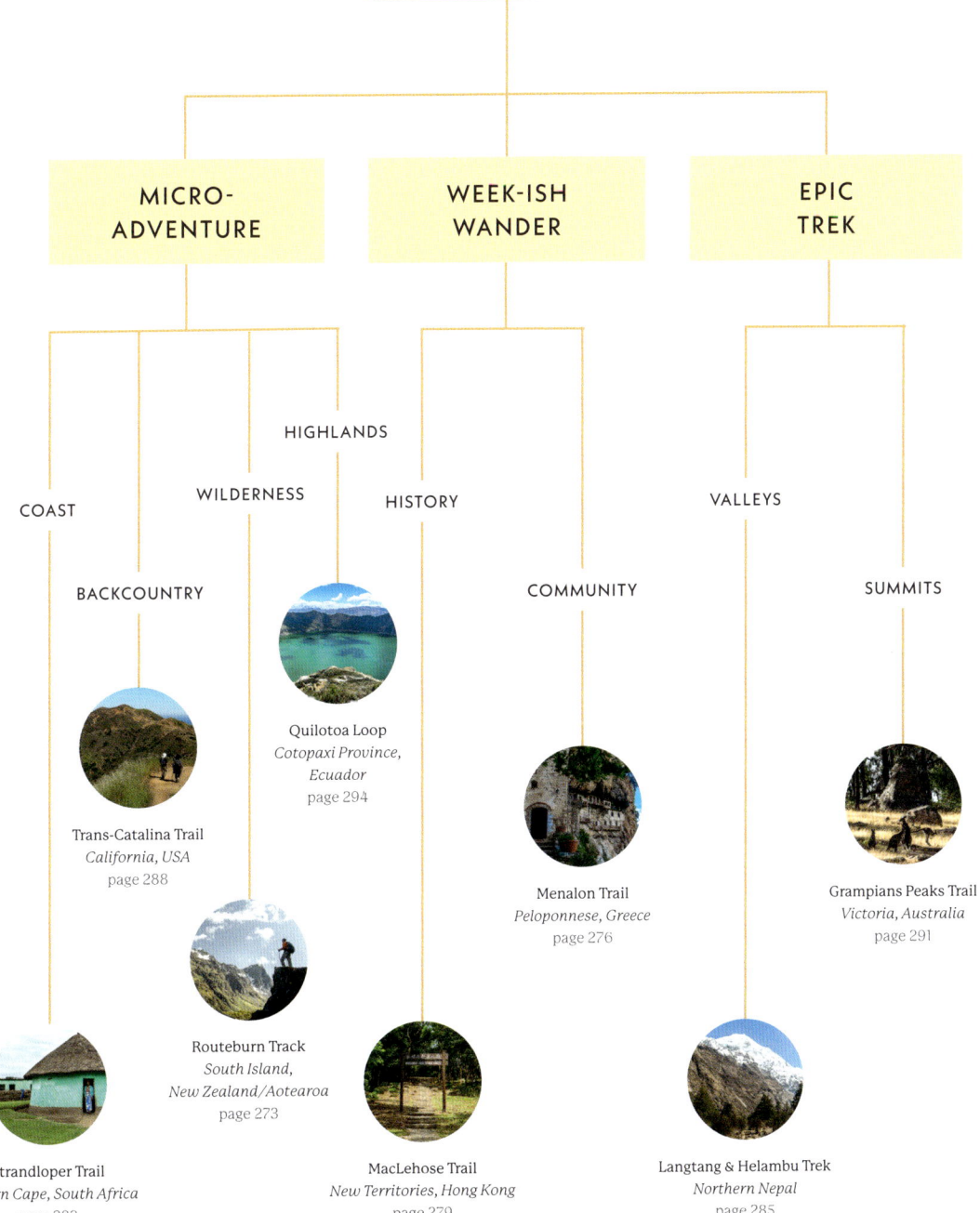

MICRO-ADVENTURE

- COAST — Strandloper Trail, *Eastern Cape, South Africa*, page 282
- BACKCOUNTRY — Trans-Catalina Trail, *California, USA*, page 288
- WILDERNESS — Routeburn Track, *South Island, New Zealand/Aotearoa*, page 273

WEEK-ISH WANDER

- HIGHLANDS — Quilotoa Loop, *Cotopaxi Province, Ecuador*, page 294
- HISTORY — MacLehose Trail, *New Territories, Hong Kong*, page 279
- COMMUNITY — Menalon Trail, *Peloponnese, Greece*, page 276

EPIC TREK

- VALLEYS — Langtang & Helambu Trek, *Northern Nepal*, page 285
- SUMMITS — Grampians Peaks Trail, *Victoria, Australia*, page 291

271

NATURE / MOUNTAINS / CAMPING

Routeburn Track

SOUTH ISLAND, NEW ZEALAND/AOTEAROA

Tramp one of New Zealand's most aspirational Great Walks, exploring both dense rainforest and lofty mountain trails on a mini-adventure through the Southern Alps.

What makes one hike better than another? Is it widescreen views, well-maintained paths, rich cultural interactions, varied wildlife encounters, a challenging summit, unforgettable food? Or maybe it's simply reputation and bragging rights?

If the idea of ranking treks seems faintly absurd, there's no denying that New Zealand's 11 Great Walks (which, curiously enough, include one canoe expedition, the Whanganui Journey) deserve the label based on those criteria. Certainly, that's the opinion of the avid trampers who rush to snag hen's-teeth places in huts and campsites as soon as bookings open (usually in late May) for the November–April Great Walks Season. At the start of that season, forests are lush and mountainsides green, summits still snowcapped, and paths, campsites and huts a little less busy than at the height of summer.

The Routeburn Track is one of the most aspirational Great Walks, an alpine epic that – appropriately enough – straddles Mt Aspiring and Fiordland National Parks in the far southwest of South Island. True, it's not so very long – in fact, a fit hiker could complete it in one long day – but its varied ecosystems, rock formations and grand mountain vistas mean that taking it slowly, and tackling the trek over three days (with time for worthwhile side trips to nearby peaks and cascades), is the way to go.

The trail can be hiked in either direction, heading southwest from the Routeburn Shelter trailhead or northeast from the Divide. The former is a little steeper but slightly easier to access, and the views down towards Lake Mackenzie from the Harris

START
Routeburn Shelter

FINISH
The Divide (or vice versa)

DISTANCE
32km (20 miles)

DURATION
Two to four days

CHALLENGE LEVEL

WHEN TO WALK
November–April

LEFT Superlative Routeburn views from Harris Saddle shelter in Mt Aspiring National Park.

NEW ZEALAND/AOTEAROA

Prized pounamu

OVER MANY centuries, Māori people trekked through this region in search of *pounamu* – greenstone, super-hard nephrite jade or serpentine rock used for making sharp blades, the short but hefty clubs called *meres*, and ornately carved jewellery. More precious than gold, it was classified in different ways, reflecting variations in colour and usage: for example, *kahurangi* is a translucent light green, while *kawakawa* is dark green, often with flecks, and commonly crafted into jewellery.

'KEEP EYES AND EARS PEELED FOR BIRDLIFE ALONG THE TRAIL, INCLUDING THE COLOURFUL YELLOWHEAD/MOHUA OR BUSH CANARY, AND THE YELLOW-CROWNED PARAKEET/KĀKĀRIKI.'

Saddle are arguably more impressive – though the Routeburn is sensational whichever way you walk it, and is achievable by moderately fit hikers.

But we're getting ahead of ourselves. Starting at the northeastern Routeburn trailhead, the first day crosses, then follows, the Route Burn (river) along a well-made stony path through magically moss-clad beech forest, beneath Bridal Veil Falls. Emerging into a plain where the river ribbons beneath conical peaks, you'll bed down at Routeburn Flats, enjoying the camaraderie of the comfortable hut or chatting around benches in the camping area. Or continue to the Routeburn Falls Hut, its veranda perched above those namesake roaring cascades.

Wave goodbye to the trees here: you're now ascending steadily among rocks and tussocks, the mountains increasingly craggy all around. It's a testing haul past gorgeous Lake Harris

TOP Uncut pounamu, long used by Māori people to make blades and jewellery. **LEFT** Forests of red and mountain beech shade rivers along the track. **RIGHT** Hiking the Routeburn in Mt Aspiring National Park.

NEW ZEALAND/AOTEAROA

ACCOMMODATION
Comfortable heated huts with bunks in shared rooms, plus toilets and water; campsites with cooking shelters.

FOOD
Bring all supplies and cooking utensils.

GETTING THERE
Trailheads are only 32km/20 miles apart on foot but 322km/200 miles by road. Transfer packages available from Queenstown to the Routeburn Shelter, and the Divide to Te Anau (both around an hour).

PLANNING
Book huts and camping pitches well in advance (via bookings.doc.govt.nz).

SAFETY
Weather can change rapidly. Prepare for all eventualities. If hiking May–October, particularly, prepare for very cold, windy and wet or snowy conditions.

INFO
doc.govt.nz

and around rocky bluffs to Harris Saddle/Tarahaka Whakatipu (1255m/4117ft) – but what a payoff: expect to join a parade of slack-jawed faces gazing across the Hollyford Valley and, as you progress, over the Darran Mountains. Take your time and drink in the morphing views as you descend to lovely, jewel-like Lake Mackenzie, site of another welcoming hut and camping area.

Day three traverses more emerald forest and ribbonwood stands to reach magnificent Earland Falls, crashing down 174m (570ft). Past the tip of Lake Howden, make time for the detour up Key Summit for a final panoramic photo-stop before dropping down to the Divide – and the end of a Great Walk that more than earns that plaudit.

NATURE / FOOD & DRINK / CULTURE

Menalon Trail

PELOPONNESE, GREECE

START
Stemnitsa

FINISH
Lagkadia

DISTANCE
75km (47 miles)

DURATION
Four to five days

CHALLENGE LEVEL

WHEN TO WALK
April–June
& September–November

Hike forested Arcadia on a trail that promises mythology, mountains and making a difference to local communities.

Welcome to a land of age-old myths, singing shepherds, fertile valleys and, more recently, officially wonderful walks. Arcadia's Menalon Trail, running through the heart of the Peloponnese, was the first hike in Greece to be awarded Leading Quality Trails status by the European Ramblers Association, an accolade awarded to high-standard routes that have a positive impact on local communities. The well-signed and serviced Menalon is a social enterprise that aims to bring hikers (and their euros) to this rural region, showing them just how beautiful it is.

It's a particularly good choice for an autumn amble. This far south in Europe, temperatures remain pleasant for walking – November highs can still hit 20°C (68°F) – while autumn colours still shine; you might even catch the end of the Arcadian grape harvest. It's a peaceful and uncrowded time, too.

The trail winds around the western edge of 1981m (6499ft) Mt Menalon, Arcadia's loftiest peak and the legendary home of Pan – god of nature, shepherds, flocks and mountain wilds. Using a network of timeworn paths and mule tracks, it's broken into eight sections; most hikers tackle it in a northward direction, taking four or five days to walk from Stemnitsa, known as the goldsmiths' village, to Lagkadia, the stonemasons' village. Along the way lie old stone settlements perched on hillsides, dramatic limestone folds, forests of fir and pine, small country churches and steep-sided valleys. Most spectacular is the walk along the Lousios Gorge, where Prodromos Monastery clings to the cliffs. The route also passes tavernas where, if the autumn weather turns chilly, you can warm up with hearty goat stews and *galaktoboureko* (custard pie), washed down with local Mantinia wine.

ACCOMMODATION
Hotels, guesthouses and rooms in villages en route.

FOOD
Cafes, shops and taverns in villages. Try *trahana* (a type of pasta).

GETTING THERE
Stemnitsa is 240km (150 miles) from Athens. Take a train to Corinth, then a taxi to Stemnitsa. Or catch a bus to Tripoli, from where you can get a bus (infrequent) or taxi to Stemnitsa.

PLANNING
Book accommodation in advance.

SAFETY
Snow and flooding can affect the route. Check trail status updates before hiking.

INFO
menalontrail.eu

LEFT Hiking the Menalon's well-maintained trails. **TOP** Goggle at cliff-clinging Prodromos Monastery on the Menalon section through Lousios Gorge.

NATURE / CULTURE / MOUNTAINS / COAST

MacLehose Trail

NEW TERRITORIES, HONG KONG

Travel across the New Territories on Hong Kong's longest hike, admiring native wildlife, historic relics and the views from the region's tallest peak.

Think you know Hong Kong? The hyper-modern, 100-miles-per-hour, densely populated forest of gleaming skyscrapers overlooking its namesake harbour? Well, yes — that's Hong Kong. But not only.

Stretching north of uber-urban Kowloon are the so-called New Territories (though, as they became part of Hong Kong in 1898, they're not so new). In this surprisingly verdant, undulating expanse, country parks host a range of wildlife as well as fascinating pockets of history: ghost villages, traditional cemeteries, trenches and pillboxes left over from WWII. And snaking almost all the way across the peninsula is the longest hiking route in the Special Administrative Region.

Named for colonial governor Murray MacLehose, who championed the protection of Hong Kong's remaining countryside and spearheaded the creation of its country parks, the MacLehose Trail opened in 1979. Winding first almost 360 degrees through the Sai Kung Peninsula, the trail then veers west along the ridge above Kowloon before tackling the region's highest peak and descending to end at the coast once more.

Handily, 200 numbered distance posts sporting the distinctive backpacker-silhouette logo stud the trail at 500m (1640ft) intervals. Adding fingerposts and other signage, navigation is pretty straightforward, path surfaces largely smooth and clear. Simple campsites are available, though many trekkers use excellent public transport or cheap taxis to hop off the trail each night and sleep in the city. Some hardy souls tackle the entire route in one day, notably during the annual Oxfam Trailwalker event

START
Pak Tam Chung

FINISH
Tuen Mun

DISTANCE
100km (62 miles)

DURATION
Four to eight days

CHALLENGE LEVEL

WHEN TO WALK
October–March

LEFT Trailside views of High Island Reservoir along the MacLehose Trail through Hong Kong's New Territories.

ACCOMMODATION
Simple campsites on the route; hostels and hotels nearby.

FOOD
Few food stores and cafes along the way; carry supplies.

GETTING THERE
Frequent buses run Kowloon–Sai Kung for connections to Pak Tam Chung (under 1¼ hours total). Tuen Mun MTR is 10 minutes from central Kowloon.

PLANNING
Many walkers travel between trailheads and Kowloon (or other urban areas) to sleep in comfy beds each night. Check bus times or book taxis.

SAFETY
Heat is the biggest concern. Wear sunscreen and a hat, and carry ample water. Trekking poles are helpful for the steep ups and downs.

INFO
discoverhongkong.com

in mid-November (best avoided by casual walkers) and Hong Kong 100 Ultra Marathon (mid-January). But with over 5000m (16,400ft) of ascent, this hike is no walk in the park – and definitely not in the heat and humidity that plagues the middle of the year, from April to September, when rain is likely and typhoons possible. The cooler, drier, clearer days of November are ideal.

You'll certainly be thankful for mild conditions on the initial sections through Sai Kung East Country Park, with little shade and plenty of climbs. Skirting the High Island Reservoir, and pausing to admire the extraordinary hexagonal basalt organ-pipe rock formations, you'll also be thankful to encounter a succession of white-sand beaches, first Long Ke Wan, then Sai Wan and Ham Tin Wan. Paddle in the cooling waters of the South China Sea before ploughing uphill again, blessing the shade-giving cover of casuarinas and acacias.

LEFT Long Ke Wan is the first of three paradisiacal white-sand beaches along the trail route. **BELOW** Hop on a ferry for a side-trip to Tap Mun Chau. **RIGHT** Stride past spectacular organ-pipe basalt cliffs in Sai Kung East Country Park.

'DISCOVER WWII HISTORY ON THE TRAIL'S SHING MUN WAR RELICS SECTION, VISITING TUNNELS, TRENCHES, BUNKERS AND PILLBOXES BUILT TO DEFEND AGAINST JAPANESE INVASION.'

Turning west, the route weaves through Sai Kung West Country Park, through isolated hamlets cradled in the foliage, with water buffalos grazing sleepily nearby. If you're lucky, you might encounter some wilder inhabitants: the parks are home to porcupines, pangolins, civets, Burmese pythons and barking deer, though you're more likely to spot macaques and the hundreds of butterfly and bird species.

Ascending 702m (2303ft) Ma On Shan in its namesake country park, the trail bucks and weaves along the ridge to Lion Rock for panoramic views across Kowloon and the harbour, then heads north to conquer Hong Kong's tallest peak, 957m (3140ft) Tai Mo Shan. From there it's (mostly) downhill all the way to the end at Tuen Mun, and a return to modernity.

Detour to Tap Mun Chau

A SHORT *kaido* (small ferry) ride from Chek Keng Pier, on Stage 2 of the MacLehose Trail, laid-back Tap Mun Chau (Grass Island) retains some of the languor of old Hong Kong, and is a good spot to chow down on Cantonese seafood. It's home to a small community of 'Boat Dwellers' – seafaring folk formerly known as Tanka – and, above the boat-bobbed harbour, a 17th-century temple to the sea goddess known here as Tin Hau.

SOUTH AFRICA

NATURE / CULTURE / COAST

Strandloper Trail

EASTERN CAPE, SOUTH AFRICA

START
Kei Mouth

FINISH
Gonubie

DISTANCE
60km (37 miles)

DURATION
Four days

CHALLENGE LEVEL

WHEN TO WALK
Year-round

Navigate the aptly named Wild Coast through the heartland of the Xhosa people, watching for whales offshore.

Whoever named South Africa's Wild Coast wasn't kidding. The Eastern Cape shoreline between East London and the KwaZulu-Natal border at Port Edward is pounded by surf, its pitiless swells wrecking numerous ships over the years. The going's pretty untamed on land, too: a lush emerald coast bucking and rearing between wide beaches and river mouths where waters surge out into the Indian Ocean. Untamed, but far from uninhabited: this has long been home to South Africa's Indigenous peoples, particularly Xhosa, whose distinctive rondavels still stud the landscape, and who welcome hikers to this little-touristed corner.

Of the various coastal hikes hereabouts, arguably the pick of the bunch is the Strandloper Trail – taking its name from the Dutch for 'beach walker'. This moderate trek between the seaside village of Kei Mouth and Gonubie, a pleasant resort just northeast of handy hub East London, offers small groups a chance to roam the coast in relative comfort, with overnight stops pre-booked. It's still a good test of fitness – and swimming or wading: a succession of river crossings demand careful planning to avoid high tide (tables are issued at the initial briefing). The Wild Coast is fairly temperate weather-wise, and the trail can be walked year-round (though heat and humidity rise as year's end approaches). In the second half of the year, you might spot migrating cetaceans (commonly southern right whales), and perhaps bottlenose dolphins.

Over four days, you'll pass through coastal forest, along sandy beaches and across rocky ledges, past centuries-old shellfish middens and shipwreck sites, up to clifftop viewpoints and into friendly seaside hamlets where a cooling dip – or even a surf – beckons at trail's end.

NOV

ACCOMMODATION
Shared rooms in simple cabins and guesthouses, equipped with braais (BBQs), toilets and (mostly cold) showers.

FOOD
Bring snacks; you can buy supplies and meals at shops and pubs on the walk.

GETTING THERE
Gonubie is around 20 minutes' drive from East London and its airport. Shuttles to Kei Mouth are available.

PLANNING
Book spots in advance; minimum group size four.

SAFETY
Several river crossings require swimming/wading; bring waterproof bags.

INFO
strandlopertrails.org.za

LEFT The Strandloper Trail loops through the heartland of the Xhosa people, whose distinctive rondavels dot the landscape here. **TOP** The Gonubie River mouth at route's end.

NATURE / CULTURE / MOUNTAINS

Langtang & Helambu Trek

NORTHERN NEPAL

Head out among the lush forests, sacred lakes, mountain villages and imposing peaks of the Langtang Himal and Helambu Valley on a sky-scraping epic.

Fringed by the planet's tallest mountains, its Himalayan uplands studded with traditional villages, rainbow-hued prayer flags and Buddhist monasteries, it's no mystery why Nepal is a hot ticket for hikers. After arriving in Kathmandu, most head swiftly east to the Big One – Everest (or Sagarmatha, as it's known locally), the behemoth that lords it over every other peak – or west to the well-established routes of the Annapurna range.

Yet other regions that are much closer and more accessible from the vibrant capital offer sensational hiking without the hordes. It's less than a day's drive north of Kathmandu to the trailhead for the Langtang Valley, centrepiece of its namesake national park. A heartland of the Tamang people, the area is suffused with Tibetan culture, and is also well on the way to recovering from the devastation wreaked by the 2015 earthquake – your visit can help revive communities.

Just to the south lies sacred Gosainkund Lake, said to have been created when the Hindu god Shiva pierced the earth with his trident to tap water, and surrounded by dozens more sparkling alpine tarns. Still nearer Kathmandu spreads the verdant Helambu Valley, renowned for its dazzling wildflowers and riotous rhododendrons. Those blossoms peak in summer – but that's also the hottest, wettest season, when paths become treacherously slippery and peaks are often shrouded in cloud. Early spring and, particularly, autumn are best for dry, clear, warmish days, ideal for trekking and for drinking in superlative views of those snowcapped Himalayan summits.

START
Syabru Besi

FINISH
Sundarijal

DISTANCE
132km (82 miles)

DURATION
10–15 days

CHALLENGE LEVEL
★ ★ ★ ★ ★

WHEN TO WALK
October–November & February–May

LEFT Heady Himalayan views on the trek through the Langtang Valley.

Wild Nepal

LANGTANG NATIONAL Park was the first designated in Nepal's Himalayan region, a diverse mix of tropical and old-growth forest — including distinctive deciduous larch — wildflower-strewn meadows and a dozen or so other ecosystems. Listen for cuckoos, barbets, nightjars and owls among the trees, along with langur monkeys. If you're incredibly lucky, you might spot an endangered red panda — actually unrelated to the better-known giant panda, though it shares the pseudothumb used to grasp bamboo when feeding.

'HINDU PILGRIMS MAKE THE TREK NORTH FROM KATHMANDU DURING THE AUGUST FESTIVAL OF JANAI PURNIMA TO BATHE IN THE ICY, PURIFYING WATERS OF THE SACRED LAKE AT GOSAINKUND.'

Each of these three hiking regions can be explored on individual out-and-back routes, but they're also easily combined into a triple-treat trek showcasing their scenic and cultural diversity. As a bonus, each night is spent in a simple but comfortable teahouse — don't expect luxury, but do anticipate warming, hearty food and cheerful chitchat with fellow hikers around the stove in the heated dining room.

An entertaining itinerary starts a day's drive north of Kathmandu, at the trailhead in the village of Syabru Besi. From here, you'll delve immediately east into Langtang National Park, crossing the gushing Bhote Kosi River on the first of many suspension bridges. Entering the narrow gorge of the Langtang Valley, keep eyes open for langur monkeys and elusive red pandas among the bamboo stands. Allow time for acclimatisation as you ascend alongside the Langtang Khola River, past yak-herders' huts to the

TOP Elusive red pandas number among the varied wildlife of Langtang National Park. **LEFT** Gosainkund Lake, a sacred place for Hindu pilgrims. **RIGHT** The rushing course of the Langtang Khola River.

ACCOMMODATION
Simple teahouses (lodges) with basic bathroom facilities.

FOOD
Hearty fare at teahouses, usually *dal bhat* — vegetable curries, lentil dal, rice and poppadom. Purify drinking water.

GETTING THERE
Syabru Besi is a seven-hour drive north of Kathmandu, Sundarijal just an hour away.

PLANNING
Fees apply for Langtang National Park, usually included in tour prices. Solo trekking isn't permitted — hire a guide or join an organised tour.

SAFETY
Altitude sickness — or at least breathlessness and headaches — are a risk on this high-altitude route. Walk slowly, drink plenty of water and always follow your guide's advice.

Buddhist monastery of Kyanjin Gompa and its namesake village; from here you can mount a testing but non-technical summit attempt on Tsergo Ri (4984m/16,352ft), for panoramas of the peaks ranged along the northern horizon.

Returning down the valley, it's another stiff climb to the main Gosainkund Lake, at around 4400m (14,440ft), where Hindu pilgrims flock in August. Then comes the toughest stage of the trek: the Laurebina La, a lofty pass at a breath-snatching 4610m (15,125ft). Rather than dashing straight for Kathmandu, weave through the warmer Himalayan foothills of the Helambu Valley, discovering the distinctive culture and costume of the region's Yolmo sherpa, to end up at Sundarijal.

USA

NATURE / CAMPING / COAST

Trans-Catalina Trail

CALIFORNIA, USA

START
Avalon

FINISH
Two Harbors

DISTANCE
62km (38.5 miles)

DURATION
Four days

CHALLENGE LEVEL
★★★

WHEN TO WALK
Year-round

Discover the rugged backcountry and gloriously lonely beaches of an island that once lured the Hollywood elite.

Catalina Island is full of surprises. First inhabited at least 7000 years ago, then colonised by the Spanish, in 1919 William Wrigley Jr (of chewing-gum fame) took control. He developed it into a getaway for residents of nearby LA, and a Hollywood filming location – one result being the establishment of a free-roaming herd of bison, transported here for a movie in 1925.

So far, so quirky. Today the Catalina Island Conservancy is restoring habitats and caring for wild denizens including more than 50 endemic species and subspecies of mammals, seabirds, herpetofauna, songbirds and plants. Visitors might well encounter those introduced bison, plus bald eagles or the Catalina Island fox.

The Conservancy also established the well-maintained Trans-Catalina Trail, snaking north-to-south through the island's rugged interior. Thanks to a mild climate, it can be tackled year-round – though early spring and late autumn/early winter are pleasant and quieter than summer. It's not technically difficult, but you need a degree of fitness and solo-hiking savvy.

Starting from Avalon's Trailhead Visitor Center, climb southwest onto Catalina's undulating spine and follow it northwest. The first day ends at remote-feeling, tree-shaded Black Jack Campground, affording dramatic views down to the Pacific. Day two passes a 2000-year-old soapstone quarry, then the airport (fuel up at the Airport in the Sky Restaurant), and traverses Cottonwood Canyon, descending to the idyllic beachfront Little Harbor Campground. Tackle the haul back to the highlands on day three, passing Two Harbors (stock up on supplies) and continuing on a challenging westerly loop to lovely Parsons Landing Campground. It's a fairly short, easy stretch back to Two Harbors to round off your trip.

NOV

ACCOMMODATION
Basic campsites, some with water. Hotels and B&Bs in Avalon and Two Harbors.

FOOD
Carry supplies for day one; there are sufficent options on subsequent stages.

GETTING THERE
Boats sail between Long Beach and Avalon, and San Pedro and both Avalon and Two Harbors, in about an hour.

PLANNING
Book campsites and collect hiking permits and maps from Avalon's Trailhead Visitor Center.

SAFETY
Be wary of bison, rattlesnakes (less common in cooler months) and poison oak.

INFO
catalinaconservancy.org

LEFT The Trans-Catalina Trail runs along the island's undulating spine. **TOP** Coastal villas near the hike's start point in Avalon.

NATURE / CULTURE / CAMPING / MOUNTAINS

Grampians Peaks Trail

VICTORIA, AUSTRALIA

Take on the 'Big Mountains' in an adventure that immerses hikers in the wild beauty and ancient Aboriginal culture of Victoria's Grampians (Gariwerd) National Park.

Names reveal a lot about a place — and a hike. Take the Indigenous Jardwadjali word for central-west Victoria's Grampians Range: Gariwerd — 'Big Mountain'. Encompassing peaks with daunting monikers such as Mt Abrupt and Mt Difficult, this 1672-sq-km (645-sq-mile) national park is a rugged, wild expanse of sandstone summits and crags.

Unsurprisingly, the Grampians Peaks Trail that snakes north-to-south through the park isn't to be taken lightly — not least because it was designed to tackle many of the highest mountains in the range. Tellingly, it's designated mostly Grade 4 or 5, suitable for experienced bushwalkers with a good level of fitness. And such passionate outdoors folk won't want to miss its hard-won delights.

This 13-stage trek finally opened in 2021 after years of work constructing many miles of trails and creating walk-in campsites with flat pitches, long-drop toilets and shelters. The result is a perambulating showreel of the park's greatest hits — its dramatic sandstone ridges and cliffs, its ancient Aboriginal rock art, its varied wildlife and, of course, its inspiring views.

Hikers encounter the region's main town, Halls Gap, at the end of Stage 4 — offering a welcome chance to slumber in a comfy bed and feast on meals someone else has cooked — but for the rest of the trek you must be fully self-sufficient. That means carrying food, camping and cooking gear plus plenty of water. In the hottest months the region is prone to drought, with water tanks running low, and sometimes bushfires — check forecasts and track conditions before setting out. Winter brings the risk

START
Mt Zero Picnic Area

FINISH
Dunkeld

DISTANCE
162km (101 miles)

DURATION
13 days

CHALLENGE LEVEL

WHEN TO WALK
March–May
& September–November

LEFT Midway through the hike, the trail summits Mt William, the highest peak in the Grampians range.

AUSTRALIA

ACCOMMODATION
Walk-in campsites; midway Halls Gap has camping, hostels, lodges and hotels.

FOOD
Carry all supplies, cooking kit and plenty of water, which may be scarce in dry periods (and should always be purified).

GETTING THERE
Halls Gap is the main hub, a 40-minute bus ride from Ararat (2½ hours by train from Melbourne). Book a transfer to Mt Zero Picnic Area (via grampianspeaks.com.au); food drops are also possible. Buses link Dunkeld with Halls Gap in 45 minutes.

PLANNING
Book campsite spots well in advance (fees payable).

SAFETY
Bring printed maps; check for wildfire warnings; prepare for all weather conditions.

INFO
parks.vic.gov.au

of ice at higher levels, too. So visit in autumn or, better still, in spring when the weather is mild and wildflowers bloom.

You'll likely encounter a cross-section of the park's native species: grey kangaroos, red-necked and swamp wallabies, emus and perhaps echidnas snuffling for ants. The region is home to at least 230 bird species, too: you may be woken by the cackling laughs of kookaburras or squawking cockatoos at your campsite. And you'll tramp through forests of stringybark and manna gums, relish the shade of banksias and she-oaks, and admire luxuriant tree ferns.

But the headline act here is geology: the quartz-gleaming sandstone sculpted and carved by wind, ice and rain over millions of years into sheer escarpments, soaring pinnacles and curious rock formations. The route tackles high peaks right from the off: the climb up Mt Stapylton comes at the start of Stage 1, Mt Difficult tests trekkers on Stage 3, and 1167m (3829ft)

LEFT MacKenzie Falls, signature sight of Grampians (Gariwerd) National Park. **RIGHT** Wallaby on the summit of Mt Abrupt, along the Grampians Peaks Trail route.

'ENJOY COUNTLESS SPRING FLOWERS CARPETING THE LAND AROUND DJARDJI-DJAWARA – ADMIRE ORCHIDS, BUSH-PEAS, GREVILLEAS AND THE STAR-SHAPED BLOOMS OF BLUE TINSEL-LILY.'

Mt William – the highest summit in the Grampians – awaits midway through the hike.

If completing the whole route in one go sounds too much, take on a shorter section. The 50km (31-mile) northern stretch, from Mt Zero Picnic Area to Halls Gap, yields marvellous views across its four days. The central five-day section between Halls Gap and Yarram is tougher, while the southern four-day leg to Dunkeld is the gentlest. However far you hike, you'll gain a rich understanding of this land of Big Mountains.

Indigenous heritage

THIS MOUNTAINOUS area of western Victorian has been the home of Aboriginal Australians, notably the Jardwadjali and Djab Wurrung peoples, for many thousands of years. Find out more about their heritage at Brambuk National Park and Cultural Centre in Halls Gap, which provides insights into what Gariwerd means to these peoples. Staff can also help you locate and understand some of the fine rock art near the route, including Gulgurn Manja Shelter near Mt Zero Picnic Area.

ECUADOR

NATURE / CULTURE / MOUNTAINS

Quilotoa Loop

COTOPAXI PROVINCE, ECUADOR

START
Sigchos

FINISH
Quilotoa

DISTANCE
34km (21 miles)

DURATION
Three days

CHALLENGE LEVEL
★★☆☆☆

WHEN TO WALK
April–November

Roam Ecuador's Andean highlands to reach attractive, culture-rich villages and a gorgeous emerald crater lake.

The Quilotoa Loop isn't quite what you'd expect. Yes, it visits a photogenically circular volcanic crater, but the hike itself is typically a point-to-point route (albeit with numerous variants). Yet though you're not completing a circuit, the endpoint — jewel-like Laguna Quilotoa — will leave you round-eyed.

This alluring body of water, cradled in an extinct volcano at close to 4000m (13,120ft), has become a focal point of a region known for its Indigenous culture, notably the Thursday bazaar at Saquisilí, thronged by Kichwa-speaking people sporting brightly coloured ponchos or shawls and felt hats. But for a more interactive insight into the lives of local people, discovering (and supporting) traditional lifestyles, tackle the three-day Quilotoa Loop.

The driest season in Ecuador's Andean highlands — June to September — is also the busiest; go April to May or October to November to enjoy the walk and the crater's mysterious beauty in relative peace. Expect clear mornings with blue skies and lush green mountainsides, and prepare for afternoon showers and chilly spells.

Most popular of the approaches to Quilotoa starts from Sigchos, following red-and-yellow signposts. It's a short route but, with many tempting detours and experiences, expect to take it slow. The first stage south to Isinliví is mostly gentle descent between fields; allow time in the village to visit cheesemakers or artisan craft workshops producing prized woodcarvings and Tigua paintings. The next day is tougher, trekking down to the Toachi Canyon, then climbing to the little village of Chugchilán — from here, a hike or horseback ride to lush cloudforest is possible. Then it's a steep zigzag haul up to the crater — circuit the rim in five or six hours, or (cautiously) duck down to the lake and kayak those turquoise waters.

NOV

ACCOMMODATION
Homestays, *hostales* (simple hotels) and lodges.

FOOD
Available at accommodation; cheese made in the high *páramo* is a speciality.

GETTING THERE
Frequent buses from capital Quito to Latacunga take around 1½ hours; local Latacunga–Sigchos and Quilotoa–Latacunga buses a little longer.

PLANNING
A small hike fee supports communities around Quilotoa. Hiring a local guide enhances your experience.

SAFETY
Be wary of altitude sickness at the crater rim, and bring warm clothing; it can get chilly.

INFO
quilotoaloop.com

LEFT Tackle the tough trek down to Toachi Canyon on the second stage of the Quilotoa Loop. **TOP** Laguna Quilotoa, cradled jewel-like in the crater of an extinct volcano.

DECEMBER

Freshwater pools at Wadi Bani Khalid, start of the E35 hike through Oman's Eastern Hajar (page 310).

DECEMBER

I WANT A HIKE THAT'S A...

- **MICRO ADVENTURE**
  - BACKCOUNTRY
    - WILDLIFE
      - Rakiura Track
        Stewart Island/Rakiura, New Zealand/Aotearoa
        page 313
  - CHALLENGE
    - Huemul Circuit
      Patagonia, Argentina
      page 298
    - Outer Mountain Loop
      Texas, USA
      page 304
  - OASES
    - E35: Wadi Bani Khalid to Wadi Tiwi
      Eastern Hajar, Oman
      page 310

- **WEEK-ISH WANDER**
  - HISTORY
    - Batongguan Traversing Trail
      Yushan National Park, Taiwan
      page 316
  - ISLAND
    - Santo Antão Trails
      Cabo Verde
      page 307

- **EPIC TREK**
  - CULTURE
    - Via Algarviana
      Algarve, Portugal
      page 319
  - COAST
    - GR92 Sendero del Mediterráneo Cataluña
      Catalonia, Spain
      page 301

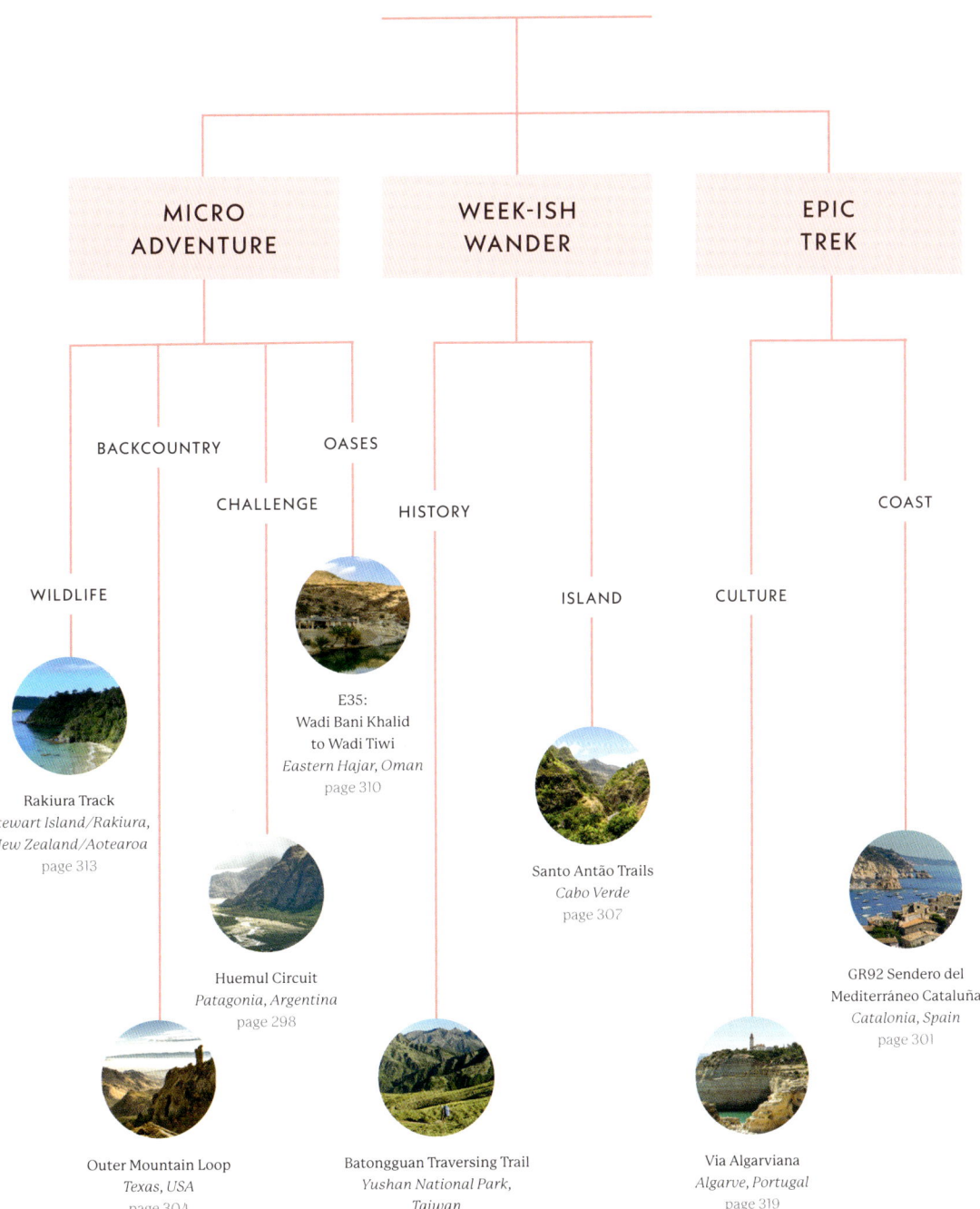

297

ARGENTINA

NATURE / CAMPING / MOUNTAINS

Huemul Circuit

PATAGONIA, ARGENTINA

START/FINISH
El Chaltén

DISTANCE
66km (41 miles)

DURATION
Four days

CHALLENGE LEVEL
★★★★★

WHEN TO WALK
November–March

This backcountry loop promises crevasse-sliced glaciers, angry rivers, violent winds – and the adventure of a lifetime.

Strap in – quite literally: this is a truly tough trek. Venturing into the icy, windy wilds of Parque Nacional Los Glaciares, the Huemul Circuit takes only four days to complete but has gained a reputation as one of Patagonia's most challenging hikes. It requires navigating shifting glaciers, unforgiving mountains and turbulent rivers, twice by means of a Tyrolean traverse – a harness-and-pulley system for which you must click in and haul yourself across a gorge on a wire, dangling over frothing whitewater.

And all of this in the face of the notoriously fickle Patagonian weather – which invariably means relentless wind: tugging at tent pegs, whipping your face, pushing you backwards like it doesn't want you here at all. You'll be blustered year-round, but the peak summer months – December to February – also bring clear, sunny, warmer days, with highs of around 17°C (62°F). This is the busiest season but, as the Huemul is more strenuous and lesser-known than many of the region's routes, it remains relatively quiet.

From El Chaltén's visitor centre, you'll cut through cattle-grazed pampas fields and lenga forest, follow the Tunel Glacier, skirt clear-blue lakes and cross two high, hard, gusty passes – the first called Paso del Viento (Windy Pass). You'll need good navigation skills (or to book an experience guide). And you'll need to take great care, especially when walking on glaciers, completing the harnessed traverses and descending from Paso Huemul, which is exceptionally steep. Yet the whole loop is breathtaking. Days are packed with vistas: up to a battalion of razor-sharp peaks (including mighty Mt Fitz Roy), over Viedma Glacier (Argentina's biggest), across the Southern Patagonian Icefield. And at night you'll be lulled to sleep by the sound of calving bergs, camping beneath a billion stars.

ACCOMMODATION
Backcountry camping. Use heavy-duty stakes.

FOOD
Pack all supplies. There are plenty of natural water sources.

GETTING THERE
El Calafate Airport is 200km (124 miles) from El Chaltén. Buses from El Calafate city to El Chaltén take three hours.

PLANNING
Permit required. Bring/hire a harness, sling, rope and carabiners for Tyrolean traverses.

SAFETY
It's mandatory to inform the El Chaltén visitor centre when you finish. Take trekking poles.

INFO
elchalten.com

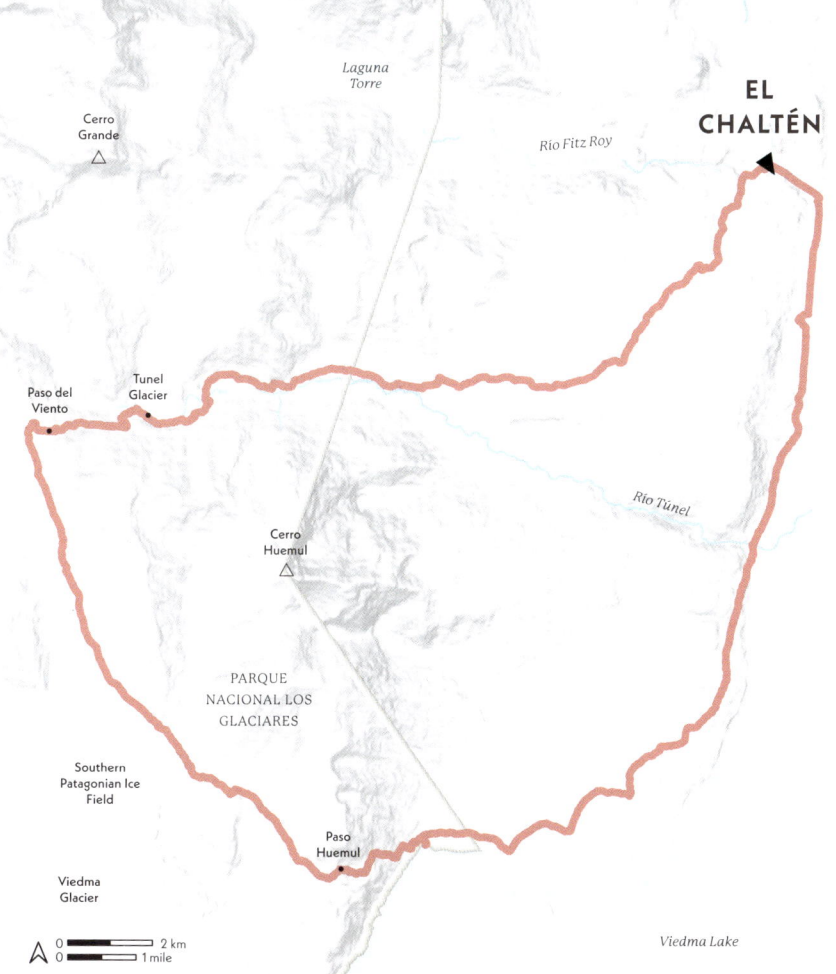

LEFT Hiking the Huemul Circuit through Parque Nacional Los Glaciares. **TOP** Looking back from Paso del Viento, the first of many high passes along the challenging Huemul route.

NATURE / FOOD & DRINK / CULTURE / COAST

GR92 Sendero del Mediterráneo Cataluña

CATALONIA, SPAIN

Wend your way from the French border along the Mediterranean coast, sampling the distinctive flavours of this singular and spectacular Spanish region.

Catalonia does things differently. It speaks its own language, cooks its own dishes, flies its own flag, practises its own traditions. It does tourism differently, too. Sure, Barcelona is besieged by tourists but, outside this overloved city, this autonomous community isn't as heavily visited or developed as many other parts of Spain. Even the coast is surprisingly unspoilt, in the main – especially the far north. Here, instead of high-rise hotels and identikit cafes serving British-style fried breakfasts, you'll find pine-clad foothills rolling down to quiet coves, traditional fishing villages, seafood restaurants and family-run guesthouses.

The Sendero del Mediterráneo Cataluña runs the length of the region and, in doing so, reveals both its independent-minded character and its estimable good looks. This relatively long trail is only one section of the GR92, an ambitious project to carve a continuous walking route from Tarifa, at the southernmost point of the Iberian Peninsula, all the way to Portbou, where Spain meets France. And even that's part of a much bigger picture: the full GR92 will ultimately become part of the European Hiking Federation's mammoth E10 long-distance path, which aims to finish in northern Finland. For now, though, be content with walking the Catalonian chunk.

It's certainly a fine hike. Divided into 31 stages, the trail begins in Portbou and ends on the Olivar Bridge across the Sénia River,

START
Portbou

FINISH
Ulldecona

DISTANCE
571km (355 miles)

DURATION
25–31 days

CHALLENGE LEVEL
★★☆☆☆

WHEN TO WALK
September–June

LEFT Stage 2 of the GR92 follows the Camí de Ronda, an old coast-guard path along the Costa Brava.

SPAIN

ACCOMMODATION
Campgrounds, guesthouses, hostels and hotels; not all sections end near accommodation, so extra walking or transfers may be necessary.

FOOD
Plentiful shops, cafes and restaurants on most stages. Try fish and seafood dishes like *esqueixada* (salt-cod salad) and paella-like *arròs negre*, rice cooked in squid ink.

GETTING THERE
Portbou has train connections to Catalan and French cities including Girona (one hour) and Perpignan (45 minutes).

PLANNING
Accessing the route is relatively easy from coastal settlements, so it's possible to tackle shorter sections or day-hikes. Book accommodation in advance.

SAFETY
Wear sun protection.

INFO
turismeamposta.cat

the natural border between Catalonia and Valencia. You'll largely stay close to the sea, skirting glorious golden beaches and tempting bays. The stretch from Portbou to the ancient town of Blanes (roughly stages 1–12) is the renowned Costa Brava – 'Wild Coast' – encompassing some of the trail's finest sections. On Stage 2 you'll follow the old Camí de Ronda coastguard path, passing through the rugged, herb-scented Parc Natural del Cap de Creus to reach the beautiful sweeping bay and whitewashed houses of Cadaqués. On Stage 8, you'll trace the Palafrugell Coast, studded with idyllic, clear-water coves and charming fishing villages such as Llafranc and Tamariu.

The trail also veers off to explore the fascinating hinterland. So you'll discover the wetlands of Parc Natural dels Aiguamolls de l'Empordà, where you might spot flamingos, storks and an array of other birds; the rugged massifs of Montgrí and Cadiretes; the pine- and holm-oak-cloaked Parc Montnegre-Corredor;

LEFT The Costa Brava section of the GR92 weaves through Parc Natural del Cabo de Creus. BELOW Port Lligat's Casa Museu Dali, set in the artist's former home. RIGHT The fortified, medieval Old Town at beach-blessed Tossa de Mar.

'THE GR92 SECTION BETWEEN BLANES AND PORTBOU IS KNOWN AS THE CAMÍ DE RONDA, AN ANCIENT PATH FORGED ALONG THE COAST TO CONNECT FISHING VILLAGES AND INTERCEPT SMUGGLERS.'

Parc Natural de Collserola, with its fine views over Barcelona; the limestone hills of the Garraf Massif; the Ebro Delta's bird-rich wetlands. You'll also encounter impressive settlements: the Old Town, towers and ramparts of Tossa de Mar; medieval, mountain-hugged Begur; and UNESCO-listed Tarragona, with its wealth of Roman sites.

Most tourists come to this coast in summer, but walkers should opt for the cooler spring/autumn months or even winter. This season is pleasantly mild and sunny here, with coastal temperatures in December hovering at 10°C–15°C (50°F–59°F); the sea (around 14°C/57°F) will appeal to colder-water swimmers. Prices are lower, too, and best of all it's sublimely quiet – you might find your footprints are the only ones on the beach.

Artistic ambling

THE DREAMY light of the Costa Brava has attracted many artists, including Joan Miró, Pablo Picasso and, most famously, the surrealist Salvador Dali. From 1930 to 1982, Dali lived in the tiny village of Port Lligat near Cadaqués, in a maze-like house cobbled together from multiple fishers' huts. It's now a museum filled with his eccentric oddments. One of his favourite spots was nearby Cap de Creus: the peninsula's rugged rock formations feature prominently in his work.

USA

NATURE / CAMPING / MOUNTAINS

Outer Mountain Loop

TEXAS, USA

START/FINISH
Chisos Basin

DISTANCE
48km (30 miles)

DURATION
Three days

CHALLENGE LEVEL
★★★★☆

WHEN TO WALK
November–April

Hike Big Bend National Park for a challenging circuit via hot deserts, cool rocks and a profusion of plants and birds.

Just getting to Big Bend is an adventure. Sprawled across far west Texas on the USA–Mexico border, this remote park lies in the heart of the Chihuahuan Desert, where the Rio Grande River makes a sudden turn between the Chisos Mountains and the north end of Mexico's Sierra Madre Oriental. Encompassing a vastness of desert, canyons and juniper woodlands, it's awash with complex geology, ancient fossils, an enormous diversity of plants and around 450 bird species, plus Native American, Spanish and rancher history – and some of North America's best stargazing.

The Outer Mountain Loop is the ultimate way to explore. It's an extremely strenuous hike, with significant and repeated ups and downs, scarce water and a hot, arid climate to contend with. So winter is a good time to walk, offering pleasantly mild, dry, sunny days – December highs range from 15°C (59°F) at altitude to 23°C (74°F) at lower elevations. But even at this cooler time of year, the arid desert air can leave you dehydrated.

The route begins at 1646m (5400ft) elevation with a stiff climb out of Chisos Basin – which sets the tone for the rest of the loop. On day one, you're headed for the campground at Juniper Canyon, via magnificent views of rocky pinnacles, Boot Canyon's shady Arizona cypress trees and, to end, a steep descent. Day two follows the Dodson Trail across the merciless open desert – the route's most challenging, hot and hard-to-follow section – before picking up the Blue Creek Canyon Trail to the ruins of Homer Wilson Ranch and campsite two. On day three, you haul back up into High Chisos woodland, through a swathe of timeworn red rock and across the Laguna Meadows before dropping back down to the basin where your adventure began.

ACCOMMODATION
Basic backcountry camping.

FOOD
Carry supplies, including water – desert sources are not reliable.

GETTING THERE
The closest airport is Midland/Odessa, 378km (235 miles) away. There's no public transport to the park; you'll need to drive or arrange transfers.

PLANNING
Backcountry permit required. Cache water at Homer Wilson (Blue Creek) Ranch before starting out. Check if natural springs are flowing.

SAFETY
Wear long trousers to protect legs from spiky plants.

INFO
nps.gov

LEFT Trek through Big Bend National Park's Boot Canyon on day one of the Outer Mountain Loop. **TOP** Backcountry camping along the route, in the shadow of the craggy Chisos Mountains.

NATURE / CULTURE / MOUNTAIN / COAST

Santo Antão Trails

SANTO ANTÃO ISLAND, CABO VERDE

Head to the wild 'hiking island' of this windswept Atlantic archipelago to explore its outrageous landscapes as the locals do – on foot.

Cast away in the remote Atlantic off the West African coast, Cabo Verde lies at the mercy of the northeast trade winds and the open ocean. It's always warm, but sometimes doesn't receive rain for months – even years – making it a challenging place to live. But it's a wonderful place to visit, especially in winter – December temperatures hover around a pleasant 20°C–25°C (68°F–77°F), and skies are largely clear and dry. (The rain, if it does come, tends to fall between August and October.)

There are 10 islands in the archipelago, most geared more towards beach holidays than hiking. But Santo Antão, the northwesternmost isle, is a different proposition. It's a place of extremes, with scarcely a flat bit. Every inch seems to rear up or collapse down in a mishmash of sharp shards, steep ravines and raw volcanic innards; some areas are as barren as the moon, others overspill with greenery.

The topography makes getting around difficult, with footpaths the only way to reach places in the island's remote corners. Now trails long trod by locals are being enjoyed by hikers, too. There's no one continuous thru-hike, and paths can be rough and rugged, but a handful of well-worn, showstopping day-walks will happily fill a hiking break.

You could start with the classic 5-mile-ish (8km) route through the Vale do Paúl, which reveals Santo Antão at its lushest: craggy flanks hewn with terraces of flourishing sugarcane, banana palms, sweet potatoes and manioc. From seaside Vila das Pombas, a trail climbs up amid the crops, between the looming

START/FINISH
Various

DISTANCE
8km–15km (5–9 miles)

DURATION
Five to six days

CHALLENGE LEVEL
★★★☆☆

WHEN TO WALK
Year-round

LEFT The snaking, vertiginous coast path from Ponta do Sol to of Cruzinha is a Santo Antão hikers' highlight.

CABO VERDE

Footsteps of the flogged

FAILED RAINS and famine loom large in Cabo Verde's history. In the 1940s, some 45,000 people died here as a result of drought; thousands more were driven to emigrate. Manuel Lopes' 1960 novel *Os Flagelados do Vento Leste* (Victims of the East Wind), a classic of the country's literature, describes the struggles faced in the Ribeira das Patas, the remote Santo Antão valley accessed via the chillingly named 'Route of the Flogged'.

'SANTO ANTÃO SWAYS TO THE RHYTHMS OF *MORNA*, THE SOUL OF THE ISLAND IN MUSICAL FORM, COVERING THEMES OF LOVE, LEAVING AND MELANCHOLIC LONGING KNOWN AS *SAUDADE*.'

valley sides, to reach a ridge-top hamlet where you can buy coffee made from beans grown nearby, and take in views stretching up to the crater rim of mighty Cova do Paúl. Finish in the village of Chã de João Vaz with a shot of *grogue* (sugarcane spirit) from the bar/rum factory while you wait for a pick-up. Alternatively, for a longer hike hereabouts (14km/8.5 miles), catch a ride to the edge of the Cova crater rim to look down into this impressive caldera, then hike down through the Vale do Paúl to the sea.

Another must-do is the coast path from the northeasterly town of Ponta do Sol to the fishing village of Cruzinha (15km/ 9 miles). The trail is audacious, cut right into the mighty cliffs, at points seeming to defy gravity. A few miles in lies Fontainhas, a village of candy-coloured houses that somehow balances on a

TOP Abandoned Aranhas, on Santo Antão's northeast coast. **LEFT** Colourful Fontainhas, on the coastal hike to Cruzinha. **RIGHT** Pathways connect the peaks and valleys of Santo Antão's scarped interior.

CABO VERDE

ACCOMMODATION
Hotels and guesthouses at trailheads such as Ponta do Sol and Curral das Vacas.

FOOD
Pack snacks and lunches; refreshment stops on some trails. Purify water.

GETTING THERE
The nearest airport is on neighbouring São Vicente Island. Ferries between Mindelo (São Vicente) and Porto Novo (Santo Antão) take one hour. Access trailheads by taxi or *alugueres* (shared minibuses).

PLANNING
Travel companies can organise hiking tours, transfers and guides. Independent hikers can book taxis to trailheads.

SAFETY
Waymarking is variable – download GPX files and take maps. The ferry crossing can be rough.

INFO
visitsantoantao.net

narrow ridge. Later, you'll pass through abandoned, crumbling Aranhas, where long-neglected terraces score the peaks behind.

Perhaps most dramatic of all is the 15km (9-mile) hike up the Bordeira do Norte, which bookends the Ribeira das Patas. It's a long, switchbacking climb up this forbidding wall of rock to reach a wild plateau, weave through a small canyon and tramp on crusted lava. Drink in vistas from a grand *miradouro* (viewpoint) before descending towards Curral das Vacas along the zigzagging path of rough black basalt known as the 'Route of the Flogged', heavily used by farmers who struggled to raise crops here during the droughts – and resulting catastrophic famines – of the 1940s.

NATURE / CAMPING / MOUNTAINS

E35: Wadi Bani Khalid to Wadi Tiwi

EASTERN HAJAR, OMAN

START
Wadi Bani Khalid

FINISH
Wadi Tiwi

DISTANCE
42km (26 miles)

DURATION
Two days

CHALLENGE LEVEL
★★★★☆

WHEN TO WALK
October–April

Tackle a tough but classic trek over the Hajar Mountains to link two magical oases and camp out under a trillion stars.

The Hajar Mountains are some of the highest in Arabia, and provide a perfect backdrop for winter walkers. Even in December, Oman's 'coldest' month, temperatures in Sur and Muscat average 26°C–28°C (79°F–82°F). It's cooler higher up, and definitely chilly at night, but still: perfect hiking weather.

The E35 trail is an iconic crossing of a high Hajar plateau along an ancient donkey track, linking the two lush oases of Wadi Bani Khalid and Wadi Tiwi. It can be hiked in either direction – there are steep ascents and descents, whichever way you choose. If you're crazy-fit, you might attempt the route in a day. Much better to take two days, camping halfway on the top of the plateau at around 2000m (6560ft). The night will be chilly, but the sunsets, sunrises, stars and solitude offer spectacular compensation.

Wadi Bani Khalid is one of Oman's most popular oases, largely because this 'dry' riverbed has permanent water. It's a beautiful spot, with pools fringed with date palms and mango trees; there's even a small restaurant here, handy for fuelling up. Energy will certainly be required for the steady ascent, which follows painted waymarks and cairns to climb up to the plateau. The rewards are immense views over the barren ravines and fertile date plantations, south to rippling Sharqiya Sands and north to the Gulf of Oman.

What goes up must come down, via a winding, scramble-y trail – look out for eagles overhead. Eventually, the route reaches Wadi Tiwi and the villages of Sooee, Al Aqur and Mybam. The wadi's emerald waters sparkle invitingly, perfect for a refreshing swim.

ACCOMMODATION
Camping – bring a thick sleeping bag, as nights are cold.

FOOD
Pack supplies, including plenty of water.

GETTING THERE
A car, taxi or other transfer is required to reach both wadis.

PLANNING
Consider using a tour company to arrange logistics and a food/water drop – the trail crosses a road, where supplies could be picked up.

SAFETY
Wear a hat and sun protection. Trekking poles are advisable.

LEFT Crystal-clear waters at the year-round oasis of Wadi Bani Khalid, start point of the E35.
TOP The turquoise pools at Wadi Tiwi, perfect for a post-hike swim.

NATURE / CULTURE / CAMPING / COAST

Rakiura Track

STEWART ISLAND/RAKIURA, NEW ZEALAND/AOTEAROA

Venture through the verdant primal forest and along the empty beaches and pristine shorelines of New Zealand's other south island, keeping eyes peeled for kiwis.

One oft-cited factoid about New Zealand is that it's home to more sheep than people – five times as many, more or less. Here's another: there are far more kiwis than humans on Stewart Island/Rakiura – perhaps 15,000–20,000 southern tokoeka, but just 440 people in an area of 1746 sq km (674 sq miles).

Over 85% of the island is protected as national park, a paradise for birds – and not just the flightless, fuzzy, long-billed kiwi. Vast numbers thrive here, including many rare and endangered native species, enjoying the rich pickings offshore and on. Trampers are fewer but equally well catered for: walking tracks total 280km (174 miles) – 10 times the distance of roads on the island. In short, it's heaven for hikers and birders.

Many come to do the Rakiura Track. This circular route in the island's far northeast is one of New Zealand's designated Great Walks. Yes, it's pretty magnificent – but it's also relatively short, a comfortable three days at a gentle pace. There are no really challenging climbs, with the highest elevation only about 200m (656ft), and daily distances all well under 15km (9 miles). Yet within that modest mileage you can savour a rich taster of the natural, scenic, cultural and historic delights of this isle some 30km (19 miles) across the Foveaux Strait from South Island.

The avian fauna isn't the only aspect that's wild on Rakiura: lying slap in the Roaring Forties latitude, its weather is unpredictable: come in summer, when days are longer and conditions more likely to favour hiking, but prepare for any eventuality and you can enjoy the experience year-round.

START
Lee Bay

FINISH
Fern Gully car park (or vice versa)

DISTANCE
32km (20 miles), plus 7km (4 miles) to/from Oban

DURATION
Three days

CHALLENGE LEVEL:
★★☆☆☆

WHEN TO WALK
Year-round

LEFT Shoreline sections of the Rakiura Track take in the island's gloriously undeveloped beaches.

NEW ZEALAND/AOTEAROA

ACCOMMODATION
Simple park huts with bunks and shared facilities at Port William and North Arm; basic campsites at these spots plus Māori Beach. Lodges and B&Bs in Oban.

FOOD
Bring supplies. Oban has a supermarket, cafes and fish-and-chips takeaway. Purify drinking water, even at huts.

GETTING THERE
Flights from Invercargill (20 minutes) and ferries from Bluff (one hour) serve Oban, from where it's a 5km (3-mile) walk to Lee Bay, and 2km (1.2 miles) back from Fern Gully car park.

PLANNING
Book DOC huts and campsites well in advance.

SAFETY
Trails may be slippery or boggy after rain.

INFO
doc.govt.nz

The official trail starts at Lee Bay, a short amble north of compact township Oban, where the ferry from Bluff docks. You can't miss the start of the track: almost as soon as you leave the road, you stride through a gateway in the form of a chain link. This imposing sculpture represents the anchor-chain of the trickster demigod Māui, who used South Island as his *waka* (canoe) and Rakiura as the anchor.

The track winds above the shore through luxuriant forest thick with rimu stands and tree ferns, opening out periodically to yield glimpses of surf against grey rocks. Descending to cross the footbridge at Little River and rounding Peter's Point for views across Wooding Bay, the path emerges onto glorious Māori Beach. Here you'll find not only one of New Zealand's loveliest little campsites, but also remnants of early 20th-century sawmilling operations. Most hikers push on north to Magnetic Beach and another scenic campsite at Port William, with a simple hut nearby.

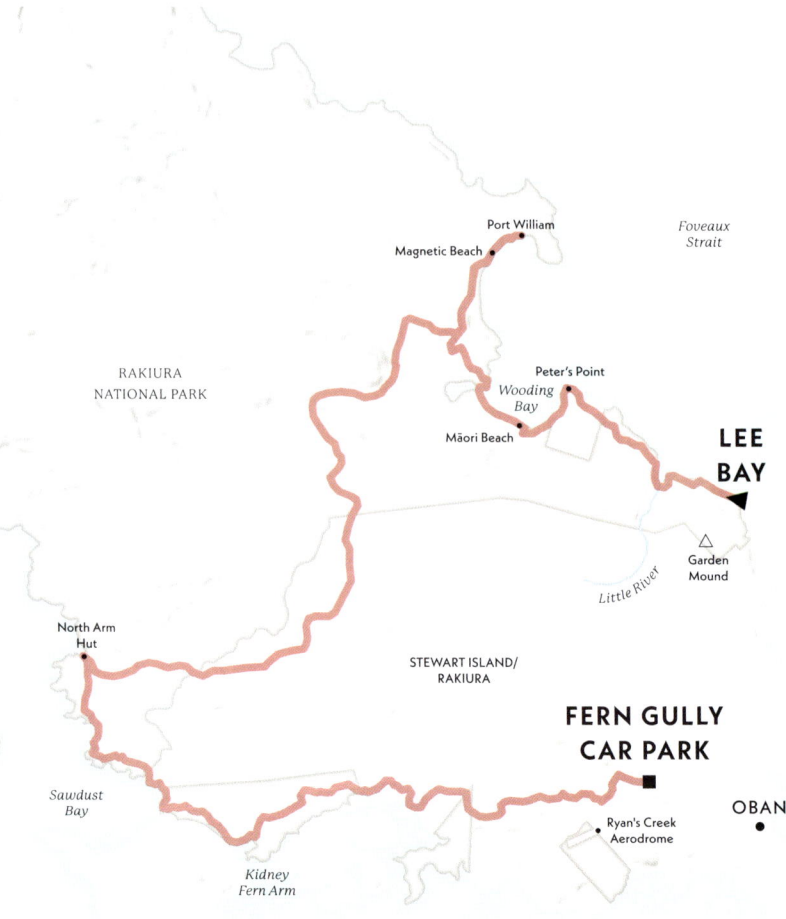

LEFT The start of the track weaves above the coast, with glimpses to the shore through the rimu stands and tree ferns. **BELOW** Active during the day, Rakiura's southern tokoeka are a common sight. **RIGHT** Tramping the track near Lee Bay.

'WATCH FOR THE ENDANGERED, ENDEMIC NEW ZEALAND SEA LIONS – *RĀPOKA/ WHAKAHAO* TO MĀORI – HAULED UP ON BEACHES AROUND RAKIURA DURING THE SUMMER BREEDING SEASON.'

Days two and three head south and then east, traversing podocarp, rimu and kāmahi forest, and passing more reminders of sawmilling including tramlines and the disused wharf at aptly named Sawdust Bay, past the hut at North Arm.

Finally, hike the connecting leg back to Oban to enjoy a warm welcome – possibly from the cheeky weka and kākā birds that lay claim to this wildest of islands.

Rakiura's kiwis

RAKIURA/STEWART Island is *the* place to spot New Zealand's vulnerable national bird. An estimated 15,000–20,000 southern tokoeka live in family groups here; unlike their northern cousins, they're active during the day. With long, curved bills and fluffy red-brown plumage, these chicken-sized birds are unmistakable. Watch for them foraging for sand-hoppers among kelp, or for other invertebrates in grassy clearings. At night, listen for their calls – shrill and repetitive from males, throaty screeches from females.

TAIWAN

NATURE / CULTURE / CAMPING / MOUNTAINS

Batongguan Traversing Trail

YUSHAN NATIONAL PARK, TAIWAN

START
Dongpu

FINISH
Shanfeng

DISTANCE
96km (60 miles)

DURATION
Eight days

CHALLENGE LEVEL
★★★☆☆

WHEN TO WALK
March–May
& October–December

Hike a trail blazed through Taiwan's lush Central Mountains over a century ago, rich in both cultural and natural history.

In 1875, China's Qing Dynasty built an east–west highway across Taiwan's mountainous spine in order to better control the people living in the remote interior – forging a route now known as the Batongguan Historic Trail. When the Japanese later took control of the island, they had a similar idea: in 1921 they completed a second route – the Batongguan Traversing Trail – designed to make access over the Central Mountains as easy as possible.

Though it's over a century old, the Traversing Trail is still partly navigable, providing a fascinating hike through history. Along its length lie reminders of the Japanese occupation, from remnants of the police stations they constructed to stone walls, hand-carved tunnels, artillery depots and memorials marking sites of conflict between Japanese officials and the Indigenous Bunun people.

The scenery is as enthralling as the history. The trail cuts though Yushan National Park, home to Taiwan's highest summit – 3952m (12,966ft) Jade Mountain – plus many more massive peaks, sheer cliffs, deep river valleys (crossed on suspension bridges) and a profusion of plants. It's also one of the best places in the country to catch a glimpse of the rare Formosan black bear.

The trail roughly splits into three: the west section, from the Indigenous village of Dongpu to Dashuiku Lake; the wild, remote central section; and the lower-elevation, more jungly east, from Baoyai to Shanfeng, which is better developed for hikers. Taiwan's subtropical climate means mild winters and hot, rainy summers – so drier, cooler October to December is particularly good for hiking.

ACCOMMODATION
Wilderness camping, plus some basic cabins.

FOOD
Pack all supplies.

GETTING THERE
Yushan National Park is remote. A bus runs to Dongpu Hot Springs, but there's no public transport to Shanfeng, near the park's Nan-an Visitor Centre.

PLANNING
Mountain permits are required. Check the national park website for updates on which sections of the trail are open.

SAFETY
There are some narrow, vertiginous sections – trekking poles are advisable. Summer rains and seasonal typhoons (mostly May–October) can play havoc with the route – landslides are frequent, particularly affecting the central section. Keep tabs on the situation.

INFO
ysnp.gov.tw

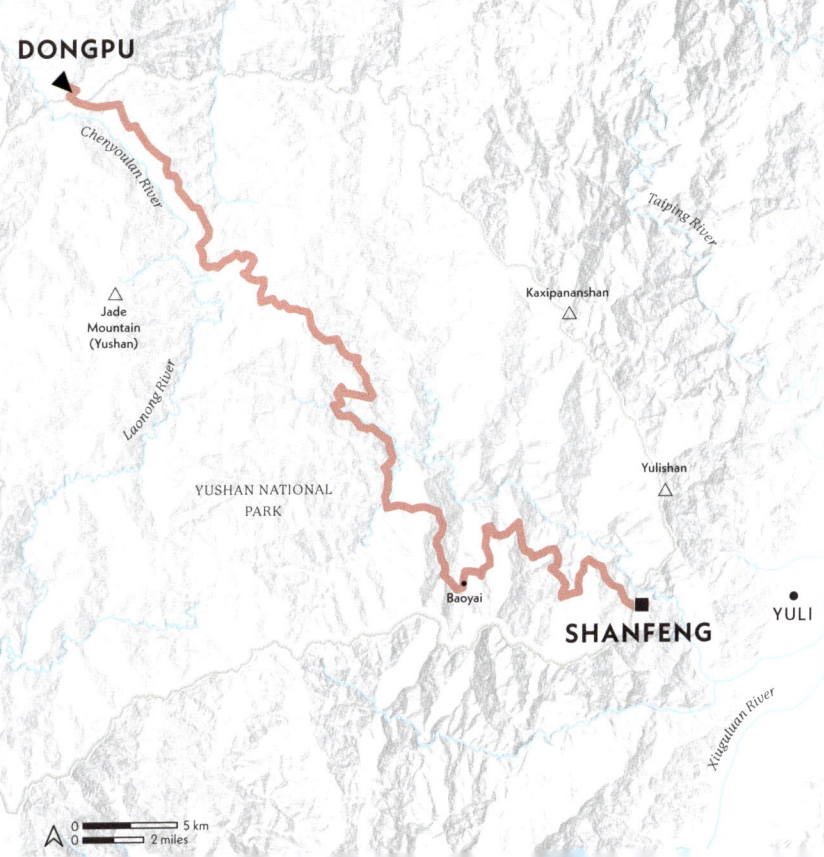

LEFT Forest-swathed temple in Yushan National Park. **TOP** The Batongguan Traversing Trail offers stellar views of Jade Mountain, Taiwan's highest peak.

NATURE / FOOD & DRINK / CULTURE

Via Algarviana

ALGARVE, PORTUGAL

Forget your beach towel and pull on your walking boots for a very different take on Portugal's sunny, mild and surprisingly wild far south.

There's the popular image of the Algarve: golf courses, beach resorts, sun-seeking sightseers. Then there's the Via Algarviana (GR13): a region-spanning route that shuns the touristy coast until its very end — in the process revealing a very different side to southern Portugal.

A modern version of the Algarve Way was first walked in 1998, and officially opened in 2009. But its origins date back to 304 CE, when Vincent of Saragossa was imprisoned in Valencia and tortured for his Christian faith on the orders of the Roman emperor. After his death, Vincent's supporters sailed his body west out of the Mediterranean, burying it near the cape that now bears his name — Cabo de São Vicente. Subsequently, Mozarabs (Spanish Christians) started to make pilgrimages to his grave, crossing into what's now Portugal over the Guadiana River and walking from Alcoutim to the sacred promontory at mainland Europe's southwesternmost point.

In 1173, Vincent's body was moved to Lisbon, where he was made the city's patron saint, and the pilgrimage trail faded from memory. But when, in the 1990s, thoughts turned to creating a trans-Algarve thru-hike, the ancient route was used as the blueprint. Today the trail explores cultural heritage and varied landscapes, as well as giving an economic boost to rural communities.

The Via Algarviana also lengthens the tourist season. High summer might be best for living it up in Lagos, but the blistering temperatures make it the worst time for hikers. Much better to visit in wildflower-y spring, balmy autumn or even midwinter. In December, the Algarve is uncrowded, yet daytime temperatures

START
Alcoutim

FINISH
Cabo de São Vicente

DISTANCE
300km (186 miles)

DURATION
14–24 days

CHALLENGE LEVEL
★★★☆☆

WHEN TO WALK
October–May

LEFT The final section of the Via Algarviana traces the coast through glorious Parque Natural do Sudoeste Alentejano e Costa Vicentina.

PORTUGAL

Smugglers' stroll

AS WELL as the Via Algarviana, four additional themed routes have been created that connect with the main trail. One is the 5.5km (3.4-mile) Rota do Contrabandista (Smugglers' Route), comprising two walking paths from Alcoutim. Smuggling began in this border region in the 13th century, and peaked in the 1930s during the Spanish Civil War. These short trails explore that history, passing old Fiscal Guard surveillance posts and barracks, and affording excellent views over the Guadiana River.

'THE INLAND ALGARVE IS SWATHED IN FIG, ALMOND, CAROB AND OLIVE TREES, THEIR FRUITS USED TO CREATE MOORISH-INFLUENCED CAKES LIKE *TRÊS DELÍCIAS DO ALGARVE* AND *QUEIJO DE FIGO*.'

hover at 10°C–18°C (50°F–65°F), with plenty of sunshine; rain isn't uncommon but tends to come in short showers. There's also the chance to spot some of the birds that overwinter here, including marsh harriers, booted eagles and greater flamingos.

Divided into 14 stages, the route kicks off with a stroll through the cobbled streets of riverside Alcoutim, on the Spanish border. From there it heads southwest, negotiating the rolling, wooded uplands before descending to the *barrocal* – the Algarve's fecund agricultural region, squeezed between the

LEFT The hike ends at Cabo de São Vicente, Europe's southwestern-most point. **RIGHT** Terraced fields near Cachopo, on Section 5 of the Via Algarviana.

ACCOMMODATION
Guesthouses bookend each stage. Wild camping is illegal.

FOOD
Carry food for the day – not all stages have shops or cafes on the route. You may need to order a picnic lunch from your guesthouse.

GETTING THERE
Trains serve Vila Real de Santo António, from where buses run to Alcoutim. Cabo de São Vicente is close to Sagres, from where buses run to Lagos.

PLANNING
Book accommodation and evening meals in advance. Some businesses close in low season.

SAFETY
Many stages pass hunting areas – consider wearing a fluorescent bib. Pack layers and waterproof clothing: winter mornings can be cold.

INFO
viaalgarviana.org

coast and the hills. Along the route, you'll experience a peaceful unfurling of rural life. You'll follow sections through cork oak forests, almond orchards and strawberry trees, used to make Medronho brandy. You'll visit a succession of whitewashed villages clinging to the mountainsides, and pass Moorish castles, historic convents and churches, ancient dolmen and menhirs, lonely windmills. And you'll encounter beguiling communities such as Cachopo, where traditional farming practices, including cheesemaking and wool-weaving, have been preserved. Only on stage 6 do you enjoy your first glimpse of the sea.

The route culminates in the Parque Natural do Sudoeste Alentejano e Costa Vicentina, verdant with endemic plants and home to the Iberian Peninsula's largest concentration of megalithic monuments (near Vila do Bispo). The grand finale comes on the craggy tip of Cabo de São Vicente itself, where you can look out from what the Romans believed was the end of the world.

Index

A

Argentina
 Huemul Circuit, Patagonia 298
Australia
 Cape to Cape Track, Western Australia 233
 Dolomite Walk, Northern Territory 207
 Gold Coast Hinterland Great Walk, Queensland 114
 Grampians Peaks Trail, Victoria 291
 Kangaroo Island Wilderness Trail, South Australia 260
 Larapinta Trail, Northern Territory 205
 Ormiston Pound Circuit, Northern Territory 207
 Scenic Rim Trail, Queensland 98
 Snowies Alpine Walk, New South Wales 42
 Thorsborne Trail, Queensland 156
 Three Capes Track, Tasmania 78
Austria
 Adlerweg durch Osttirol 188
 Adlerweg, Tyrol 187

B

Bhutan
 Jomolhari Trek 133
Bosnia & Hercegovina
 Via Dinarica 147

C

Cabo Verde
 Santo Antão Trails 307
Canada
 East Coast Trail, Newfoundland 159
 Island Walk, Prince Edward Island 254
 Pacific Crest Trail 171
 Traversée de Charlevoix, Québec 236
 West Coast Trail, British Columbia 184

canyon hikes
 Dana to Petra Trail, Jordan 95
 Fish River Canyon Trail, Namibia 178
 Grand Canyon Rim-to-Rim, USA 130
 Larapinta Trail, Australia 205
 Tiger Leaping Gorge, China 124
Chile
 W Trek, Patagonia 36
China 124
 MacLehose Trail, Hong Kong 279
 Tiger Leaping Gorge, Yunnan 124
city hikes
 Berliner Mauerweg, Germany 39
coastal hikes
 Archipelago Trail, Denmark 181
 Baltic Coastal Hiking Trail, Lithuania 211
 Cape to Cape Track, Australia 233
 Dingle Way, Ireland 153
 Dry Stone Route (GR221), Mallorca 75
 East Coast Trail, Canada 159
 Fishermen's Trail, Portugal 63
 GR92 Sendero del Mediterráneo Cataluña, Spain 301
 GR132 Circular, Canary Islands 13
 Island Trails, Madeira 29
 Island Walk, Canada 254
 Jeju Olle Trail, South Korea 227
 Kalalau Trail, Hawai'i 230
 Kangaroo Island Wilderness Trail, Australia 260
 Lycian Way, Türkiye 81
 Mare è Monti Nord, Corsica 141
 MacLehose Trail, Hong Kong, China 279
 Michinoku Coastal Trail, Japan 150
 Queen Charlotte Track, New Zealand/Aotearoa 19
 Rakiura Track, New Zealand/Aotearoa 313
 Santa Barbara Cammino, Sardinia 84
 Santo Antão Trails, Cabo Verde 307
 Sentier du Douanier, Corsica 143
 Shikoku 88 Temple Pilgrimage, Japan 69

 South West Coast Path, England 101
 Strandloper Trail, South Africa 282
 Thorsborne Trail, Australia 156
 Three Capes Track, Australia 78
 Trans-Catalina Trail, USA 288
 Waitukubuli Trail, Dominica 16
 West Coast Trail, Canada 184
Colombia
 Ciudad Perdida Trek, Santa Marta Mountains 23
Costa Rica
 Camino de Costa Rica 32
Croatia
 Premužić Trail, Velebit Mountains 224
culture-rich hikes
 Adlerweg, Austria 187
 Baltic Coastal Hiking Trail, Lithuania 211
 Berliner Mauerweg, Germany 39
 Camino de Costa Rica 32
 Camino Francés, Spain 55
 Cape to Cape Track, Australia 233
 Ciudad Perdida Trek, Colombia 23
 Dana to Petra Trail, Jordan 95
 Dingle Way, Ireland 153
 Dry Stone Route (GR221), Mallorca 75
 Fishermen's Trail, Portugal 63
 GR92 Sendero del Mediterráneo Cataluña, Spain 301
 Grampians Peaks Trail, Australia 291
 Island Walk, Canada 254
 Jeju Olle Trail, South Korea 227
 Jomolhari Trek, Bhutan 133
 Juliana Trail, Slovenia 127
 Kumano Kodō, Japan 263
 Lake Waikaremoana Track, New Zealand/Aotearoa 48
 Langtang & Helambu Trek, Nepal 285
 Manaslu Circuit, Nepal 51
 Mare è Monti Nord, Corsica 141
 Markha Valley Trek, India 172
 Menalon Trail, Greece 276
 Michinoku Coastal Trail, Japan 150
 Pekoe Trail, Sri Lanka 26

Queen Charlotte Track,
    New Zealand/Aotearoa 19
Quilotoa Loop, Ecuador 294
Rakiura Track, New Zealand/
    Aotearoa 313
Shikoku 88 Temple Pilgrimage,
    Japan 69
Singalila Ridge, India 110
South West Coast Path,
    England 101
Strandloper Trail,
    South Africa 282
Toubkal Circuit, Morocco 121
Via Algarviana, Portugal 319
Via Dinarica, Bosnia &
    Hercegovina/Montenegro 147
Via Francigena, Italy 257
Via Transilvanica, Romania 162
Waitukubuli Trail, Dominica 16
Czechia
Lužnice Valley Trail, Bohemia 202

D

day hikes
Berliner Mauerweg, Germany 39
Dolomite Walk, Australia 207
Fimmvörðuháls Trail, Iceland 200
GR92 Sendero del Mediterráneo
    Cataluña, Spain 301
Grand Canyon Rim-to-Rim,
    USA 130
Historical Way, Portugal 65
Island Trails, Madeira 29
Kaiserjäger, Italy 240
Kalalau Trail, Hawai'i 230
Malerweg, Germany 267
Ormiston Pound Circuit,
    Australia 207
PS PR1 Porto Santo, Portugal 30
Rota do Contrabandista,
    Portugal 320
Santo Antão Trails,
    Cabo Verde 307
Denmark
Archipelago Trail,
    Fyn Archipelago 181
Dominica
Waitukubuli Trail 16

E

Ecuador
Quilotoa Loop, Cotopaxi
    Province 294
England
Coast to Coast, Cumbria &
    Yorkshire 245
South West Coast Path 101
Estonia
Baltic Coastal Hiking Trail 211
Baltic Forest Hiking Trail 212
extreme trails
Cordillera Huayhuash Circuit,
    Peru 136
Huemul Circuit, Argentina 298
John Muir Trail, USA 169
K2 Base Camp & Concordia,
    Pakistan 208
Kilimanjaro, Tanzania 9

F

family-friendly hikes
Archipelago Trail, Denmark 181
Berliner Mauerweg, Germany 39
Dutch Mountain Trail,
    Netherlands 92
Island Trails, Madeira 29
Moselsteig, Germany 107
Finland
Karhunkierros Trail 218
food & drink hikes
Adlerweg, Austria 187
Andros Route, Greece 251
Archipelago Trail, Denmark 181
Camino Francés, Spain 55
Cape to Cape Track, Australia 233
Dingle Way, Ireland 153
Fishermen's Trail, Portugal 63
GR92 Sendero del Mediterráneo
    Cataluña, Spain 301
Island Trails, Madeira 29
Juliana Trail, Slovenia 127
Kumano Kodō, Japan 263
Lycian Way, Türkiye 81
Malerweg, Germany 267
Menalon Trail, Greece 276
Moselsteig, Germany 107
Pekoe Trail, Sri Lanka 26
Toubkal Circuit, Morocco 121

ViaBerna, Switzerland 166
Via Dinarica, Bosnia &
    Hercegovina/Montenegro 147
Via Francigena, Italy 257
Via Transilvanica, Romania 162
West Highland Way, Scotland 117
France
Chemin de Stevenson, Massif
    Central 175
Mare à Mare, Corsica 143
Mare è Monti Nord, Corsica 141
Mare è Monti Sud, Corsica 143
Mare Sud, Corsica 143
Sentier du Douanier, Corsica 143

G

Germany
Berliner Mauerweg 39
Malerweg, Saxony 267
Moselsteig, Moselle Valley 107
glacier hikes
Huemul Circuit, Argentina 298
K2 Base Camp & Concordia,
    Pakistan 208
Kungsleden, Sweden 193
W Trek, Chilean Patagonia 36
Greece
Andros Route, Cyclades 251
Menalon Trail, Peloponnese 276
Guatemala
El Mirador Trek, Petén 66
guided hikes
Camino de Costa Rica 32
Ciudad Perdida Trek,
    Colombia 23
Cordillera Huayhuash Circuit,
    Peru 136
Dana to Petra Trail, Jordan 95
El Mirador Trek, Guatemala 66
Jomolhari Trek, Bhutan 133
Kilimanjaro, Tanzania 9
Manaslu Circuit, Nepal 51
Mt Kenya Traverse, Kenya 45
Mt Kinabalu, Malaysian Borneo 58
Santo Antão Trails,
    Cabo Verde 307
Scenic Rim Trail, Australia 98
Singalila Ridge, India 110
Strandloper Trail,
    South Africa 282

INDEX

guided hikes (cont)
   Toubkal Circuit, Morocco 121
   Waitukubuli Trail, Dominica 16

H

history-rich hikes
   Alta Via 1, Italy 239
   Andros Route, Greece 251
   Archipelago Trail, Denmark 181
   Batongguan Traversing Trail, Taiwan 316
   Berliner Mauerweg, Germany 39
   Camino Francés, Spain 55
   Cape to Cape Track, Australia 233
   Chemin de Stevenson, France 175
   Choquequirao Trek, Peru 221
   Dana to Petra Trail, Jordan 95
   Dingle Way, Ireland 153
   Dry Stone Route (GR221), Mallorca 75
   Dutch Mountain Trail, Netherlands 92
   Fishermen's Trail, Portugal 63
   GR92 Sendero del Mediterráneo Cataluña, Spain 301
   Island Walk, Canada 254
   Jeju Olle Trail, South Korea 227
   Kumano Kodō, Japan 263
   Lužnice Valley Trail, Czechia 202
   Lycian Way, Türkiye 81
   MacLehose Trail, Hong Kong, China 279
   Malerweg, Germany 267
   Malmveien Historical Trail, Norway 214
   Moselsteig, Germany 107
   Queen Charlotte Track, New Zealand/Aotearoa 19
   Rogue River Trail, USA 104
   Santa Barbara Cammino, Sardinia 84
   Shikoku 88 Temple Pilgrimage, Japan 69
   South West Coast Path, England 101
   Three Capes Track, Australia 78
   Via Algarviana, Portugal 319
   ViaBerna, Switzerland 166
   Via Dinarica, Bosnia & Hercegovina/Montenegro 147
   Via Francigena, Italy 257
   Via Transilvanica, Romania 162
   West Highland Way, Scotland 117

I

Iceland
   Fimmvörðuháls Trail 200
   Laugavegur 199
India
   Markha Valley Trek, Ladakh 172
   Singalila Ridge, West Bengal 110
Ireland
   Dingle Way, County Kerry 153
Italy
   Alta Via 1, Dolomites 239
   Kaiserjäger, Dolomites 240
   Santa Barbara Cammino, Sardinia 84
   Via Francigena 257

J

Japan
   88 Temple Pilgrimage, Shikoku 69
   Kumano Kodō, Honshū 263
   Michinoku Coastal Trail, Honshū 150
Jordan
   Dana to Petra Trail 95

K

Kenya
   Mt Kenya Traverse 45

L

Lithuania
   Baltic Coastal Hiking Trail 211
   Baltic Forest Hiking Trail 212
long-distance hikes
   Adlerweg, Austria 187
   Appalachian Trail, USA 248
   Baltic Coastal Hiking Trail, Lithuania 211
   Baltic Forest Hiking Trail, Lithuania & Estonia 212
   Berliner Mauerweg, Germany 39
   Camino de Costa Rica 32
   Camino de Invierno, Spain 56
   Camino Francés, Spain 55
   Chemin de Stevenson, France 175
   Coast to Coast, England 245
   Dingle Way, Ireland 153
   East Coast Trail, Canada 159
   Fishermen's Trail, Portugal 63
   GR92 Sendero del Mediterráneo Cataluña, Spain 301
   Grampians Peaks Trail, Australia 291
   Historical Way, Portugal 65
   John Muir Trail, USA 169
   Juliana Trail, Slovenia 127
   K2 Base Camp & Concordia, Pakistan 208
   Langtang & Helambu Trek, Nepal 285
   Larapinta Trail, Australia 205
   Lycian Way, Türkiye 81
   Manaslu Circuit, Nepal 51
   Michinoku Coastal Trail, Japan 150
   Moselsteig, Germany 107
   Pacific Crest Trail, USA & Canada 171
   Pekoe Trail, Sri Lanka 26
   Shikoku 88 Temple Pilgrimage, Japan 69
   South West Coast Path, England 101
   Via Algarviana, Portugal 319
   ViaBerna, Switzerland 166
   Via Francigena, Italy 257
   Via Transilvanica, Romania 162
   Waitukubuli Trail, Dominica 16
   West Highland Way, Scotland 117

M

Malaysia
   Mt Kinabalu, Sabah, Borneo 58
Montenegro
   Via Dinarica 147

Morocco
   Toubkal Circuit, Atlas
     Mountains 121
mountain hikes
   Adlerweg, Austria 187
   Alta Via 1, Italy 239
   Andros Route, Greece 251
   Appalachian Trail, USA 248
   Batongguan Traversing Trail,
     Taiwan 316
   Camino de Costa Rica 32
   Chemin de Stevenson,
     France 175
   Choquequirao Trek, Peru 221
   Ciudad Perdida Trek,
     Colombia 23
   Coast to Coast, England 245
   Cordillera Huayhuash Circuit,
     Peru 136
   Dry Stone Route (GR221),
     Mallorca 75
   E35, Oman 310
   Giant's Cup Trail, South Africa 89
   Gold Coast Hinterland Great
     Walk, Australia 114
   GR132 Circular, Canary Islands 13
   Grampians Peaks Trail,
     Australia 291
   Huemul Circuit, Argentina 298
   Island Trails, Madeira 29
   John Muir Trail, USA 169
   Jomolhari Trek, Bhutan 133
   K2 Base Camp & Concordia,
     Pakistan 208
   Kaiserjäger, Italy 240
   Kilimanjaro, Tanzania 9
   Kungsleden, Sweden 193
   Langtang & Helambu Trek,
     Nepal 285
   Larapinta Trail, Australia 205
   Laugavegur, Iceland 199
   Malerweg, Germany 267
   Manaslu Circuit, Nepal 51
   Mare è Monti Nord, Corsica 141
   Markha Valley Trek, India 172
   Menalon Trail, Greece 276
   Mt Kenya Traverse, Kenya 45
   Mt Kinabalu, Malaysian
     Borneo 58
   Outer Mountain Loop, USA 304
   Premužić Trail, Croatia 224
   Quilotoa Loop, Ecuador 294

   Routeburn Track, New Zealand/
     Aotearoa 273
   Santo Antão Trails,
     Cabo Verde 307
   Scenic Rim Trail, Australia 98
   Singalila Ridge, India 110
   Snowies Alpine Walk,
     Australia 42
   Toubkal Circuit, Morocco 121
   ViaBerna, Switzerland 166
   Via Dinarica, Bosnia &
     Hercegovina/Montenegro 147
   Waitukubuli Trail,
     Dominica 16
   West Highland Way, Scotland 117
   Wonderland Trail, USA 196

N

Namibia
   Fish River Canyon Trail 178
Nepal
   Langtang & Helambu Trek 285
   Manaslu Circuit 51
Netherlands
   Dutch Mountain Trail,
     Zuid-Limburg 92
New Zealand/Aotearoa
   Lake Waikaremoana Track,
     North Island 48
   Queen Charlotte Track,
     South Island 19
   Rakiura Track, Stewart Island/
     Rakiura 313
   Routeburn Track, South
     Island 273
Norway
   Malmveien Historical Trail,
     Trøndelag 214

O

Oman
   E35, Eastern Hajar 310

P

Pakistan
   K2 Base Camp & Concordia 208

Peru
   Choquequirao Trek 221
   Cordillera Huayhuash
     Circuit 136
pilgrimage routes
   88 Temple Pilgrimage, Japan 69
   Camino de Invierno, Spain 56
   Camino Francés, Spain 55
   Via Francigena, Switzerland &
     Italy 257
Portugal
   Fishermen's Trail, Alentejo &
     Algarve 63
   Historical Way, Alentejo 65
   Island Trails, Madeira 29
   PS PR1, Porto Santo 30
   Rota do Contrabandista,
     Algarve 320
   Via Algarviana, Algarve 319

R

Romania
   Via Transilvanica 162

S

Scotland
   West Highland Way 117
Slovenia
   Breginjski Trail 129
   Juliana Trail 127
South Africa
   Giant's Cup Trail, KwaZulu-
     Natal 89
   Otter Trail, Western &
     Eastern Cape 72
   Strandloper Trail,
     Eastern Cape 282
South Korea
   Jeju Olle Trail, Jeju-do 227
Spain
   Camino Francés 55
   Dry Stone Route, Mallorca 75
   GR92 Sendero del Mediterráneo
     Cataluña 301
   GR131, Canary Islands 14
   GR132 Circular, Canary Islands 13
Sri Lanka
   Pekoe Trail, Central Highlands 26

INDEX

Sweden
Kungsleden, Lapland 193
Switzerland
ViaBerna 166
Via Francigena 257

T

Taiwan
Batongguan Traversing Trail 316
Tanzania
Machame Route, Kilimanjaro 9
Türkiye
Lycian Way 81

U

USA
Appalachian Trail, Tennessee & North Carolina 248
Grand Canyon Rim-to-Rim, Arizona 130
Greenstone Ridge Trail, Michigan 144
John Muir Trail, California 169
Kalalau Trail, Hawai'i 230
Outer Mountain Loop, Texas 304
Pacific Crest Trail 171
Rogue River Trail, Oregon 104
Trans-Catalina Trail, California 288
Wonderland Trail, Washington State 196

W

wilderness hikes
Ciudad Perdida Trek, Colombia 23
Cordillera Huayhuash Circuit, Peru 136
Dana to Petra Trail, Jordan 95
E35, Oman 310
El Mirador Trek, Guatemala 66
Fish River Canyon Trail, Namibia 178
Giant's Cup Trail, South Africa 89
Gold Coast Hinterland Great Walk, Australia 114

Grampians Peaks Trail, Australia 291
Greenstone Ridge Trail, USA 144
John Muir Trail, USA 169
Jomolhari Trek, Bhutan 133
K2 Base Camp & Concordia, Pakistan 208
Kalalau Trail, Hawai'i 230
Kangaroo Island Wilderness Trail, Australia 260
Kilimanjaro, Tanzania 9
Kungsleden, Sweden 193
Larapinta Trail, Australia 205
Laugavegur, Iceland 199
Mt Kenya Traverse, Kenya 45
Mt Kinabalu, Malaysian Borneo 58
Outer Mountain Loop, USA 304
Routeburn Track, New Zealand/Aotearoa 273
Scenic Rim Trail, Australia 98
Snowies Alpine Walk, Australia 42
Thorsborne Trail, Australia 156
Three Capes Track, Australia 78
Traversée de Charlevoix, Canada 236
West Coast Trail, Canada 184
Wonderland Trail, USA 196
W Trek, Chilean Patagonia 36
wildlife-rich hikes 214
Adlerweg, Austria 187
Alta Via 1, Italy 239
Andros Route, Greece 251
Appalachian Trail, USA 248
Baltic Coastal Hiking Trail, Lithuania 211
Batongguan Traversing Trail, Taiwan 316
Camino de Costa Rica 32
Cape to Cape Track, Australia 233
Ciudad Perdida Trek, Colombia 23
Dana to Petra Trail, Jordan 95
Dingle Way, Ireland 153
East Coast Trail, Canada 159
El Mirador Trek, Guatemala 66
Fishermen's Trail, Portugal 63
Fish River Canyon Trail, Namibia 178
Giant's Cup Trail, South Africa 89
Gold Coast Hinterland Great Walk, Australia 114

GR92 Sendero del Mediterráneo Cataluña, Spain 301
Grampians Peaks Trail, Australia 291
Greenstone Ridge Trail, USA 144
Island Walk, Canada 254
John Muir Trail, USA 169
Jomolhari Trek, Bhutan 133
Juliana Trail, Slovenia 127
Kangaroo Island Wilderness Trail, Australia 260
Karhunkierros Trail, Finland 218
Kungsleden, Sweden 193
Lake Waikaremoana Track, New Zealand/Aotearoa 48
Langtang & Helambu Trek, Nepal 285
MacLehose Trail, Hong Kong, China 279
Markha Valley Trek, India 172
Mt Kenya Traverse, Kenya 45
Mt Kinabalu, Malaysian Borneo 58
Otter Trail, South Africa 72
Outer Mountain Loop, USA 304
Pekoe Trail, Sri Lanka 26
Queen Charlotte Track, New Zealand/Aotearoa 19
Rakiura Track, New Zealand/Aotearoa 313
Rogue River Trail, USA 104
Scenic Rim Trail, Australia 98
Singalila Ridge, India 110
Snowies Alpine Walk, Australia 42
Thorsborne Trail, Australia 156
Three Capes Track, Australia 78
Trans-Catalina Trail, USA 288
Waitukubuli Trail, Dominica 16
West Coast Trail, Canada 184
Wonderland Trail, USA 196
W Trek, Chilean Patagonia 36

Photo Credits

5: Jan Jerman/Shutterstock; **6:** Stian Klo for Lonely Planet; **7:** Ellen Ryan/Lonely Planet, Dronoptera/Shutterstock, Stian Klo for Lonely Planet, Pandora Pictures/Shutterstock, Photosbypatrik/Shutterstock, Matt Munro for Lonely Planet, Stefan Neumann/Shutterstock, Marie-Soleil Chabot/Shutterstock; **8:** Aboubakar Malipula/Shutterstock; **10:** VisualStories/Getty Images; **11:** Bossa Art/Shutterstock; **12:** Stian Klo for Lonely Planet; **14:** Stian Klo for Lonely Planet; **15:** Stian Klo for Lonely Planet; **16:** Micheal Lees/Lonely Planet; **17:** Rieger Bertrand/hemis.fr/Alamy; **18:** Dmitry Naumov/Getty Images; **20:** Brian Scantlebury/Shutterstock; **21:** Patrick McGrath/500px, Wolfgang Kaehler/Getty Images; **22:** Artush/Shutterstock; **24:** dunn4040/Shutterstock; **25:** David Vargas F/Shutterstock, Joerg Steber/Shutterstock; **26:** Matt Munro for Lonely Planet; **27:** Oleh_Slobodeniuk/Getty Images; **28:** Thomas Marchhart/Shutterstock; **30:** Curioso.Photography/Shutterstock, Jon Sparks/Alamy; **31:** Photosbypatrik/Shutterstock; **32:** Toh Gouttenoire/The New York Times/Redux; **33:** Javier Fernández Sánchez/Getty Images; **34:** Ophe/Shutterstock; **35:** Kondoruk/Getty Images, Westend61/Getty Images, Greens and Blues/Shutterstock, tolobalaguer.com/Shutterstock, Jonathan Stokes for Lonely Planet, Andrey Josephs/Shutterstock, Aleksandr Degtiarev/Shutterstock, Sandra Ophorst/Shutterstock; **36:** tolobalaguer.com/Shutterstock; **37:** Krista Lance/Shutterstock; **38:** Jonathan Stokes for Lonely Planet; **40:** LordRunar/Getty Images, 41: Peeradontax/Shutterstock, benstevens/Getty Images; **42:** Greens and Blues/Shutterstock; **43:** Willowtreehouse/Shutterstock; **44:** WanderingNomad/Getty Images; **46:** Eric Lafforgue/Lonely Planet, guenterguni/Getty Images; **47:** elisolidum/Shutterstock; **48:** Karin Wassmer/Shutterstock; **49:** Jiri Foltyn/Shutterstock; **50:** Punnawit Suwattananun/Shutterstock; **52:** Ganesh Bastola/Getty Images; **53:** Darya Ufimtseva/Alamy, Aleksandr Degtiarev/Shutterstock; **54:** Brester Irina/Shutterstock; **56:** jarcosa/Getty Images; **57:** Hemis/Alamy; **58:** Boyloso/Shutterstock; **59:** Pintai Suchachaisri/Getty Images; **60:** Amehime/Shutterstock; **61:** Massimo Corda/Shutterstock, Catherine Sutherland/Lonely Planet, TravelNerd/Shutterstock, Raphael Rivest/Shutterstock, PhotoSky/Shutterstock, mtnmichelle/Getty Images, Sanga Park/Getty Images, Kerry Murray for Lonely Planet; **62:** Olga Gudumac/Getty Images; **64:** Marlene Marques/Lonely Planet; **65:** Martin Schuetz/Shutterstock; **66:** David Ducoin/Getty Images; **67:** Carlos Alonzo/Getty Images; **68:** Sanga Park/Shutterstock; **70:** Sanga Park/Getty Images, David Madison/Getty Images; **71:** Alex Saurel/Getty Images; **72:** DV8OR/Stocksy; **73:** Image Professionals GmbH/Alamy; **74:** Kris Hoobaer/Getty Images; **76:** tolobalaguer.com/Shutterstock; **77:** tolobalaguer.com/Shutterstock, Kris Hoobaer/Getty Images; **78:** Catherine Sutherland/Lonely Planet; **79:** Catherine Sutherland/Lonely Planet; **80:** Quinn Martin/Shutterstock; **82:** Yasemin Ozdemir/Getty, Photo Volcano/Shutterstock; **83:** GrelaFoto/Getty Images; **84:** Markus Lange/robertharding; **85:** Atzori Riccardo/Shutterstock; **86:** Tom Mackie for Lonely Planet; **87:** Pete Seaward/Lonely Planet, Lorena Montoya/Shutterstock, Erik Isakson/Getty Images, Tom Mackie for Lonely Planet, Michael Heffernan/Lonely Planet, zakir1346/Shutterstock, GAPS/Getty Images, alfotokunst/Shutterstock; **88:** Michael Heffernan/Lonely Planet; **90:** Yasmine DG/500px; **91:** Michael Heffernan/Lonely Planet, EcoPrint/Shutterstock; **92:** Lorena Montoya/Shutterstock; **93:** Wut_Moppie/Shutterstock; **94:** Tom Mackie for Lonely Planet; **96:** Justin Foulkes for Lonely Planet; **97:** Iwanami Photos/Shutterstock; **98:** janetteasche/Getty Images; **99:** Jakub Maculewicz/Shutterstock; **100:** Devon and Cornwall Photography/Getty Images; **102:** Justin Paget/Getty Images; **103:** Rolf E. Staerk/Shutterstock, Myles New/Lonely Planet; **104:** Cavan Images/Alamy; **105:** JKendall/Shutterstock; **106:** foto-select/Shutterstock; **108:** Ina Peters/Getty Images, Nachteule/Getty Images; **109:** LianeM/Shutterstock; **110:** suprabhat/Shutterstock; **111:** David Ducoin/Getty Images; **112:** Beto Santillan/Shutterstock; **113:** Matt Munro for Lonely Planet, Ngo Ho/Shutterstock, THPStock/Shutterstock, Rene Baars/Shutterstock, Maleo Photography/Shutterstock, Ducoin David/Getty Images, Tomas1706/Getty Images, Kesterhu/Getty Images; **114:** Enrique Diaz/Getty Images; **115:** FiledIMAGE/Shutterstock; **116:** Larissa Chilanti/Shutterstock; **118:** Louis-Michel Desert/Getty Images; **119:** Renata Kilinskaite/Shutterstock; **120:** Alberto Loyo/Shutterstock; **122:** Jan Jerman/Shutterstock; **123:** Lukas Hodon/Getty Images; **124:** Andrew Murray/Getty Images; **125:** Martinho Smart/Shutterstock; **126:** ZGPhotography/Shutterstock; **128:** Justin Foulkes for Lonely Planet; **129:** Vaclav Volrab/Shutterstock, Pecold/Shutterstock; **130:** Mark Read for Lonely Planet; **131:** Matt Munro for Lonely Planet; **132:** Wan Kum Seong/Shutterstock; **134:** Dylan Haskin/Shutterstock, Romulo Rejon/Getty Images; **135:** Alex Treadway/Getty Images; **136:** Mikadun/Shutterstock; **137:** Mikadun/Shutterstock; **138:** Ondrej Prochazka/Shutterstock; **139:** Coral Brunner/Shutterstock, Timothy Mulholland/Alamy, Hokiyu/Shutterstock, SuperFlo/Shutterstock, Mikadun/Shutterstock, Pete Seaward/Lonely Planet, Agent Wolf/Shutterstock, Lucy Hewett/Lonely Planet; **140:** Rolf E. Staerk/Shutterstock; **142:** Jon Ingall/Shutterstock; **143:** Agent Wolf/Shutterstock, Andreas Zeitler/Shutterstock; **144:** RichardSeeley/Getty Images; **145:** Timothy Mulholland/Alamy; **146:** Slavica Stajic/Alamy; **148:** PhotoBajone/Shutterstock, Lukas_Vejrik/Shutterstock; **149:** SuperFlo/Shutterstock; **150:** H_Yasui/Getty Images; **151:** Teerasak Chinnasot/Shutterstock; **152:** maydays/Getty Images; **154:** Bailey Freeman for Lonely Planet; **155:** Nick Fox/Shutterstock; **156:** Nick Galvin/Shutterstock; **157:** Andrew Bain/Alamy; **158:** Lucy Hewett/Lonely Planet; **160:** chrisontour84/Shutterstock; **161:** Paul Brady Photography/Shutterstock; **162:** rechitansorin/Getty Images; **163:** Catalin Lazar/Shutterstock; **164:** szefei/Shutterstock; **165:** Serge Goujon/Shutterstock, Chess Ocampo/Shutterstock, LGieger/Shutterstock, imageBROKER/Moritz Wolf/Getty Images, Fat Jackey/Shutterstock, Alfredo Maiquez/Getty Images, Hemis/Alamy, Nirian/Getty Images; **166:** YueStock/Shutterstock; **167:** DaLiu/Shutterstock; **168:** Nicholas Motto/Getty Images; **170:** John Couture/Shutterstock; **171:** Juancat/Shutterstock; **172:** beibaoke/Shutterstock; **173:** xerazed/Shutterstock; **174:** Hemis/Alamy; **176:** Hemis/Alamy; **177:** Hemis/Alamy; **178:** Felix Lipov/Shutterstock; **179:** Gunter Nuyts/Shutterstock; **180:** LGieger/Shutterstock; **182:** TasfotoNL/Shutterstock; **183:** Nick Brundle Photography/Getty Images, Oliver Hoffmann/Shutterstock; **184:** Tomas Kulaja/Shutterstock; **185:** Anton Bielousov/Shutterstock; **186:** imageBROKER/Moritz Wolf/Getty Images; **188:** imageBROKER.com/Shutterstock, imageBROKER/Mara Brandl/Getty Images; **189:** adisa/Adobe Stock; **190:** Alan Kearney/Getty Images; **191:** Gorodisskij/Shutterstock, Matyas Rehak/Alamy, jacquesvandinteren/Getty Images, Yevgen Belich/Shutterstock, Johner Images/Getty Images, Hussain Warraich/Shutterstock, puyalroyo/Shutterstock, Nat Chittamai/Shutterstock; **192:** Viktorishy/Shutterstock; **194:** blueflanker/Shutterstock; **195:** Natasa Kirin/Shutterstock; **196:** Kelly vanDellen/Alamy; **197:** Spring Images/Alamy; **198:** SayuDaygo/Shutterstock; **200:** travelwild/Shutterstock, imageBROKER.com/Alamy; **201:** Marek Bieganski/Getty Images; **202:** Pecold/Shutterstock; **203:** Sergey Fedoskin/Shutterstock; **204:** Bryce Thomas/Getty Images; **206:** janetteasche/Getty Images; **207:** Artie Photography/Getty Images; **208:** Peter John Watson/Shutterstock; **209:** Naveed Hussain/Alamy; **210:** A. Aleksandravicius/Shutterstock; **212:** bassaran/Shutterstock, Vaidotas Grybauskas/Shutterstock; **213:** asta.sabonyte/Shutterstock; **214:** PhotoVisions/Shutterstock; **215:** Patricia Hamilton/Getty Images; **216:** Matt Munro for Lonely Planet; **217:** Filipa Beros/Shutterstock, Tec Petaja/Lonely Planet, Mazur Travel/Shutterstock, Rafal Cichawa/Getty Images, Natalia Natapova/Shutterstock, Tom Jastram/Shutterstock, Sanga Park/Shutterstock, ClickAlps Srls/Alamy; **218:** Ilona Bradacova/Shutterstock; **219:** Mazur Travel/Shutterstock; **220:** Narongsak Nagadhana/Shutterstock; **222:** Yuri Zvezdny/Shutterstock; **223:** DanielPrudek/Getty Images, Jekaterina Sahmanova/Getty Images; **224:** Richard Rajnai/Shutterstock; **225:** Vedrana Sucic/Getty Images; **226:** JIPEN/Shutterstock; **228:** Jeju Olle Foundation; **229:** wisdom32/Shutterstock; **230:** bluestork/Shutterstock; **231:** Matt Munro for Lonely Planet; **232:** Abstract Aerial Art/Getty Images; **234:** Sam Jeffs/Shutterstock; **235:** FiledIMAGE/Getty Images, Elsalass/Shutterstock; **236:** David Boutin/Shutterstock; **237:** Sergio Canobbio/Getty Images; **238:** Alberto Masnovo/Shutterstock; **240:** Alex Treadway/Getty Images; **241:** Fabio Lotti/Shutterstock; **242:** olgagorovenko/Shutterstock; **243:** Zack Frank/Shutterstock, Jonathan Stokes for Lonely Planet, robynbrody/Getty Images, Emilie Nguyen/Shutterstock, ZGPhotography/Shutterstock, bob davis photography/Getty Images, Lemonan/Getty Images, StevanZZ/Shutterstock; **244:** joe daniel price/Getty Images; **246:** Julie Pigulav/Getty Images; **247:** Ron Evans/Alamy, stanciuc/Getty Images; **248:** ZakZeinert/Shutterstock; **249:** William Silver/Shutterstock; **250:** Mazur Travel/Shutterstock; **252:** Poike/iStock; **253:** Lemonan/Getty Images; **254:** Vadim.Petrov/Shutterstock; **255:** Emilie Nguyen/Shutterstock; **256:** Laura Edwards/Lonely Planet; **258:** Marco Scataglini/UCG/Universal Images Group via Getty Images; **259:** Federrame/Shutterstock; **260:** bmphotographer/Shutterstock; **261:** Danita Delimont/Alamy; **262:** Cristi Croitoru/Shutterstock; **264:** M Andy/Shutterstock, Jonathan Stokes for Lonely Planet; **265:** Sean Pavone/Shutterstock; **266:** Neunerphotography/Shutterstock; **268:** Annabell Gsoedl/Shutterstock; **269:** ZGPhotographyShutterstock; **270:** Philip Lee Harvey for Lonely Planet; **271:** Michael Heffernan/Lonely Planet, Tandem Ride Photography/Shutterstock, Philip Lee Harvey for Lonely Planet, Jon Chica/Shutterstock, Whitworth Images/Getty Images, Andronos Haris/Shutterstock, Niti Thanomsri/Shutterstock, Marvin Minder/Shutterstock; **272:** Philip Lee Harvey for Lonely Planet; **274:** kmh72/Shutterstock, Philip Lee Harvey for Lonely Planet; **275:** Philip Lee Harvey for Lonely Planet; **276:** Ioannis Mantas/Alamy; **277:** andronos/Alamy; **278:** Adrienne Pitts/Lonely Planet; **280:** Tina Zhou/Shutterstock; **281:** Dragon Claws/Shutterstock, TungCheung/Shutterstock; **282:** Luke Schmidt/Shutterstock; **283:** Madele/Shutterstock; **284:** VANESSAL/Shutterstock; **286:** Sander Meertins/Alamy, filrom/Getty Images; **287:** mezzotint/Shutterstock; **288:** Brian Swanson/Shutterstock; **289:** raphoto/Getty Images; **290:** josh.tagi/Shutterstock; **292:** Peter Nguyen/500px; **293:** Andrew Bain/Alamy; **294:** Labetaa Andre/Shutterstock; **295:** Ludmila Ruzickova/Shutterstock; **296:** bonn bonn foto/Shutterstock; **297:** R. Vickers/Shutterstock, Kelly vanDellen/Shutterstock, Jan Jerman/Shutterstock, Frans Sellies/Getty Images, VII-photo/Getty Images, Susana_Martins/Shutterstock, vane_hinausindiewelt/Shutterstock, Robert Ahner/Shutterstock; **298:** Jan Jerman/Shutterstock; **299:** Jan Jerman/Shutterstock; **300:** ikumaru/Shutterstock; **302:** Toniflap/Shutterstock; **303:** Robert Ahner/Shutterstock, nito/Shutterstock; **304:** Kelly vanDellen/Alamy; **305:** Eric Poulin/Shutterstock; **306:** na.knoe/Shutterstock; **308:** africa2008st/Shutterstock, Ulrich Hollmann/Getty Images; **309:** ChrisNoe/Shutterstock; **310:** Damian Ryszawy/Shutterstock; **311:** trabantos/Shutterstock; **312:** LH11/Shutterstock; **314:** R. Vickers/Shutterstock; **315:** Jinhee Jung/Shutterstock, Harvepino/Shutterstock; **316:** Josh Lu photography/Shutterstock; **317:** elwynn1130/iStock; **318:** slege/Shutterstock; **320:** Kris Hoobaer/Shutterstock; **321:** Sopotnicki/Shutterstock

Where to Go When Hiking
May 2026
Published by Lonely Planet Global Limited
CRN 554153
www.lonelyplanet.com
10 9 8 7 6 5 4 3 2 1

Printed in Malaysia
ISBN 978 18375 8875 6
© Lonely Planet 2025
© photographers as indicated 2025

Publisher & VP, Print Piers Pickard
Publisher, Gift & Illustrated Becca Hunt
Senior Editor Robin Barton
Senior Designer Emily Dubin
Book Designer Taylor Miles Hopkins
Image Research Sharon Dortenzio, Elena Noel Santos
Cartographers Daniela Machova, Bohumil Ptacek, Katerina Pavkova
Editors Polly Thomas, Cliff Wilkinson
Authors Sarah Baxter & Paul Bloomfield
Print Production Nigel Longuet

Although the authors and Lonely Planet have taken all reasonable care in preparing this book, we make no warranty about the accuracy or completeness of its content and, to the maximum extent permitted, disclaim all liability from its use.

All rights reserved. No part of this publication may be reproduced, stored in a retrieval system or transmitted in any form by any means, electronic, mechanical, photocopying, recording or otherwise except brief extracts for the purpose of review, without the written permission of the publisher. Lonely Planet and the Lonely Planet logo are trademarks of Lonely Planet and are registered in the US patent and Trademark Office and in other countries.

STAY IN TOUCH lonelyplanet.com/contact

Lonely Planet Global Limited
Digital Depot, Roe Lane (off Thomas St),
Digital Hub, Dublin 8,
D08 TCV4
Ireland
(EU authorised representative)

Mapping data sources: © Lonely Planet, © OpenStreetMap, © Natural Earth, © USGS-ASTER, © GEBCO

Cover, top to bottom: MarinaTP/Shutterstock, Lenspiration/Shutterstock, Nattrass/Shutterstock, George KUZ/Shutterstock
Back cover, top to bottom: My Good Images/Shutterstock, Nataliia Melnychuk/Shutterstock, Dominic Meijers/Shutterstock, Ryan Richardson/Getty Images
Spine: XZD Stock/Shutterstock